# Mark Twain on Travel

## Also by Terry Mort

## Nonfiction (available from The Lyons Press)

*The Reasonable Art of Fly Fishing*

*Zane Grey on Fishing*

*Jack London on Adventure*

## Fiction

*Showdown at Verity*

*The Lawless Breed*

*Shipment to Mexico*

# MARK TWAIN

# ON TRAVEL

*Edited by*
TERRY MORT

THE LYONS PRESS
Guilford, Connecticut
An imprint of The Globe Pequot Press

The Lyons Press is an imprint of The Globe Pequot Press

10 9 8 7 6 5 4 3 2 1

Printed in the United States of America

Library of Congress Cataloging-in-Publication Data

Twain, Mark, 1835-1910.
Mark Twain on travel / edited by Terry Mort.
p. cm.
ISBN 1-59228-806-5
1. Twain, Mark, 1835-1910—Travel. 2. Authors, American—19th century—Biography. 3. Americans—Foreign countries—History—19th century. 4. Voyages and travels. I. Mort, T. A. (Terry A.) II. Title.
PS1331.A2 2005
818'.409—dc22

2005013912

# *Contents*

***Contents***

# *Introduction*

In 1888 Samuel Clemens, then in his early fifties, received an honorary M.A. from Yale University. In his acceptance speech he explained why he was drawn to writing humor:

> Ours is a useful trade, a worthy calling . . . with all its lightness, and frivolity, it has one serious purpose, one aim, one specialty, and it is consistent to it—the deriding of shams, the exposure of pretentious falsities, the laughing of stupid superstitions out of existence; and . . . whoso is by instinct engaged in this sort of warfare is the natural enemy of royalties, nobilities, privileges and all kindred swindles, and the natural friend of human rights and human liberties.

From the lofty perch of the Yale podium and from the perspective of mature success, it was easy enough to defend the role of humorist—and to assign it a noble raison d'etre. But he was not always so sure of himself. For much of his life he was of two minds about the subject—one part of him followed his natural inclinations toward the humorous, while the other part craved the respect of the cultural elite who seemed to think that serious and smileless (to use a Twain expression) literature was the only kind of writing that mattered. That and sermons.

In *Life on the Mississippi* Sam Clemens tells us that he adopted his pen name from Captain Isaiah Sellers, a patriarch of steamboat pilots who wrote occasional pieces for the newspapers and signed them Mark Twain. It would be interesting to know at what point Clemens realized the significance of the name. Was Twain a lucky accident, or was it a sly private joke from the beginning? A laugh shared between the Siamese twins of his character? A recognition of the internal battles he was fighting with himself? Was the story about Isaiah Sellers even true, or just a way of covering up his own invention?

And he was divided by more than just ambivalence about humor. His mind was constantly roiled by differing and evolving perspectives and attitudes, competing ideas, emotions and values, enthusiasms, passions. Conventional attitudes warred with exuberant rebellion, starchy morality with a healthy bawdy streak, romanticism with practicality, imagination with reality. He was Tom and Huck, the king and the dauphin, Hank Morgan and Arthur, Mark Twain and Sam Clemens—all rolled into one complex and energetic literary Vesuvius.

Despite his success, the word "mere" dogged him through much of his career. As in "mere" humorist. He was brilliant as a platform lecturer, brilliantly entertaining, but although he enjoyed the accolades and worked hard to perfect his delivery, he came to loathe the business. It was lucrative, but it was exhausting. It was rewarding, but it was somehow degrading. It helped to make him famous but also reinforced the perception that he was a literary clown. He was placed in the same sentence as "Petroleum V. Nasby," another platform humorist whose performances the cultural elite described as rhetorical buffoonery. Clearly, the Brahmins who established the standards of taste regarded humor with more than a little disdain. Twain's humorous writing and performing teetered on the edge of vulgarity in the eyes of people for whom Henry James and his ilk were the ideal—in terms of subject, form, and tone. And yet Twain wanted their approval. It's hard to understand why, for the cultural and social elite must have looked to Twain like grown-up versions of the Model Boy:

> The Model Boy of my time—we never had but one—was perfect; perfect in manners, perfect in dress, perfect in conduct, perfect in filial piety, perfect in exterior godliness; but at bottom he was a prig; and as for the contents of his skull, they could have changed places with the contents of a pie, and nobody would have been the worse off for it but the pie. This fellow's reproachlessness was a standing reproach to every lad in the village. He was the admiration of all the mothers, and the detestation of all their sons.

But one half of him did want their approval, though he would never be able to become the literary Model Boy, himself—not that he really wanted to. He was much more in sympathy with Huck Finn—" . . . Aunt Sally she's going to adopt me and sivilize me and I can't stand it." And yet it was the Aunt Sallys and the Model Boys who were running things, in the respectable literary world.

His wife, Olivia, is sometimes regarded as the prim force behind his ambition to achieve the acceptance of the elites, as though she pushed him to become something he was not, didn't want to be, and never could be. But that seems to be a bad rap. True, she sometimes cringed at his professional and personal antics—"O, Youth!" she would say in exasperation, using her pet name for him, whenever his enthusiasm over some new idea or a particularly fine joke carried him beyond the conventional pale. And her name for him is apposite, for part of Mark Twain always remained a boy—his imagination, his mischievousness, his innocence, his energy. But it was not just Livy who wanted him to be respectable. Twain, himself, also yearned to be known as a writer of "serious" literature; or perhaps, more accurately, to be taken seriously as a writer. And his attempts in that direction, such as *Joan of Arc*, did garner him some of the praise he wanted, though today that book hardly compares to Huck Finn or the Connecticut Yankee. But still he was drawn to humor, as though his other self kept calling him, like a voice urging Tom Sawyer to climb out his bedroom window and go off into the night, looking for adventure. And giving in to it must have been a relief—the kind of relief Huck felt when he could escape from "sivilization" for a while and have a peaceful smoke.

None of this is to suggest that Twain was, to use the popular phrase, "bipolar." He did have periods of elation and periods of depression, but there was nothing pathological about any of that. There were good reasons. He had more than his share of family tragedies—his wife, infant son, and two of his three daughters all died during his lifetime, so that the pleasure he derived from his enormous popular success was counterbalanced by successive waves of bitterness and grief. And there were financial upheavals along the way. At times he was wealthy beyond his dreams, while at others he was bankrupt—variously, a prince and a pauper. He was a complicated man with multiple sensibilities; a southerner who lived in the north, a thorough American who spent eleven years of his life abroad, a businessman with a passion for wealth and inventions and yet a romantic with a deep and abiding nostalgia for the agrarian past, an extrovert buffeted by episodes of darkness and despair, a traveler who liked to stay at home. Indeed, his well loved home in Hartford—a mansion incorporating many different architectural ideas—is a wonderful reflection of the man. The style is—incredible. Twain's biographer, Justin Kaplan, says, "It was part steamboat, part Medieval stronghold and part cuckoo clock."

His lifelong friend, William Dean Howells (a Brahmin who nonetheless appreciated him), called Twain "the Lincoln of our literature." But unlike Lincoln, Twain had doubts about the wisdom of the common man and about the wisdom of letting everyone—the dolts as well as the accomplished—vote. And in a similar vein he thought trial by jury was more likely to result in injustice than the other way around. Both of these attitudes reflected his skepticism about the human race: "I believe that our Heavenly Father invented man because he was disappointed in the monkey." Or, as he says in a letter to Howells, "Is [man] really fit for anything but to be stood up on the street corner as a convenience for dogs?"

As an insouciant boy, he lived—along with his family and friends—quite comfortably with slavery in the days before the Civil War, and he looked back upon those days with sentimental warmth and drew a distinction between the treatment and condition of a domestic house slave and the wretched field hand on a plantation: " . . . there was nothing about the slavery of the Hannibal region to rouse one's dozing humane instincts to activity." And he did serve, albeit briefly, in the Confederate army, in Missouri, a state in which there were large pockets of abolitionist and unionist sentiment. In other words, he had a choice, and he chose the South. Yet when the evils of racism came home to him, he never deviated from his antagonism toward it. His "humane instincts," once roused, remained that way and reached their finest expression in *Huckleberry Finn*, which is, in part, a thorough indictment of the South's racial attitudes and practices and one that is all the more powerful because of the irony imbedded in the innocent voice of a boy.

In that same book he introduces us to the king and the dauphin, charlatans who reflect two other recurrent themes in the mature Mark Twain—the absurdity of royalty and its attendant hierarchies and privileges, which by definition violate everyone else's human rights, and the pernicious effects of Southern traditions of "chivalry," which he thought stemmed from the popularity in the South of Sir Walter Scott: "Admiration of his fantastic heroes and their grotesque chivalry doings and romantic juvenalities still survives here . . . " He blamed those traditions for the Civil War and for the postwar South's slow recovery, for their "windy humbuggeries" acted as a drag on the modernizing and entrepreneurial spirit that led to social and economic mobility and dynamism. He would return to those themes in *A Connecticut Yankee in King Arthur's Court*, although the horrific climax also reflects Twain's ambivalence toward modern ingenuity and technology that can produce not only progress, but mass destruction.

As a young man, Mark Twain had an eye for the ladies, although he wondered if he would ever marry, for the only women who would have him were not the sort to bring home to mother. ("I wouldn't *have* a girl that *I* was worthy of. *She* wouldn't do. She wouldn't be respectable enough.") Apparently, he doubted his fitness for polite society, and those doubts may have stemmed in part from his high spirited adventures in the freewheeling towns out west, where the only available women were "no better than they should be." But ultimately he did marry, and by all accounts his relationship with the eminently proper and conventional Olivia Langdon was loving, faithful, supportive, and sexually fulfilling. There was evidently more to Livy than met the public eye.

Despite the vivacity of his early bohemian days, the mature Twain had an almost prissy aversion to what he considered sexual immorality—he detested the French, for example, because of what he saw as their unblushing adulterous mores; he called them "the connecting link between man and monkey." This seems a bit out of synch with his lifelong fondness for bawdy stories and tales that he would tell and listen to during the all-male dinners he frequently attended. Of course, there is an obvious difference between a fondness for bawdy jokes and a fondness for loose women. Still, for a man with a bit of a past, his virulent public pronouncements on sexual matters seem almost like something the Model Boy might say. Perhaps that was the point; perhaps it was a way, however unconscious, to strengthen his credentials and kinship with the respectable class, for whom a Victorian double standard was neither inconsistent nor ironic.

Mark Twain had a taste for whiskey, too, and we get the impression that he lived pretty hard during his bachelor days out west. (When he heard that Mark Twain was getting married, Ambrose Bierce wrote that it was too bad Twain's "long bright smile will no longer greet the early barkeeper.") Yet he embraced the unthirsty values of his wife's family and circle of friends once he came east. At least some of the time. When he married Livy, he even took the pledge. For a while. But he was experienced at taking pledges and valued them accordingly. As a boy he had taken a pledge against smoking, so that he could be privileged to wear a red sash and march in holiday parades in Hannibal: ". . . the pledge part of the matter was of no consequence. It was so small in importance that, contrasted with the sash, it was in effect non-existent." He soon returned to smoking, for there were not enough parades to compensate for the sacrifice, and he recollects in his autobiography the heavenly pleasure of that first post-pledge cigar, even though: "It was probably not choice, or the previous smoker would not have thrown it away so soon." So, too, after his marriage, he was not long in returning to his evening hot Scotches, and Livy, not so prim after all, kept him company with a glass of beer. Even a cocktail before breakfast was not unheard of. But there is no suggestion that Twain ever suffered from any dependency—except perhaps on cigars or a pipe.

So, Twain—former steamboat pilot, printer, prospector, journalist, wanderer—was a complicated man with a number of conflicting ambitions, viewpoints, and facets to his personality—as well as some strong opinions on the important matters of the day. It's not surprising, then, that the travel books and articles he wrote throughout his career reflect that complexity. In fact, that is one of their chief virtues.

Twain traveled extensively and wrote about it extensively throughout his life. But after his initial wanderings as a young man through the west and his first transatlantic trip, travel became more a matter of business than pleasure. He wanted and needed the money. His various financial disasters, mostly stemming from a fascination with mechanical inventions that almost worked, periodically created a desperate financial pinch, and that led him back to the detested lecture circuit and to the writing of travel books—a way to get two sources of income from one trip. His early success on the lecture circuit and the great success of his first travel book, *The Innocents Abroad*, meant that he could always return to those markets when he needed to—which was oftener than he liked.

The books were sold by subscription, that is, by salesmen going door to door in rural areas selling to people who only rarely bought books. (Twain once said that if a book of his sold sixty thousand copies, fifty thousand would be bought by people who had never seen the inside of a bookstore, and it's easy to imagine *The Innocents Abroad* standing on a small bookshelf accompanied only by a family Bible and *Pilgrim's Progress*.) When they did buy, therefore, they wanted something substantial for their money—six hundred pages plus illustrations. More, if possible.

Subscription sales generated more money than Twain could get from traditional publishing; but this method of marketing also affected the content and form of the books themselves. For example, there was no need to be concise; quite the contrary, for the buyers wanted bulk. Length was the object. Twain could therefore let his prose bounce from one subject to another without worrying about whether any of it hung together, and that suited his energetic imagination and his love of storytelling and conversation. The reader tags along as Twain and his various travel partners wander here and there, talking all the while. As he says in *A Tramp Abroad*:

> Now the true charm of pedestrianism does not lie in the walking, or in the scenery, but in the talking. The walking is good to time the movement of the tongue by, and to keep the blood and brain stirred up and active; the scenery and the woodsy smells are good to bear in upon a man an unconscious and unobtrusive charm and solace to the eye and soul and sense; but the supreme pleasure comes from the talk. It

> is no matter whether one talks wisdom or nonsense, the case is the same; the bulk of the enjoyment lies in the wagging of the gladsome jaw and the flapping of the sympathetic ear.

He might have been describing the structure of his travel books, for that is how they are organized—a series of episodes, adventures, digressions, tall tales, reminiscences, conversations. In many cases the foreign country is not the subject but rather just the context or backdrop for the telling of colorful stories, anecdotes, and memories. In these episodes the actual location is almost irrelevant.

But Twain also knew that his readers expected some information on the exotic locales most of them would never see; they wanted local color. That, plus the need to deliver substantial volumes to his readers, led Twain to lard his travel books with long quotations from other writers and with his own bits and pieces of guidebook information and description. It was an easy way to add pages. And sometimes not so easy, as when Twain couldn't borrow from others and had to write the stuff himself. It was a struggle whenever he was forced to subdue his imagination and stick to the realities of the journeys. Here again is the split between Twain following his natural instincts toward humor and grudgingly giving in to the need to play it straight and give the reader some information.

To the modern reader these dollops of filler can be not only uninteresting, but annoying or boring, depending. Twain didn't like them much, either. Worse, these additions shoulder aside the thing that gives the books their charm—Twain's unique voice.

And what a sublime voice it can be. Often filled with gorgeous language and constructions, generally veined with irony, his voice is quite simply inimitable. Consider this well-known selection from *Pudd'nhead Wilson's Calendar*:

> There is no character, howsoever good and fine, but can be destroyed by ridicule, howsoever poor and witless. Observe the ass, for instance; his character is about perfect, he is the

> choicest spirit among all the humbler animals, yet see what ridicule has brought him to. Instead of being complimented when we are called an ass, we are left in doubt.

A reasonably adept writer might come up with the first two and a half sentences, but only Mark Twain would have written that final phrase. Happily, Twain's travel writing is filled with nuggets similar to this one. The real gold often lies in the digressions or reminiscences, such as in the story of his boyhood Hannibal when the "fragrant" town drunk, Jimmy Finn, sells a future interest in his own skeleton to get a jug of whiskey that hastens the "change of ownership" in the property. Obviously memory is an important aspect of Twain's art, and in his travel books he wanders back in time as enjoyably as he wanders through foreign lands—more so, probably.

The travel books are also filled with glimpses and foreshadowing of important themes and story lines that appear in his fiction. There is the raft trip down the Neckar River in Germany during which he talks about the tranquility of being on a raft while alternately experiencing some broadly comic adventures. And of course *Life on the Mississippi* presages *Huckleberry Finn*, too—indeed contains a chapter from the novel, since he was working on both books more or less at the same time, off and on. This could hardly be considered filler, but it is hardly travel writing either. Certainly it's another example of Twain's need to add bulk to his book.

The voice of what will be the Connecticut Yankee also pops up frequently, as in the story of the "scientific knight" who uses a fire extinguisher to dispatch a fire-breathing dragon, or in Twain's comparison of the Vatican to the US Patent Office—the Vatican being the storehouse of art, the Patent Office the storehouse of practical genius—the ancient and the modern, each with its separate virtues. In fact, this juxtaposition of the Yankee modernity and dynamism with the old world's high art, ancient culture, slow pace, and suffocating institutions is a consistent theme, with Twain typically alternating between viewpoints—sometimes for comic effect, sometimes in perfect seriousness. Sometimes the American rube loose in the temples of high art, sometimes the practical Yankee seeing the warts on a decaying culture, sometimes the wide-eyed boy with a Sawyer-esque taste for color and romance, sometimes the fool, sometimes the critic who exposes the fool, sometimes the good-hearted observer who sympathizes with the wretched victims of religion or politics, sometimes the self-made individualist who despises them for accepting their misery—Twain catalogues what he came to call "the damned human race" in all its absurdity, confusion, genius, bigotry, diversity, venality, achievement, and continually interesting foolishness. His own included.

Mark Twain wrote five travel books—*The Innocents Abroad* (1869), *Roughing It* (1872), *A Tramp Abroad* (1880), *Life on the Mississippi* (1883), and *Following the Equator* (1897).

*The Innocents Abroad*, subtitled *A New Pilgrim's Progress*, solidified Twain's national reputation. The subtitle is apt, because it is the story of a chartered ship that stops at several European ports on the way to the Holy Land. And aside from Twain and one or two of his pals, the excursion consists of a group of straitlaced religious "Pilgrims," who represent conventional American middle-class values—values Twain always regarded with amused and sometimes angry skepticism. The "Model Boy" pieties of the Pilgrims naturally brought out the mischievous and satiric strain that was much stronger in Twain than the conventional faith he tried, now and then, to accept. Religion never quite "took" with Twain, although he gave it a good try during his courtship and early married days in an effort to become worthy of Livy. But, ironically, over the years it was Livy who lost her faith, partly as a result of Twain's increasing belief that the world he saw could hardly be guided by a Divine Providence. The Pilgrims were "innocent," but of what? Perceptiveness, perhaps.

Then, too, Twain could pose as the innocent Yank adrift in the capitals of high art and culture and do so for comic effect. In this he created a character—himself—who was the opposite of Henry James's Americans in Europe. And while the contrast was intended to be funny, he was also genuinely incapable of going into raptures over the dark smudges of Leonardo's "Last Supper" or galleries full of paintings of monks and martyrs gazing heavenward while being shot full of arrows.

*Roughing It* came next. It is a reminiscence of his travels in the west, to which was added his trip to Hawaii. Out west he was in his element; there was no need to pose as an outsider, for he was very much an insider in the mining camps of Nevada. The humor stems not from drawing contrasts between the old world and the new but from his own misadventures in trying to strike it rich and from the cast of odd and colorful characters who are there trying to do the same thing, and generally failing.

*A Tramp Abroad* takes him back to Europe, this time in company of his friend from Hartford, the Reverend Joseph Twichell, in the guise of "Harris," Twain's so-called agent. This book is a combination of the earlier two in its approach, because Twain returns to the device of contrasting his Yankee "innocence" against the high culture of Europe (as in his reactions to Wagner's music) and also acting as a character undergoing episodes of misadventure while interspersing the text with tall tales and reminiscences.

Then came *Life on the Mississippi.* By this time Twain was getting older, and revisiting the scenes of his boyhood and traveling the great river in a steamboat, just as he had for five years as a pilot before the Civil War, aroused his longing for the past. Being back on the eternal yet endlessly changing Mississippi was the stimulus he needed to carry on with what would become his greatest novel.

*Following the Equator* emerged after his round-the-world lecture tour undertaken to repair his disastrous financial condition. He wrote it with a heavy heart, just after his daughter Susy died at the age of twenty-four. The book is understandably more subdued in tone, although somehow he was able to inject some of his characteristic humor: "I wrote my last travel book in hell; but I let on, the best I could, that is was an excursion through heaven. Someday I will read it, and if its lying cheerfulness fools me, then I shall believe it fooled the reader."

Those five books were the sources for this volume. The object was to select pieces that highlight Twain's incomparable style and also reflect his views on the important matters of his day and ours—race, politics, morality, art and culture, religion, and the human condition in all its odd configurations. Written over time, in periods of success as well as travail and tragedy, and filtered through his multiple sensibilities and matchless eye and ear for humor and irony, these pieces display at least a portion of Mark Twain's fathomless genius.

# *A Note on the Edition*

The episodic nature of the books made it somewhat easier to select pieces and put them together into a structure of a kind. Geography is of course the most obvious way to organize something like this, but I also used a device that I hope Twain would have approved of—I started him in Hannibal, then headed him west and from there and sent him around the world as though the sections in the book were chapters in one great excursion. The idea was to fit these various pieces, written at various times, into something like a coherent whole. And within a few of the individual selections I cut some guidebook padding in order to keep the focus on the main story line. Here and there I added a footnote to clarify a situation or a reference that seemed to me obscure. And finally, very occasionally, I adjusted some of Twain's punctuation. (Twain's own footnotes are identified by "M.T.") He had a mild addiction to the semicolon, for example, and used it in places where modern readers are used to seeing commas.

In all of this I was keenly aware of the potential sin of lese majesty, but I believe the result is a fair presentation of Twain's travel writing at its best. That was the intention, certainly.

# Mark Twain on Travel

# Part One

## *Along the Big River*

*When I was younger I could remember anything, whether it had happened or not; but my faculties are decaying now and soon I shall be so I cannot remember any but the things that never happened. It is sad to go to pieces like this but we all have to do it.*

from *The Autobiography of Mark Twain*

# The Boys' Ambition

When I was a boy, there was but one permanent ambition among my comrades in our village on the west bank of the Mississippi River. That was, to be a steamboatman. We had transient ambitions of other sorts, but they were only transient.

When a circus came and went, it left us all burning to become clowns; the first Negro minstrel show that came to our section left us all suffering to try that kind of life; now and then we hoped that if we lived and were good, God would permit us to become pirates. These ambitions faded out, each in its turn; but the ambition to be a steamboatman always remained.

Once a day a cheap, gaudy packet arrived upward from St. Louis, and another downward from Keokuk. Before these events, the day was glorious with expectancy; after them, the day was a dead and empty thing. Not only the boys, but the whole village, felt this. After all these years I can picture that old time to myself now, just as it was then: the white town drowsing in the sunshine of a summer's morning; the streets empty, or pretty nearly so; one or two clerks sitting in front of the Water Street stores, with their splint-bottomed chairs tilted back against the wall, chins on their breasts, hats slouched over their faces, asleep—with shingle shavings enough around to show what broke them down; a sow and a litter of pigs loafing along the sidewalk, doing a good business in watermelon rinds and seeds; two or three lonely little freight piles scattered around the "levee"; a pile of "skids" on the slope of the stone-paved wharf, and the fragrant town drunkard asleep in the shadow of them; two or three wood flats at the head of the wharf, but nobody to listen to the peaceful lapping of the wavelets against them; the great Mississippi, the majestic, the magnificent Mississippi, rolling its mile-wide tide along, shining in the sun; the dense forest away on the other side; the "point" above the town, and the "point" below, bounding the river-glimpse and turning it into a sort of sea, and withal a very still and brilliant and lonely one. Presently a film of dark smoke appears above one of these remote "points"; instantly a Negro drayman, famous for his quick eye and prodigious voice, lifts up the cry, "S-t-e-a-m-boat a-comin'!"and the scene changes! The town drunkard stirs, the clerks wake up, a furious clatter of drays follows, every house and store pours out a human contribution, and all in a twinkling the dead town is alive and moving. Drays, carts, men, boys, all go hurrying from many quarters to a common center, the wharf. Assembled there, the people fasten their eyes upon the coming boat as upon a wonder they are seeing for the first time. And the boat *is* rather a handsome sight, too. She is long and sharp and trim and pretty; she has two tall, fancy-topped chimneys, with a gilded device of some kind swung between them; a fanciful pilothouse, all glass and "gingerbread," perched on top of the "texas" deck behind them; the paddle-boxes are gorgeous with a picture or with gilded rays above the boat's name; the boiler deck, the hurricane deck, and the texas deck are fenced and ornamented with clean white railings; there is a flag gallantly flying from the jack-staff; the furnace doors are open and the fires glaring bravely; the upper decks are black with passengers; the captain stands by the big bell, calm, imposing, the envy of all; great volumes of the blackest smoke are rolling and tumbling out of the chimneys—a husbanded grandeur created with a bit of pitch pine just before arriving at a town; the crew are grouped on the forecastle; the broad stage is run far out over the port bow, and an envied deck hand stands picturesquely on the end of it with a coil of rope in his hand; the pent steam is screaming through the gauge cocks; the captain lifts his hand, a bell rings, the wheels stop; then they turn back, churning the water to foam, and the steamer is at rest. Then such a scramble as there is to get aboard, and to get ashore, and to take in freight and to discharge freight, all at one and the same time; and such a yelling and cursing as the mates facilitate it all with! Ten minutes later the steamer is under way again, with no flag on the jack-staff and no black smoke issuing from the chimneys. After ten more minutes the town is dead again, and the town drunkard asleep by the skids once more.

My father was a justice of the peace, and I supposed he possessed the power of life and death over all men and could hang anybody that offended him. This was distinction enough for me as a general thing; but the desire to be a steamboatman kept intruding, nevertheless. I first wanted to be a cabin boy, so that I could come out with a white apron on and shake a tablecloth over the side, where all my old comrades could see me; later I thought I would rather be the deck hand who stood on the end of the stage plank with the coil of rope in his hand, because he was particularly conspicuous. But these were only daydreams—they were too heavenly to be contemplated as real possibilities. By and by one of our boys went away. He was not heard of for a long time. At last he turned up as apprentice engineer or "striker" on a steamboat. This thing shook the bottom out of all my Sunday-school teachings. That boy had been notoriously worldly, and I just the reverse; yet he was exalted to this eminence, and I left in obscurity and misery. There was nothing generous about this fellow in his greatness. He would always manage to have a rusty bolt to scrub while his boat tarried at our town, and he would sit on the inside guard and scrub it, where we could all see him and envy him and loathe him. And whenever his boat was laid up he would come home and swell around the town in his blackest and greasiest clothes, so that nobody could help remembering that he was a steamboatman; and he used all sorts of steamboat technicalities in his talk, as if he were so used to them that he forgot common people could not understand them. He would speak of the "labboard" side of a horse in an easy, natural way that would make one wish he was dead. And he was always talking about "St. Looy" like an old citizen; he would refer casually to occasions when he "was coming down Fourth Street," or when he was "passing by the Planter's House," or when there was a fire and he took a turn on the brakes of "the old Big Missouri"; and then he would go and lie about how many towns the size of ours were burned down there that day. Two or three of the boys had long been persons of consideration among us because they had been to St. Louis once and had a vague general knowledge of its wonders, but the day of their glory was over now. They lapsed into humble silence, and learned to disappear when the ruthless "cub" engineer approached. This fellow had money, too, and hair oil. Also an ignorant silver watch and a showy brass watch chain. He wore a leather belt and used no suspenders. If ever a youth was cordially admired and hated by his comrades, this one was. No girl could withstand his charms. He "cut out" every boy in the village. When his boat blew up at last, it diffused a tranquil contentment among us such as we had not known for months. But when he came home the next week, alive, renowned, and appeared in church all battered up and bandaged, a shining hero, stared at and wondered over by everybody, it seemed to us that the partiality of Providence for an undeserving reptile had reached a point where it was open to criticism.

This creature's career could produce but one result, and it speedily followed. Boy after boy managed to get on the river. The minister's son became an engineer. The doctor's and the postmaster's sons became "mud clerks"; the wholesale liquor dealer's son became a barkeeper on a boat; four sons of the chief merchant, and two sons of the county judge, became pilots. Pilot was the grandest position of all. The pilot, even in those days of trivial wages, had a princely salary—from a hundred and fifty to two hundred and fifty dollars a month, and no board to pay. Two months of his wages would pay a preacher's salary for a year. Now some of us were left disconsolate. We could not get on the river—at least our parents would not let us.

So by and by I ran away. I said I never would come home again till I was a pilot and could come in glory. But somehow I could not manage it. I went meekly aboard a few of the boats that lay packed together like sardines at the long St. Louis wharf, and very humbly inquired for the pilots, but got only a cold shoulder and short words from mates and clerks. I had to make the best of this treatment for the time being, but I had comforting daydreams of a future when I should be a great and honored pilot, with plenty of money, and could kill some of these mates and clerks and pay for them.

* * *

Months afterward the hope within me struggled to a reluctant death, and I found myself without an ambition. But I was ashamed to go home. I was in Cincinnati, and I set to work to map out a new career. I had been reading about the recent exploration of the River Amazon by an expedition sent out by our government. It was said that the expedition, owing to difficulties, had not thoroughly explored a part of the country lying about the headwaters, some four thousand miles from the mouth of the river. It was only about fifteen hundred miles from Cincinnati to New Orleans, where I could doubtless get a ship. I had thirty dollars left; I would go and complete the exploration of the Amazon. This was all the thought I gave to the subject. I never was great in matters of detail. I packed my valise and took passage on an ancient tub called the *Paul Jones,* for New Orleans. For the sum of sixteen dollars I had the scarred and tarnished splendors of "her" main saloon principally to myself, for she was not a creature to attract the eye of wiser travelers.

When we presently got under way and went poking down the broad Ohio, I became a new being, and the subject of my own admiration. I was a traveler! A word had never tasted so good in my mouth before. I had an exultant sense of being bound for mysterious lands and distant climes which I never have felt in so uplifting a degree since. I was in such a glorified condition that all ignoble feelings departed out of me, and I was able to look down and pity the untraveled with a compassion that had hardly a trace of contempt in it. Still, when we stopped at villages and woodyards, I could not help lolling carelessly upon the railings of the boiler deck to enjoy the envy of the country boys on the bank. If they did not seem to discover me, I presently sneezed to attract their attention, or moved to a position where they could not help seeing me. And as soon as I knew they saw me I gaped and stretched, and gave other signs of being mightily bored with traveling.

I kept my hat off all the time, and stayed where the wind and sun could strike me, because I wanted to get the bronzed and weatherbeaten look of an old traveler. Before the second day was half-gone, I experienced a joy which filled me with the purest gratitude; for I saw that the skin had begun to blister and peel off my face and neck. I wished that the boys and girls at home could see me now.

We reached Louisville in time—at least the neighborhood of it. We stuck hard and fast on the rocks in the middle of the river, and lay there four days. I was now beginning to feel a strong sense of being a part of the boat's family, a sort of infant son to the captain and younger brother to the officers. There is no estimating the pride I took in this grandeur, or the affection that began to swell and grow in me for those people. I could not know how the lordly steamboatman scorns that sort of presumption in a mere landsman. I particularly longed to acquire the least trifle of notice from the big stormy mate, and I was on the alert for an opportunity to do him a service to that end. It came at last. The riotous powwow of setting a spar was going on down on the forecastle, and I went down there and stood around in the way—or mostly skipping out of it—till the mate suddenly roared a general order for somebody to bring him a capstan bar. I sprang to his side and said: "Tell me where it is—I'll fetch it!"

If a ragpicker had offered to do a diplomatic service for the Emperor of Russia, the monarch could not have been more astounded than the mate was. He even stopped swearing. He stood and stared down at me. It took him ten seconds to scrape his disjointed remains together again. Then he said impressively: "Well, if this don't beat hell!" and turned to his work with the air of a man who had been confronted with a problem too abstruse for solution.

I crept away, and courted solitude for the rest of the day. I did not go to dinner; I stayed away from supper until everybody else had finished. I did not feel so much like a member of the boat's family now as before. However, my spirits returned, in installments, as we pursued our way down the river. I was sorry I hated the mate so, because it was not in (young) human nature not to admire him. He was huge and muscular, his face was bearded and whiskered all over; he had a red woman and a blue woman tattooed on his right arm—one on each side of a blue anchor with a red rope to it; and in the matter of profanity he was sublime. When he was getting out cargo at a landing, I was always where I could see and hear. He felt all the majesty of his great position, and made the world feel it, too. When he gave even the simplest order, he discharged it like a blast of lightning, and sent a long, reverberating peal of profanity thundering after it. I could not help contrasting the way in which the average landsman would give an order with the mate's way of doing it. If the landsman should wish the gangplank moved a foot farther forward, he would probably say: "James, or William, one of you push that plank forward, please"; but put the mate in his place, and he would roar out: "Here, now, start that gangplank for'ard! Lively, now! *What*'re you about!

Snatch it! *Snatch* it! There! There! Aft again! Aft again! Don't you hear me? Dash it to dash! Are you going to *sleep* over it! '*Vast* heaving! 'Vast heaving, I tell you! Going to heave it clear astern? Where're you going with that barrel! *For-ard* with it 'fore I make you swallow it, you dash-dash-dash-*dashed* split between a tired mud turtle and a crippled hearse horse!"

I wished I could talk like that.

When the soreness of my adventure with the mate had somewhat worn off, I began timidly to make up to the humblest official connected with the boat—the night watchman. He snubbed my advances at first, but I presently ventured to offer him a new chalk pipe, and that softened him. So he allowed me to sit with him by the big bell on the hurricane deck, and in time he melted into conversation. He could not well have helped it; I hung with such homage on his words and so plainly showed that I felt honored by his notice. He told me the names of dim capes and shadowy islands as we glided by them in the solemnity of the night, under the winking stars, and by and by got to talking about himself. He seemed oversentimental for a man whose salary was six dollars a week—or rather he might have seemed so to an older person than I. But I drank in his words hungrily, and with a faith that might have moved mountains if it had been applied judiciously. What was it to me that he was soiled and seedy and fragrant with gin? What was it to me that his grammar was bad, his construction worse, and his profanity so void of art that it was an element of weakness rather than strength in his conversation? He was a wronged man, a man who had seen trouble, and that was enough for me. As he mellowed into his plaintive history his tears dripped upon the lantern in his lap, and I cried, too, from sympathy. He said he was the son of an English nobleman—either an earl or an alderman, he could not remember which, but believed was both; his father, the nobleman, loved him, but his mother hated him from the cradle; and so while he was still a little boy he was sent to "one of them old, ancient colleges"—he couldn't remember which; and by and by his father died and his mother seized the property and "shook" him, as he phrased it. After his mother shook him, members of the nobility with whom he was acquainted used their influence to get him the position of "lob-lolly-boy in a ship"; and from that point on my watchman threw off all trammels of date and locality and branched out into a narrative that bristled all along with incredible adventures; a narrative that was so reeking with bloodshed and so crammed with hairbreadth escapes and the most engaging and unconscious personal villainies, that I sat speechless, enjoying, shuddering, wondering, worshiping.

It was a sore blight to find out afterward that he was a low, vulgar, ignorant, sentimental, half-witted humbug, an untraveled native of the wilds of Illinois, who had absorbed wildcat literature and appropriated its marvels, until in time he had woven odds and ends of the mess into this yarn, and then gone on telling it to fledglings like me, until he had come to believe it himself.

# A Pilot's Needs

But I am wandering from what I was intending to do, that is, make plainer than perhaps appears in the previous chapters some of the peculiar requirements of the science of piloting. First of all, there is one faculty which a pilot must incessantly cultivate until he has brought it to absolute perfection. Nothing short of perfection will do. That faculty is memory. He cannot stop with merely thinking a thing is so and so; he must *know* it, for this is eminently one of the "exact" sciences. With what scorn a pilot was looked upon, in the old times, if he ever ventured to deal in that feeble phrase "I think," instead of the vigorous one "I know!" One cannot easily realize what tremendous thing it is to know every trivial detail of twelve hundred miles of river and know it with absolute exactness. If you will take the longest street in New York, and travel up and down it, conning its features patiently until you know every house and window and door and lamppost and big and little sign by heart, and know them so accurately that you can instantly name the one you are abreast of when you are set down at random in that street in the middle of an inky black night, you will then have a tolerable notion of the amount and the exactness of a pilot's knowledge who carries the Mississippi River in his head. And then if you will go on until you know every street crossing, the character, size, and position of the crossing stones, and the varying depth of mud in each of those numberless places, you will have some idea of what the pilot must know in order to keep a Mississippi steamer out of trouble. Next, if you will take half of the signs in that long street, and *change their places* once a month, and still manage to know their new positions accurately on dark nights, and keep up with these repeated changes without making any mistakes, you will understand what is required of a pilot's peerless memory by the fickle Mississippi.

I think a pilot's memory is about the most wonderful thing in the world. To know the Old and New Testaments by heart, and be able to recite them glibly, forward or backward, or begin at random anywhere in the book and recite both ways and never trip or make a mistake, is no extravagant mass of knowledge, and no marvelous facility, compared to a pilot's massed knowledge of the Mississippi and his marvelous facility in the handling of it. I make this comparison deliberately, and believe I am not expanding the truth when I do it. Many will think my figure too strong, but pilots will not.

And how easily and comfortably the pilot's memory does its work; how placidly effortless is its way; how *unconsciously* it lays up its vast stores, hour by hour, day by day, and never loses or mislays a single valuable package of them all! Take an instance. Let a leadsman cry, "Half twain! Half twain! Half twain! Half twain! Half twain!" until it becomes as monotonous as the ticking of a clock; let conversation be going on all the time, and the pilot be doing his share of the talking, and no longer consciously listening to the leadsman; and in the midst of this endless string of half twains let a single "quarter twain!" be interjected, without emphasis, and then the half twain cry go on again, just as before; two or three weeks later that pilot can describe with precision the boat's position in the river when that quarter twain was uttered, and give you such a lot of head-marks, stern-marks, and side-marks to guide you, that you ought to be able to take the boat there and put her in that same spot again yourself! The cry of "quarter twain" did not really take his mind from his talk, but his trained faculties instantly photographed the bearings, noted the change of depth, and laid up the important details for future reference without requiring any assistance from *him* in the matter. If you were walking and talking with a friend, and another friend at your side kept up a monotonous repetition of the vowel sound A, for a couple of blocks, and then in the midst interjected an R, thus, A, A, A, A, A, R, A, A, A, etc., and gave the R no emphasis, you would not be able to state, two or three weeks afterward, that the R had been put in, nor be able to tell what objects you were passing at the moment it was done. But you could if your memory had been patiently and laboriously trained to do that sort of thing mechanically.

Give a man a tolerably fair memory to start with, and piloting will develop it into a very colossus of capability. But *only in the matters it is daily drilled in*. A time would come when the man's faculties could not help noticing landmarks and soundings, and his memory could not help holding on to them with the grip of a vise; but if you asked that same man at noon what he had had for breakfast, it would be ten chances to one that he could not tell you. Astonishing things can be done with the human memory if you will devote it faithfully to one particular line of business.

At the time that wages soared so high on the Missouri River, my chief, Mr. Bixby, went up there and learned more than a thousand miles of that stream with an ease and a rapidity that were astonishing. When he had seen each division *once* in the daytime and *once* at night, his education was so nearly complete that he took out a "daylight" license; a few trips later he took out a full license, and went to piloting day and night—and he ranked A-1, too.

Mr. Bixby placed me as a steersman for a while under a pilot whose feats of memory were a constant marvel to me. However, his memory was born in him, I think, not built. For instance, somebody would mention a name. Instantly Mr. Brown would break in:

"Oh, I knew *him*. Sallow-faced, red-headed fellow, with a little scar on the side of his throat, like a splinter under the flesh. He was only in the Southern trade six months. That was thirteen years ago. I made a trip with him. There was five feet in the upper river then; the *Henry Blake* grounded at the foot of Tower Island drawing four and a half; the *George Elliott* unshipped her rudder on the wreck of the *Sunflower*—"

"Why, the *Sunflower* didn't sink until—"

"*I* know when she sunk; it was three years before that, on the 2nd of December; Asa Hardy was captain of her, and his brother John was first clerk; and it was his first trip in her, too; Tom Jones told me these things a week afterward in New Orleans; he was first mate of the *Sunflower.* Captain Hardy stuck a nail in his foot the 6th of July of the next year, and died of lockjaw on the 15th. His brother John died two years after—3rd of March—erysipelas. I never saw either of the Hardys—they were Alleghany River men—but people who knew them told me all these things. And they said Captain Hardy wore yarn socks winter and summer just the same, and his first wife's name was Jane Shook—she was from New England—and his second one died in a lunatic asylum. It was in the blood. She was from Lexington, Kentucky. Name was Horton before she was married."

And so on, by the hour, the man's tongue would go. He could *not* forget anything. It was simply impossible. The most trivial details remained as distinct and luminous in his head, after they had lain there for years, as the most memorable events. His was not simply a pilot's memory; its grasp was universal. If he were talking about a trifling letter he had received seven years before, he was pretty sure to deliver you the entire screed from memory. And then without observing that he was departing from the true line of his talk, he was more than likely to hurl in a long-drawn parenthetical biography of the writer of that letter; and you were lucky indeed if he did not take up that writer's relatives, one by one, and give you their biographies, too.

Such a memory as that is a great misfortune. To it, all occurrences are of the same size. Its possessor cannot distinguish an interesting circumstance from an uninteresting one. As a talker, he is bound to clog his narrative with tiresome details and make himself an insufferable bore. Moreover, he cannot stick to his subject. He picks up every little grain of memory he discerns in his way, and so is led aside. Mr. Brown would start out with the honest intention of telling you a vastly funny anecdote about a dog. He would be "so full of laugh" that he could hardly begin; then his memory would start with the dog's breed and personal appearance; drift into a history of his owner; of his owner's family, with descriptions of weddings and burials that had occurred in it, together with recitals of congratulatory verses and obituary poetry provoked by the same; then this memory would recollect that one of these events occurred during the celebrated "hard winter" of such and such a year, and a minute description of that winter would follow, along with the names of people who were frozen to death, and statistics showing the high figures which pork and hay went up to. Pork and hay would suggest corn and fodder; corn and fodder would suggest cows and horses; cows and horses would suggest the circus and certain celebrated bareback riders; the transition from the circus to the menagerie was easy and natural; from the elephant to equatorial Africa was but a step; then of course the heathen savages would suggest religion; and at the end of three or four hours, tedious jaw, the watch would change, and Brown would go out of the pilot-house muttering extracts from sermons he had heard years before about the efficacy of prayer as a means of grace. And the original first mention would be all you had learned about that dog, after all this waiting and hungering.

A pilot must have a memory; but there are two higher qualities which he must also have. He must have good and quick judgment and decision, and a cool, calm courage that no peril can shake. Give a man the merest trifle of pluck to start with, and by the time he has become a pilot he cannot be unmanned by any danger a steamboat can get into; but one cannot say the same about judgment. Judgment is a matter of brains, and a man must *start* with a good stock of that article or he will never succeed as a pilot.

The growth of courage in the pilothouse is steady all the time, but it does not reach a high and satisfactory condition until some time after the young pilot has been "standing his own watch," alone and under the staggering weight of all the responsibilities connected with the position. When an apprentice has become pretty thoroughly acquainted with the river, he goes clattering along so fearlessly with his steamboat, night or day, that he presently begins to imagine that it is *his* courage that animates him; but the first time the pilot steps out and leaves him to his own devices he finds out it was the other man's. He discovers that the article has been left out of his own cargo altogether. The whole river is bristling with exigencies in a moment; he is not prepared for them; he does not know how to meet them; all his knowledge forsakes him; and within fifteen minutes he is as white as a sheet and scared almost to death. Therefore pilots wisely train these cubs by various strategic tricks to look danger in the face a little more calmly. A favorite way of theirs is to play a friendly swindle upon the candidate.

Mr. Bixby served me in this fashion once, and for years afterward I used to blush even in my sleep when I thought of it. I had become a good steersman; so good, indeed, that I had all the work to do on our watch, night and day; Mr. Bixby seldom made a suggestion to me; all he ever did was to take the wheel on particularly bad nights or in particularly bad crossings, land the boat when she needed to be landed, play gentleman of leisure nine-tenths of the watch, and collect the wages. The lower river was about bank full, and if anybody had questioned my ability to run any crossing between Cairo and New Orleans without help or instruction, I should have felt irreparably hurt. The idea of being afraid of any crossing in the lot, in the *daytime*, was a thing too preposterous for contemplation. Well, one matchless summer's day I was bowling down the bend above island 66, brimful of self-conceit and carrying my nose as high as a giraffe's, when Mr. Bixby said—

"I am going below a while. I suppose you know the next crossing?"

This was almost an affront. It was about the plainest and simplest crossing in the whole river. One couldn't come to any harm, whether he ran it right or not; and as for depth, there never had been any bottom there. I knew all this, perfectly well.

"Know how to *run* it? Why, I can run it with my eyes shut."

"How much water is there in it?"

"Well, that is an odd question. I couldn't get a bottom there with a church steeple."

"You think so, do you?"

The very tone of the question shook my confidence. That was what Mr. Bixby was expecting. He left, without saying anything more. I began to imagine all sorts of things. Mr. Bixby, unknown to me, of course, sent somebody down to the forecastle with some mysterious instruction to the leadsmen, another messenger was sent to whisper among the officers, and then Mr. Bixby went into hiding behind a smokestack where he could observe results. Presently the captain stepped out on the hurricane deck; next the chief mate appeared; then a clerk. Every moment or two a straggler was added to my audience; and before I got to the head of the island I had fifteen or twenty people assembled down there under my nose. I began to wonder what the trouble was. As I started across, the captain glanced aloft at me and said with a sham uneasiness in his voice—

"Where is Mr. Bixby?"

"Gone below, sir."

But that did the business for me. My imagination began to construct dangers out of nothing, and they multiplied faster than I could keep the run of them. All at once I imagined I saw shoal water ahead! The wave of coward agony that surged through me then came near dislocating every joint in me. All my confidence in that crossing vanished. I seized the bell rope; dropped it, ashamed; seized it again; dropped it once more; clutched it tremblingly once again, and pulled it so feebly that I could hardly hear the stroke myself. Captain and mate sang out instantly, and both together—

"Starboard lead there! And quick about it!"

This was another shock. I began to climb the wheel like a squirrel; but I would hardly get the boat started to port before I would see new dangers on that side, and away I would spin to the other; only to find perils accumulating to starboard, and be crazy to get to port again. Then came the leadsman's sepulchral cry:

"D-e-e-p four!"

Deep four in a bottomless crossing! The terror of it took my breath away.

"M-a-r-k three! . . . M-a-r-k three . . . Quarter less three! . . . Half twain!"

This was frightful! I seized the bell ropes and stopped the engines.

"Quarter twain! Quarter twain! *Mark* twain!"

I was helpless. I did not know what in the world to do. I was quaking from head to foot, and I could have hung my hat on my eyes, they stuck out so far.

"Quarter *less* twain! Nine and a *half*!"

We were *drawing* nine! My hands were in a nervous flutter. I could not ring a bell intelligibly with them. I flew to the speaking tube and shouted to the engineer—

"Oh, Ben, if you love me, *back* her! Quick, Ben! Oh, back the immortal *soul* out of her!"

I heard the door close gently. I looked around, and there stood Mr. Bixby, smiling a bland, sweet smile. Then the audience on the hurricane deck sent up a thundergust of humiliating laughter. I saw it all, now, and I felt meaner than the meanest man in human history. I laid in the lead, set the boat in her marks, came ahead on the engines, and said:

"It was a fine trick to play on an orphan, *wasn't* it? I suppose I'll never hear the last of how I was ass enough to heave the lead at the head of 66."

"Well, no, you won't, maybe. In fact I hope you won't; for I want you to learn something by that experience. Didn't you *know* there was no bottom in that crossing?"

"Yes, sir, I did."

"Very well, then. You shouldn't have allowed me or anybody else to shake your confidence in that knowledge. Try to remember that. And another thing: when you get into a dangerous place, don't turn coward. That isn't going to help matters any."

It was a good enough lesson, but pretty hardly learned. Yet about the hardest part of it was that for months I so often had to hear a phrase which I had conceived a particular distaste for. It was, "Oh, Ben, if you love me, back her!"

# The First "Mark Twain"

We had some talk about Captain Isaiah Sellers, now many years dead. He was a fine man, a high-minded man, and greatly respected both ashore and on the river. He was very tall, well built, and handsome; and in his old age—as I remember him—his hair was as black as an Indian's, and his eye and hand were as strong and steady and his nerve and judgment as firm and clear as anybody's, young or old, among the fraternity of pilots. He was the patriarch of the craft; he had been a keelboat pilot before the day of steamboats; and a steamboat pilot before any other steamboat pilot, still surviving at the time I speak of, had ever turned a wheel. Consequently his brethren held him in the sort of awe which illustrious survivors of a bygone age are always held by their associates. He knew how he was regarded, and perhaps this fact added some trifle of stiffening to his natural dignity, which had been sufficiently stiff in its original state.

* * *

Whenever Captain Sellers approached a body of gossiping pilots, a chill fell there, and talking ceased. For this reason: whenever six pilots were gathered together, there would always be one or two newly fledged ones in the lot, and the elder ones would always be "showing off" before these poor fellows; making them sorrowfully feel how callow they were, how recent their nobility, how humble their degree, by talking largely and vaporously of old-time experiences on the river; always making it a point to date everything back as far as they could, so as to make the new men feel their newness to the sharpest degree possible, and envy the old stagers in the like degree. And how these complacent baldheads *would* swell, and brag, and lie, and date back—ten, fifteen, twenty years—and how they did enjoy the effect produced upon the marveling and envying youngsters!

And perhaps just at this happy stage of the proceedings, the stately figure of Captain Isaiah Sellers, that real and only genuine Son of Antiquity, would drift solemnly into the midst. Imagine the size of the silence that would result on the instant. And imagine the feelings of those baldheads, and the exultation of their recent audience when the ancient captain would begin to drop casual and indifferent remarks of a reminiscent nature—about islands that had disappeared, and cutoffs that had been made, a generation before the oldest baldhead in the company had ever set foot in a pilothouse!

Many and many a time did this ancient mariner appear on the scene in the above fashion, and spread disaster and humiliation around him. If one might believe the pilots, he always dated his islands back to the misty dawn of river history; and he never used the same island twice; and never did he employ an island that still existed, or give one a name which anybody present was old enough to have heard of before. If you might believe the pilots, he was always conscientiously particular about little details; never spoke of "the State of Mississippi," for instance—no, he would say, "When the State of Mississippi was where Arkansas now is"; and would never speak of Louisiana or Missouri in a general way, and leave an incorrect impression on your mind—no, he would say, "When Louisiana was up the river farther," or, "When Missouri was on the Illinois side."

The old gentleman was not of literary turn or capacity, but he used to jot down brief paragraphs of plain practical information about the river, and sign them "Mark Twain," and give them to the New Orleans *Picayune*. They related to the stage and condition of the river, and were accurate and valuable; and thus far, they contained no poison. But in speaking of the stage of the river today, at a given point, the captain was pretty apt to drop in a little remark about this being the first time he had seen the water so high or so low at that particular point for forty-nine years; and now and then he would mention Island so and so, and follow it, in parentheses, with some such observation as "disappeared in 1807, if I remember rightly." In these antique interjections lay poison and bitterness for the other old pilots, and they used to chaff the "Mark Twain" paragraphs with unsparing mockery.

It so chanced that one of these paragraphs became the text for my first newspaper article. I burlesqued it broadly, very broadly, stringing my fantastics out to the extent of eight hundred or a thousand words. I was a "cub" at the time. I showed my performance to some pilots, and they eagerly rushed it into print in the New Orleans *True Delta*. It was a great pity; for it did nobody any worthy service, and it sent a pang deep into a good man's heart. There was no malice in my rubbish; but it laughed at the captain. It laughed at a man to whom such a thing was new and strange and dreadful. I did not know then, though I do now, that there is no suffering comparable with that which a private person feels when he is for the first time pilloried in print.

Captain Sellers did me the honor to profoundly detest me from that day forth. When I say he did me the honor, I am not using empty words. It was a very real honor to be in the thoughts of so great a man as Captain Sellers, and I had wit enough to appreciate it and be proud of it. It was a distinction to be loved by such a man; but it was a much greater distinction to be hated by him, because he loved scores of people; but he didn't sit up nights to hate anybody but me.

He never printed another paragraph while he lived, and he never again signed "Mark Twain" to anything. At the time the telegraph brought the news of his death, I was on the Pacific coast. I was a fresh new journalist, and needed a *nom de guerre*; so I confiscated the ancient mariner's discarded one, and have done my best to make it remain what it was in his hands—a sign and symbol and warrant that whatever is found in its company may be gambled on as being the petrified truth; how I have succeeded, it would not be modest in me to say.

# Part Two

## *Out West*

*And it was comfort in those succeeding days to sit up and contemplate the majestic panorama of mountains and valleys spread out below us and eat ham and hard-boiled eggs while our spiritual natures reveled alternatively in rainbows, thunderstorms, and peerless sunsets. Nothing helps scenery like ham and eggs. Ham and eggs, and after these a pipe—an old, rank, delicious pipe—ham and eggs and scenery, a "downgrade," a flying coach, a fragrant pipe and a contented heart—these make happiness. It is what all the ages have struggled for.*

from *Roughing It*

# Stage Coaching

My brother had just been appointed Secretary of Nevada Territory—an office of such majesty that it concentrated in itself the duties and dignities of Treasurer, Comptroller, Secretary of State, and Acting Governor in the Governor's absence. A salary of eighteen hundred dollars a year and the title of "Mr. Secretary" gave to the great position an air of wild and imposing grandeur. I was young and ignorant, and I envied my brother. I coveted his distinction and his financial splendor, but particularly and especially the long, strange journey he was going to make, and the curious new world he was going to explore. He was going to travel! I never had been away from home, and that word "travel" had a seductive charm for me.[1] Pretty soon he would be hundreds and hundreds of miles away on the great plains and deserts, and among the mountains of the Far West, and would see buffaloes and Indians, and prairie dogs, and antelopes, and have all kinds of adventures, and maybe get hanged or scalped, and have ever such a fine time, and write home and tell us all about it, and be a hero. And he would see the

[1] One of MT's " stretchers." He had been a steamboat pilot and, briefly, a Confederate soldier by the time of his brother's appointment.

gold mines and the silver mines, and maybe go about of an afternoon when his work was done, and pick up two or three pailfuls of shining slugs, and nuggets of gold and silver on the hillside. And by and by he would become very rich, and return home by sea, and be able to talk to talk as calmly about San Francisco and the ocean and "the isthmus" as if it was nothing of any consequence to have seen those marvels face to face. What I suffered in contemplating his happiness, pen cannot describe. And so, when he offered me, in cold blood, the sublime position of private secretary under him, it appeared to me that the heavens and the earth passed away, and the firmament was rolled together as a scroll! I had nothing more to desire. My contentment was complete. At the end of an hour or two I was ready for the journey. Not much packing up was necessary, because we were going in the overland stage from the Missouri frontier to Nevada, and passengers were only allowed a small quantity of baggage apiece. There was no Pacific railroad in those fine times of ten or twelve years ago—not a single rail of it.

I only proposed to stay in Nevada three months—I had not thought of staying longer than that. I meant to see all I could that was new and strange, and then hurry home to business. I little thought that I would not see the end of that three-month pleasure excursion for six or seven uncommonly long years!

I dreamed all night about Indians, deserts, and silver bars, and in due time, next day, we took shipping at the St. Louis wharf on board a steamboat bound up the Missouri River.

We were six days going from St. Louis to " St. Jo."—a trip that was so dull, and sleepy, and eventless that it has left no more impression on my memory than if its duration had been six minutes instead of that many days. No record is left in my mind, now, concerning it, but a confused jumble of savage-looking snags, which we deliberately walked over with one wheel or the other; and of reefs which we butted and butted, and then retired from and climbed over in some softer place; and of sandbars which we roosted on occasionally, and rested, and then got out our crutches and sparred over. In fact, the boat might almost as well have gone to St. Jo. by land, for she was walking most of the time, anyhow—climbing over reefs and clambering over snags patiently and laboriously all day long. The captain said she was a " bully" boat, and all she wanted was more "shear" and a bigger wheel. I thought she wanted a pair of stilts, but I had the deep sagacity not to say so.

* * *

The first thing we did on that glad evening that landed us at St. Joseph was to hunt up the stage-office, and pay a hundred and fifty dollars apiece for tickets per overland coach to Carson City, Nevada.

The next morning, bright and early, we took a hasty breakfast, and hurried to the starting-place. Then an inconvenience presented itself which we had not properly appreciated before, namely, that one cannot make a heavy traveling trunk stand for twenty-five pounds of baggage—because it weighs a good deal more. But that was all we could take—twenty-five pounds each. So we had to snatch our trunks open, and make a selection in a good deal of a hurry. We put our lawful twenty-five pounds apiece all in one valise, and shipped the trunks back to St. Louis again. It was a sad parting, for now we had no swallow-tail coats and white kid gloves to wear at Pawnee receptions in the Rocky Mountains, and no stovepipe hats nor patent-leather boots, nor anything else to make life calm and peaceful. We were reduced to a war-footing. Each of us put on a rough, heavy suit of clothing, woolen army shirt and "stogy" boots included; and into the valise we crowded a few white shirts, some under-clothing and such things. My brother, the Secretary, took along about four pounds of United States statutes and six pounds of Unabridged Dictionary; for we did not know—poor innocents—that such things could be bought in San Francisco on one day and received in Carson City the next. I was armed to the teeth with a pitiful little Smith & Wesson seven-shooter, which carried a ball like a homeopathic pill, and it took the whole seven to make a dose for an adult. But I thought it was grand. It appeared to me to be a dangerous weapon. It only had one fault—you could not hit anything with it. One of our "conductors" practiced awhile on a cow with it, and as long as she stood still and behaved herself she was safe; but as soon as she went to moving about, and he got to shooting at other things, she came to grief. The Secretary had a small-sized Colt's revolver strapped around him for protection against the Indians, and to guard against accidents he kept it uncapped. Mr. George Bemis was dismally formidable. George Bemis was our fellow-traveler. We had never seen him before. He wore in his belt an old original "Allen" revolver, such as irreverent people call a "pepperbox." Simply drawing the trigger back, cocked and fired the pistol. As the trigger came back, the hammer would begin to rise and the barrel to turn over, and presently down would drop the hammer, and away would speed the ball. To aim along the turning barrel and hit the thing aimed at was a feat which was probably never done with an "Allen" in the world. But George's was a reliable weapon, nevertheless, because, as one of the stage-drivers afterward said, "If she didn't get what she went after, she would fetch something else." And so she did. She went after a deuce of spades nailed against a tree, once, and fetched a mule standing about thirty yards to the left of it. Bemis did not want the mule; but the owner came out with a double-barreled shotgun and persuaded him to buy it, anyhow. It was a cheerful weapon—the "Allen." Sometimes all six barrels would go off at once, and then there was no safe place in all the region round about, but behind it.

We took two or three blankets for protection against frosty weather in the mountains. In the matter of luxuries we were modest—we took none along but some pipes and five pounds of smoking tobacco. We had two large canteens to carry water in, between stations on the Plains, and we also took with us a little shot-bag of silver coin for daily expenses in the way of breakfasts and dinners.

By eight o'clock everything was ready, and we were on the other side of the river. We jumped into the stage, the driver cracked his whip, and we bowled away and left "the States" behind us. It was a superb summer morning, and all the landscape was brilliant with sunshine. There was a freshness and breeziness, too, and an exhilarating sense of emancipation from all sorts of cares and responsibilities, that almost made us feel that the years we had spent in the close, hot city, toiling and slaving, had been wasted and thrown away. We were spinning along through Kansas, and in the course of an hour and a half we were fairly abroad on the great Plains. Just here the land was rolling—a grand sweep of regular elevations and depressions as far as the eye could reach—like the stately heave and swell of the ocean's bosom after a storm. And everywhere were cornfields, accenting with squares of deeper green, this limitless expanse of grassy land. But presently this sea upon dry ground was to lose its "rolling" character and stretch away for seven hundred miles as level as a floor!

Our coach was a great swinging and swaying stage, of the most sumptuous description—an imposing cradle on wheels. It was drawn by six handsome horses, and by the side of the driver sat the "conductor," the legitimate captain of the craft; for it was his business to take charge and care of the mails, baggage, express matter, and passengers. We three were the only passengers, this trip. We sat on the back seat, inside. About all the rest of the coach was full of mailbags—for we had three days' delayed mails with us. Almost touching our knees, a perpendicular wall of mail matter rose up to the roof. There was a great pile of it strapped on top of the stage, and both the fore and hind boots were full. We had twenty-seven hundred pounds of it aboard, the driver said—"a little for Brigham, and Carson, and 'Frisco, but the heft of it for the Injuns, which is powerful troublesome 'thout they get plenty of truck to read." But as he just then got up a fearful convulsion of his countenance which was suggestive of a wink being swallowed by an earthquake, we guessed that his remark was intended to be facetious, and to mean that we would unload the most of our mail matter somewhere on the Plains and leave it to the Indians, or whosoever wanted it.

We changed horses every ten miles, all day long, and fairly flew over the hard, level road. We jumped out and stretched our legs every time the coach stopped, and so the night found us still vivacious and unfatigued.

* * *

About an hour and a half before daylight we were bowling along smoothly over the road—so smoothly that our cradle only rocked in a gentle, lulling way, that was gradually soothing us to sleep, and dulling our consciousness—when something gave way under us! We were dimly aware of it, but indifferent to it. The coach stopped. We heard the driver and conductor talking together outside, and rummaging for a lantern, and swearing because they could not find it—but we had no interest in whatever had happened, and it only added to our comfort to think of those people out there at work in the murky night, and we snug in our nest with the curtains drawn. But presently, by the sounds, there seemed to be an examination going on, and then the driver's voice said:

"By George, the thoroughbrace is broke!"

This startled me broad awake—as an undefined sense of calamity is always apt to do. I said to myself: "Now, a thoroughbrace is probably part of a horse; and doubtless a vital part, too, from the dismay in the driver's voice. Leg, maybe—and yet how could he break his leg waltzing along such a road as this? No, it can't be his leg. That is impossible, unless he was reaching for the driver. Now, what can be the thoroughbrace of a horse, I wonder? Well, whatever comes, I shall not air my ignorance in this crowd, anyway."

Just then the conductor's face appeared at a lifted curtain, and his lantern glared in on us and our wall of mail matter. He said:

"Gents, you'll have to turn out a spell. Thoroughbrace is broke."

We climbed out into a chill drizzle, and felt ever so homeless and dreary. When I found that the thing they called a "thoroughbrace" was the massive combination of belts and springs which the coach rocks itself in, I said to the driver:

"I never saw a thoroughbrace used up like that before, that I can remember. How did it happen?"

"Why, it happened by trying to make one coach carry three days' mail—that's how it happened," said he. "And right here is the very direction which is wrote on all the newspaper-bags which was to be put out for the Injuns for to keep 'em quiet. It's most uncommon lucky, becuz it's so nation dark I should'a gone by unbeknowns if that air thoroughbrace hadn't broke."

I knew that he was in labor with another of those winks of his, though I could not see his face, because he was bent down at work; and wishing him a safe delivery, I turned to and helped the rest get out the mail-sacks. It made a great pyramid by the roadside when it was all out. When they had mended the thoroughbrace we filled the two boots again, but put no mail on top, and only half as much inside as there was before. The conductor bent all the seat-backs down, and then filled the coach just half full of mailbags from end to end. We objected loudly to this, for it left us no seats. But the conductor was wiser than we, and said a bed was better than seats, and moreover, this plan would protect his thoroughbraces. We never wanted any seats after that. The lazy bed was infinitely preferable. I had many an exciting day, subsequently, lying on it reading the statutes and the dictionary, and wondering how the characters would turn out.

The conductor said he would send back a guard from the next station to take charge of the abandoned mailbags, and we drove on.

It was now just dawn; and as we stretched our cramped legs full length on the mail sacks, and gazed out through the windows across the wide wastes of greensward clad in cool, powdery mist, to where there was an expectant look in the eastern horizon, our perfect enjoyment took the form of a tranquil and contented ecstasy. The stage whirled along at a spanking gait, the breeze flapping curtains and suspended coats in a most exhilarating way; the cradle swayed and swung luxuriously; the pattering of the horses' hoofs, the cracking of the driver's whip, and his "Hi-yi! g'lang!" were music; the spinning ground and the waltzing trees appeared to give us a mute hurrah as we went by, and then slack up and look after us with interest, or envy, or something; and as we lay and smoked the pipe of peace and compared all this luxury with the tiresome city life that had gone before it, we felt that there was only one complete and satisfying happiness in the world, and we had found it.

* * *

By and by, as the sun rose up and warmed the world, we pulled off our clothes and got ready for breakfast. We were just pleasantly in time, for five minutes afterward the driver sent the weird music of his bugle winding over the grassy solitudes, and presently we detected a low hut or two in the distance. Then the rattling of the coach, the clatter of our six horses' hoofs, and the driver's crisp commands awoke to a louder and stronger emphasis, and we went sweeping down on the station at our smartest speed. It was fascinating—that old overland stagecoaching.

We jumped out in undress uniform. The driver tossed his gathered reins out on the ground, gaped and stretched complacently, drew off his heavy buckskin gloves with great deliberation and insufferable dignity—taking not the slightest notice of a dozen solicitous inquiries after his health, and humbly facetious and flattering accostings, and obsequious tenders of service, from five or six hairy and half-civilized station-keepers and hostlers who were nimbly unhitching our steeds and bringing the fresh team out of the stables—for in the eyes of the stage-driver of that day, station-keepers and hostlers were a sort of good enough low creatures, useful in their place, and helping to make up a world, but not the kind of beings which a person of distinction could afford to concern himself with; while, on the contrary, in the eyes of the station-keeper and the hostler, the stage-driver was a hero—a great and shining dignitary, the world's favorite son, the envy of the people, the observed of the nations. When they spoke to him they received his insolent silence meekly, and as being the natural and proper conduct of so great a man; when he opened his lips they all hung on his words with admiration (he never honored a particular individual with a remark, but addressed it with a broad generality to the horses, the stables, the surrounding country *and* the human underlings); when he discharged a facetious, insulting personality at a hostler, that hostler was happy for the day; when he uttered his one jest—old as the hills, coarse, profane, witless, and inflicted on the same audience, in the same language, every time his coach drove up there—the varlets roared, and slapped their thighs, and swore it was the best thing they'd ever heard in all their lives. And how they would fly around when he wanted a basin of water, a gourd of the same, or a light for his pipe!—but they would instantly insult a passenger if he so far forgot himself as to crave a favor at their hands. They could do that sort of insolence as well as the driver they copied it from—for, let it be borne in mind, the overland driver had but little less contempt for his passengers than he had for his hostlers.

The hostlers and station-keepers treated the really powerful *conductor* of the coach merely with the best of what was their idea of civility, but the *driver* was the only being they bowed down to and worshipped. How admiringly they would gaze up at him in his high seat as he gloved himself with lingering deliberation, while some happy hostler led the bunch of reins aloft, and waited patiently for him to take it! And how they would bombard him with glorifying ejaculations as he cracked his long whip and went careering away.

The station buildings were long, low huts, made of sun-dried, mud-colored bricks, laid up without mortar (*adobes*, the Spaniards call these bricks, and the Americans shorten it to *'dobies*). The roofs, which had no slant to them worth speaking of, were thatched and then sodded or covered with a thick layer of earth, and from this sprang a pretty rank growth of weeds and grass. It was the first time we had ever seen a man's front yard on top of his house. The buildings consisted of barns, stable-room for twelve or fifteen horses, and a hut for an eating-room for passengers. This latter had bunks in it for the station-keeper and a hostler or two. You could rest your elbow on its eaves, and you had to bend in order to get in at the door. In place of a window there was a square hole about large enough for a man to crawl through, but this had no glass in it. There was no flooring, but the ground was packed hard. There was no stove, but the fireplace served all needful purposes. There were no shelves, no cupboards, no closets. In a corner stood an open sack of flour, and nestling against its base were a couple of black and venerable tin coffeepots, a tin teapot, a little bag of salt, and a side of bacon.

By the door of the station-keeper's den, outside, was a tin washbasin, on the ground. Near it was a pail of water and a piece of yellow bar soap, and from the eaves hung a hoary blue woolen shirt, significantly—but this latter was the station-keeper's private towel, and only two persons in all the party might venture to use it—the stage-driver and the conductor. The latter would not, from a sense of decency; the former would not, because he did not choose to encourage the advances of a station-keeper. We had towels—in the valise; they might as well have been in Sodom and Gomorrah. We (and the conductor) used our handkerchiefs, and the driver his pantaloons and sleeves. By the door, inside, was fastened a small old-fashioned looking-glass frame, with two little fragments of the original mirror lodged down in one corner of it. This arrangement afforded a pleasant double-barreled portrait of you when you looked into it, with one half of your head set up a couple of inches above the other half. From the glass frame hung half of a comb by a string—but if I had to describe that patriarch or die, I believe I would order some sample coffins. It had come down from Esau and Samson, and had been accumulating hair ever since—along with certain impurities. In one corner of the room stood three or four rifles and muskets, together with horns and pouches of ammunition. The station-men wore pantaloons, of course, country-woven stuff, and into the seat and the inside of the legs were sewed ample additions of buckskin, to do duty in place of leggings, when the man rode horseback—so the pants were half dull blue and half yellow, and unspeakably picturesque. The pants were stuffed into the tops of high boots, the heels whereof were armed with great Spanish spurs, whose little iron clogs and chains jingled with every step. The man wore a huge beard and mustachios, an old slouch hat, a blue woolen shirt, no suspenders, no vest, no coat—in a leathern sheath in his belt, a great long "navy" revolver (slung on right side, hammer to the front), and projecting from his boot a horn-handled bowie-knife. The furniture of the hut was neither gorgeous nor much in the way. The rocking-chairs and sofas were not present, and never had been, but they were represented by two three-legged stools, a pine-board bench four feet long, and two empty candle-boxes. The table was a greasy board on stilts, and the tablecloth and napkins had not come—and they were not looking for them, either. A battered tin platter, a knife and fork, and a tin pint cup were at each man's place, and the driver had a queensware saucer that had seen better days. Of course this duke sat at the head of the table. There was one isolated piece of table furniture that bore about it a touching air of grandeur in misfortune. This was the caster. It was German silver, and crippled and rusty, but it was so preposterously out of place there that it was suggestive of a tattered exiled king among barbarians, and the majesty of its native position compelled respect even in its degradation. There was only one cruet left, and that was a stopperless, fly-specked, broken-necked thing, with two inches of vinegar in it, and a dozen preserved flies with their heels up and looking sorry they had invested there.

The station-keeper upended a disk of last week's bread, of the shape and size of an old-time cheese, and carved some slabs from it which were as good as Nicholson pavement, and tenderer.

He sliced off a piece of bacon for each man, but only the experienced old hands made out to eat it, for it was condemned army bacon which the United States would not feed to its soldiers in the forts, and the stage company had bought it cheap for the sustenance of their passengers and employes. We may have found this condemned army bacon further out on the plains than the section I am locating it in, but we *found* it—there is no gainsaying that.

Then he poured for us a beverage which he called "*Slumgullion*," and it is hard to think he was not inspired when he named it. It really pretended to be tea, but there was too much dishrag, and sand, and old bacon-rind in it to deceive the intelligent traveler. He had no sugar and no milk—not even a spoon to stir the ingredients with.

We could not eat the bread or the meat, nor drink the "slumgullion." And when I looked at that melancholy vinegar-cruet, I thought of the anecdote (a very, very old one, even at that day) of the traveler who sat down to a table which had nothing on it but a mackerel and a pot of mustard. He asked the landlord if that was all. The landlord said:

"*All!* Why, thunder and lightning, I should think there was mackerel enough there for six."

"But I don't like mackerel."

"Oh—then help yourself to the mustard."

In other days I had considered it a good, a very good, anecdote, but there was a dismal plausibility about it, here, that took all the humor out of it.

Our breakfast was before us, but our teeth were idle.

I tasted and smelt, and said I would take coffee, I believed. The station-boss stopped dead still, and glared at me speechless. At last, when he came to, he turned away and said, as one who communes with himself upon a matter too vast to grasp:

"*Coffee!* Well, if that don't go clean ahead of me, I'm d——-d!"

We could not eat, and there was no conversation among the hostlers and herdsmen—we all sat at the same board. At least there was no conversation further than a single hurried request, now and then, from one employe to another. It was always in the same form, and always gruffly friendly. Its western freshness and novelty startled me, at first, and interested me; but it presently grew monotonous, and lost its charm. It was:

"Pass the bread, you son of a skunk!" No, I forget—skunk was not the word; it seems to me it was still stronger than that; I know it was, in fact, but it is gone from my memory, apparently. However, it is no matter—probably it was too strong for print, anyway. It is the landmark in my memory which tells me where I first encountered the vigorous new vernacular of the occidental plains and mountains.

We gave up the breakfast, and paid our dollar apiece and went back to our mailbag bed in the coach, and found comfort in our pipes. Right here we suffered the first diminution of our princely state. We left our six fine horses and took six mules in their place. But they were wild Mexican fellows, and a man had to stand at the head of each of them and hold him fast while the driver gloved and got himself ready. And when at last he grasped the reins and gave the word, the men sprang suddenly away from the mules' heads and the coach shot from the station as if it had issued from a cannon. How the frantic animals did scamper! It was a fierce and furious gallop—and the gait never altered for a moment till we reeled off ten or twelve miles and swept up to the next collection of little station-huts and stables.

* * *

In a little while all interest was taken up in stretching our necks and watching for the "pony-rider"—the fleet messenger who sped across the continent from St. Jo. to Sacramento, carrying letters nineteen hundred miles in eight days! Think of that for perishable horse and human flesh and blood to do! The pony-rider was usually a little bit of a man, brimful of spirit and endurance. No matter what time of day or night his watch came on, and no matter whether it was winter or summer, raining, snowing, hailing, or sleeting, or whether his "beat" was a level straight road or a crazy trail over mountain crags and precipices, or whether it led through peaceful regions or regions that swarmed with hostile Indians, he must be always ready to leap into the saddle and be off like the wind! There was no idling-time for a pony-rider on duty. He rode fifty miles without stopping, by daylight, moonlight, starlight, or through the blackness of darkness—just as it happened. He rode a splendid horse that was born for a racer and fed and lodged like a gentleman; kept him at his utmost speed for ten miles, and then, as he came crashing up to the station where stood two men holding fast a fresh, impatient steed, the transfer of rider and mailbag was made in the twinkling of an eye, and away flew the eager pair and were out of sight before the spectator could get hardly the ghost of a look. Both rider and horse went "flying light." The rider's dress was thin, and fitted close; he wore a "roundabout,"[2] and a skullcap, and tucked his pantaloons into his boot-tops like a race-rider. He carried no arms—he carried nothing that was not absolutely necessary, for even the postage on his literary freight was worth *five dollars a letter*. He got but little frivolous correspondence to carry—his bag had business letters in it, mostly. His horse was stripped of all unnecessary weight, too. He wore a little wafer of a racing-saddle, and no visible blankets. He wore light shoes, or none at all. The little flat mail-pockets strapped under the rider's thighs would each hold about the bulk of a child's primer. They held many and many an important business chapter and newspaper letter, but these were written on paper as airy and thin as gold-leaf, nearly, and thus bulk and weight were economized. The stagecoach traveled about a hundred to a hundred and twenty-five miles a day (twenty-four hours), the pony-rider about two hundred and fifty. There were about eighty pony-riders in the saddle all the time, night and day, stretching in a long, scattering procession from Missouri to California, forty flying eastward, and forty toward the west, and among them making four hundred gallant horses earn a stirring livelihood and see a deal of scenery every single day of the year.

We had a consuming desire, from the beginning, to see a pony-rider, but somehow or other all that passed us and all that met us

[2] A close-fitting jacket.

managed to streak by in the night, and so we heard only a whiz and a hail, and the swift phantom of the desert was gone before we could get our heads out of the windows. But now we were expecting one along every moment, and would see him in broad daylight. Presently the driver exclaims:

"HERE HE COMES!"

Every neck is stretched further, and every eye strained wider. Away across the endless dead level of the prairie a black speck appears against the sky, and it is plain that it moves. Well, I should think so! In a second or two it becomes a horse and rider, rising and falling, rising and falling—sweeping toward us nearer and nearer—growing more and more distinct, more and more sharply defined—nearer and still nearer, and the flutter of the hoofs comes faintly to the ear—another instant a whoop and a hurrah from our upper deck, a wave of the rider's hand, but no reply, and man and horse burst past our excited faces, and go winging away like a belated fragment of a storm!

So sudden is it all, and so like a flash of unreal fancy, that but for the flake of white foam left quivering and perishing on a mail-sack after the vision had flashed by and disappeared, we might have doubted whether we had seen any actual horse and man at all, maybe.

We rattled through Scott's Bluffs Pass, by and by. It was along here somewhere that we first came across genuine and unmistakable alkali water in the road, and we cordially hailed it as a first-class curiosity, and a thing to be mentioned with eclat in letters to the ignorant at home. This water gave the road a soapy appearance, and in many places the ground looked as if it had been white-washed. I think the strange alkali water excited us as much as any wonder we had come upon yet, and I know we felt very complacent and conceited, and better satisfied with life after we had added it to our list of things which *we* had seen and some other people had not. In a small way we were the same sort of simpletons as those who climb unnecessarily the perilous peaks of Mont Blanc and the Matterhorn, and derive no pleasure from it except the reflection that it isn't a common experience. But once in a while one of those parties trips and comes darting down the long mountain-crags in a sitting posture, making the crusted snow smoke behind him, flitting from bench to bench, and from terrace to terrace, jarring the earth where he strikes, and still glancing and flitting on again, sticking an iceberg into himself every now and then, and tearing his clothes, snatching at things to save himself, taking hold of trees and fetching them along with him, roots and all, starting little rocks now and then, then big boulders, then acres of ice and snow and patches of forest, gathering and still gathering as he goes, adding and still adding to his massed and sweeping grandeur as he nears a three-thousand foot precipice, till at last he waves his hat magnificently and rides into eternity on the back of a raging and tossing avalanche!

This is all very fine, but let us not be carried away by excitement, but ask calmly, how does this person feel about it in his cooler moment next day, with six or seven thousand feet of snow and stuff on top of him?

We crossed the sand hills near the scene of the Indian mail robbery and massacre of 1856, wherein the driver and conductor perished, and also all the passengers but one, it was supposed; but this must have been a mistake, for at different times afterward on the Pacific coast I was personally acquainted with a hundred and thirty-three or four people who were wounded during that massacre, and barely escaped with their lives. There was no doubt about the truth of it—I had it from their own lips. One of these parties told me that he kept coming across arrowheads in his system for nearly seven years after the massacre; and another of them told me that he was stuck so literally full of arrows that after the Indians were gone and he could raise up and examine himself, he could not restrain his tears, for his clothes were completely ruined.

# Carson City and the Genuine Mexican Plug

I resolved to have a horse to ride. I had never seen such wild, free, magnificent horsemanship outside of a circus as these picturesquely-clad Mexicans, Californians and Mexicanized Americans displayed in Carson streets every day. How they rode! Leaning just gently forward out of perpendicular, easy and nonchalant, with broad slouch-hat brim blown square up in front, and a long *riata* swinging above the head, they swept through the town like the wind! The next minute they were only a sailing puff of dust on the far desert. If they trotted, they sat up gallantly and gracefully, and seemed part of the horse; did not go jiggering up and down after the silly Miss-Nancy fashion of the riding-schools. I had quickly learned to tell a horse from a cow, and was full of anxiety to learn more. I was resolved to buy a horse.

While the thought was rankling in my mind, the auctioneer came scurrying through the plaza on a black beast that had as many humps and corners on him as a dromedary, and was necessarily uncomely; but he was "going, going, at twenty-two!—horse, saddle and bridle at twenty-two dollars, gentlemen!" and I could hardly resist.

A man whom I did not know (he turned out to be the auctioneer's brother) noticed the wistful look in my eye, and observed that that was a very remarkable horse to be going at such a price; and added that the saddle alone was worth the money. It was a Spanish saddle, with ponderous *tapidaros*,[3] and furnished with the ungainly sole-leather covering with the unspellable name. I said I had half a notion to bid. Then this keen-eyed person appeared to me to be "taking my measure"; but I dismissed the suspicion when he spoke, for his manner was full of guileless candor and truthfulness. Said he:

"I know that horse—know him well. You are a stranger, I take it, and so you might think he was an American horse, maybe, but I assure you he is not. He is nothing of the kind; but—excuse my speaking in a low voice, other people being near—he is, without a shadow of a doubt, a Genuine Mexican Plug!"

I did not know what a Genuine Mexican Plug was, but there was something about this man's way of saying it that made me swear inwardly that I would own a Genuine Mexican Plug, or die.

"Has he any other—er—advantages?" I inquired, suppressing what eagerness I could.

He hooked his forefinger in the pocket of my army-shirt, led me to one side, and breathed in my ear impressively these words:

"He can outbuck anything in America!"

"Going, going, going—at *twent-ty*-four dollars and a half, gen—"

"Twenty-seven!" I shouted, in a frenzy.

"And sold!" said the auctioneer, and passed over the Genuine Mexican Plug to me.

I could scarcely contain my exultation. I paid the money, and put the animal in a neighboring livery-stable to dine and rest himself.

In the afternoon I brought the creature into the plaza, and certain citizens held him by the head, and others by the tail, while I mounted him. As soon as they let go, he placed all his feet in a

[3] A stiff leather cover attached to the stirrup to prevent the rider's foot from falling through.

bunch together, lowered his back, and then suddenly arched it upward, and shot me straight into the air a matter of three of four feet! I came as straight down again, lit in the saddle, went instantly up again, came down, almost on the high pommel, shot up again, and came down on the horse's neck—all in the space of three or four seconds. Then he rose and stood almost straight up on his hind feet, and I, clasping his lean neck desperately, slid back into the saddle, and held on. He came down, and immediately hoisted his heels into the air, delivering a vicious kick at the sky, and stood on his forefeet. And then down he came once more, and began the original exercise of shooting me straight up again. The third time I went up I heard a stranger say:

"Oh, *don't* he buck, though!"

While I was up, somebody struck the horse a sounding thwack with a leathern strap, and when I arrived again the Genuine Mexican Plug was not there. A Californian youth chased him up and caught him, and asked if he might have a ride. I granted him that luxury. He mounted the Genuine, got lifted into the air once, but sent his spurs home as he descended, and the horse darted away like a telegram. He soared over three fences like a bird, and disappeared down the road toward the Washoe Valley.

I sat down on a stone, with a sigh, and by a natural impulse of one of my hands sought my forehead, and the other the base of my stomach. I believe I never appreciated, till then, the poverty of the human machinery—for I still needed a hand or two to place elsewhere. Pen cannot describe how I was jolted up. Imagination cannot conceive how disjointed I was—how internally, externally and universally I was unsettled, mixed up and ruptured. There was a sympathetic crowd around me, though.

One elderly-looking comforter said:

"Stranger, you've been taken in. Everybody in this camp knows that horse. Any child, any Injun, could have told you that he'd buck; he is the very worst devil to buck on the continent of America. You hear *me*. I'm Curry. *Old* Curry. Old *Abe* Curry. And moreover, he's a simon-pure, out-and-out, genuine d——d Mexican plug, and an uncommon mean one at that, too. Why, you turnip, if you had laid low and kept dark, there's chances to buy an *American* horse for mighty little more than you paid for that bloody old foreign relic."

I gave no sign; but I made up my mind that if the auctioneer's brother's funeral took place while I was in the Territory I would postpone all other recreations and attend it.

After a gallop of sixteen miles the Californian youth and the Genuine Mexican Plug came tearing into town again, shedding foam-flakes like the spume-spray that drives before a typhoon, and, with one final skip over a wheelbarrow and a Chinaman, cast anchor in front of the "ranch."

Such panting and blowing! Such spreading and contracting of the red equine nostrils, and glaring of the wild equine eye! But was the imperial beast subjugated? Indeed he was not. His lordship the Speaker of the House thought he was, and mounted him to go down to the Capitol; but the first dash the creature made was over a pile of telegraph poles half as high as a church; and his time to the Capitol—one mile and three quarters—remains unbeaten to this day. But then he took an advantage—he left out the mile, and only did the three quarters. That is to say, he made a straight cut across lots, preferring fences and ditches to a crooked road; and when the Speaker got to the Capitol he said he had been in the air so much he felt as if he had made the trip on a comet.

In the evening the Speaker came home afoot for exercise, and got the Genuine towed back behind a quartz wagon. The next day I loaned the animal to the Clerk of the House to go down to the Dana silver mine, six miles, and *he* walked back for exercise, and got the horse towed. Everybody I loaned him to always walked back; they never could get enough exercise any other way. Still, I continued to loan him to anybody who was willing to borrow him, my idea being to get him crippled, and throw him on the borrower's hands, or killed, and make the borrower pay for him. But somehow nothing ever happened to him. He took chances that no other horse ever took and survived, but he always came out safe. It was his daily habit to try experiments that had always before been considered impossible, but he always got through. Sometimes he miscalculated a little, and did not get his rider through intact, but *he* always got through himself. Of course I had tried to sell him, but that was a stretch of simplicity which met with little sympathy. The auctioneer stormed up and down the streets on him for four days, dispersing the populace, interrupting business, and destroying children, and never got a bid—at least never any but the eighteen-dollar one he hired a notoriously substanceless bummer to make. The people only smiled pleasantly, and restrained their desire to buy, if they had any. Then the auctioneer brought in his bill, and I withdrew the horse from the market. We tried to trade him off at private vendue [auction] next, offering him at a sacrifice for secondhand tombstones, old iron, temperance tracts—any kind of property. But holders were stiff, and we retired from the market again. I never tried to ride the horse any more. Walking was good enough exercise for a man like me, that had nothing the matter with him except ruptures, internal injuries, and such things. Finally I tried to *give* him away. But it was a failure. Parties said earthquakes were handy enough on the Pacific coast—they did not wish to own one. As a last resort I offered him to the Governor for the use of the "Brigade." His face lit up eagerly at first, but toned down again, and he said the thing would be too palpable.

Just then the livery-stable man brought in his bill for six weeks, keeping—stall-room for the horse, fifteen dollars; hay for the horse, two hundred and fifty! The Genuine Mexican Plug had eaten a ton of the article, and the man said he would have eaten a hundred if he had let him.

I will remark here, in all seriousness, that the regular price of hay during that year and a part of the next was really two hundred and fifty dollars a ton. During a part of the previous year it had sold at five hundred a ton, in gold, and during the winter before that there was such scarcity of the article that in several instances small quantities had brought eight hundred dollars a ton in coin! The consequence might be guessed without my telling it: people turned their stock loose to starve, and before the spring arrived Carson and Eagle valleys were almost literally carpeted with their carcasses! Any old settler will verify these statements.

I managed to pay the livery bill, and that same day I gave the Genuine Mexican Plug to a passing Arkansas emigrant whom fortune delivered into my hand. If this ever meets his eye, he will doubtless remember the donation.

Now whoever has had the luck to ride a real Mexican plug will recognize the animal depicted in this chapter, and hardly consider him exaggerated—but the uninitiated will feel justified in regarding his portrait as a fancy sketch, perhaps.

# A Prospecting Expedition

Hurry, was the word! We wasted no time. Our party consisted of four persons—a blacksmith sixty years of age, two young lawyers, and myself. We bought a wagon and two miserable old horses. We put eighteen hundred pounds of provisions and mining tools in the wagon and drove out of Carson on a chilly December afternoon. The horses were so weak and old that we soon found that it would be better if one or two of us got out and walked. It was an improvement. Next, we found that it would be better if a third man got out. That was an improvement also. It was at this time that I volunteered to drive, although I had never driven a harnessed horse before and many a man in such a position would have felt fairly excused from such a responsibility. But in a little while it was found that it would be a fine thing if the driver got out and walked also. It was at this time that I resigned the position of driver, and never resumed it again. Within the hour, we found that it would not only be better, but was absolutely necessary, that we four, taking turns, two at a time, should put our hands against the end of the wagon and push it through the sand, leaving the feeble horses little to do but keep out of the way and hold up the tongue. Perhaps it is well for one to know his fate at first, and get reconciled to it. We had learned ours in one afternoon. It was plain that we had to walk through the sand and shove that wagon and those horses two hundred miles. So we accepted the situation, and from that time forth we never rode. More than that, we stood regular and nearly constant watches pushing up behind.

We made seven miles, and camped in the desert. Young Clagett (now member of Congress from Montana) unharnessed and fed and watered the horses; Oliphant and I cut sagebrush, built the fire and brought water to cook with; and old Mr. Ballou the blacksmith did the cooking. This division of labor, and this appointment, was adhered to throughout the journey. We had no tent, and so we slept under our blankets in the open plain. We were so tired that we slept soundly.

We were fifteen days making the trip—two hundred miles; thirteen, rather, for we lay by a couple of days, in one place, to let the horses rest. We could really have accomplished the journey in ten days if we had towed the horses behind the wagon, but we did not think of that until it was too late, and so went on shoving the horses and the wagon too when we might have saved half the labor. Parties who met us, occasionally, advised us to put the horses *in* the wagon, but Mr. Ballou, through whose ironclad earnestness no sarcasm could pierce, said that that would not do, because the provisions were exposed and would suffer, the horses being "bituminous from long deprivation." The reader will excuse me from translating. What Mr. Ballou customarily meant, when he used a long word, was a secret between himself and his Maker. He was one of the best and kindest-hearted men that ever graced a humble sphere of life. He was gentleness and simplicity itself—and unselfishness, too. Although he was more than twice as old as the eldest of us, he never gave himself any airs, privileges, or exemptions on that account. He did a *young* man's share of the work; and did his share of conversing and entertaining from the general standpoint of *any* age—not from the arrogant, overawing summit-height of sixty years. His one striking peculiarity was his Partingtonian[4] fashion of loving and using big words *for their own sakes*, and independent of any bearing they might have upon the thought he was purposing to convey. He always let his ponderous syllables fall with an easy unconsciousness that left them wholly without offensiveness. In truth his air was so natural and so simple that one was always catching himself accepting his stately sentences as meaning something, when they really meant nothing in the world. If a word was long and grand and resonant, that was sufficient to win the old man's love, and he would drop that word into the most out-of-the-way place in a sentence or a subject, and be as pleased with it as if it were perfectly luminous with meaning.

We four always spread our common stock of blankets together on the frozen ground, and slept side by side; and finding that our foolish, long-legged hound pup had a deal of animal heat in him, Oliphant got to admitting him to the bed, between himself and Mr. Ballou, hugging the dog's warm back to his breast and finding great comfort in it. But in the night the pup would get stretchy and brace his feet against the old man's back and shove, grunting complacently the while; and now and then, being warm and snug, grateful and happy, he would paw the old man's back simply in excess of comfort; and at yet other times he would dream of the chase and in his sleep tug at the old man's back hair and bark in his ear. The old gentleman complained mildly about these familiarities, at last, and when he got through with his statement he said that such a dog as that was not a proper animal to admit to bed with tired men, because he was "so meretricious in his movement and so organic in his emotions." We turned the dog out.

[4] A reference to Mrs. Partington, a character in the humorous writing of B. P. Shillaber, and a nineteenth-century American version of Mrs. Malaprop.

It was a hard, wearing, toilsome journey, but it had its bright side; for after each day was done and our wolfish hunger appeased with a hot supper of fried bacon, bread, molasses, and black coffee, the pipe-smoking, song-singing, and yarn-spinning around the evening campfire in the still solitudes of the desert was a happy, carefree sort of recreation that seemed the very summit and culmination of earthly luxury. It is a kind of life that has a potent charm for all men, whether city- or country-bred. We are descended from desert-lounging Arabs, and countless ages of growth toward perfect civilization have failed to root out of us the nomadic instinct. We all confess to a gratified thrill at the thought of "camping out."

Once we made twenty-five miles in a day, and once we made forty miles (through the Great American Desert), and ten miles beyond—fifty in all—in twenty-three hours, without halting to eat, drink, or rest. To stretch out and go to sleep, even on the stony and frozen ground, after pushing a wagon and two horses fifty miles, is a delight so supreme that for the moment it almost seems cheap at the price.

We camped two days in the neighborhood of the "Sink of the Humboldt." We tried to use the strong alkaline water of the Sink, but it would not answer. It was like drinking lye, and not weak lye, either. It left a taste in the mouth, bitter and every way execrable, and a burning in the stomach that was very uncomfortable. We put molasses in it, but that helped it very little; we added a pickle, yet the alkali was the prominent taste, and so it was unfit for drinking. The coffee we made of this water was the meanest compound man has yet invented. It was really viler to the taste than the unameliorated water itself. Mr. Ballou, being the architect and builder of the beverage, felt constrained to endorse and uphold it, and so drank half a cup, by little sips, making shift to praise it faintly the while, but finally threw out the remainder, and said frankly it was "too technical for *him*."

But presently we found a spring of fresh water, convenient, and then, with nothing to mar our enjoyment, and no stragglers to interrupt it, we entered into our rest.

* * *

After leaving the Sink, we traveled along the Humboldt River a little way. People accustomed to the monster mile-wide Mississippi grow accustomed to associating the term "river" with a high degree of watery grandeur. Consequently, such people feel rather disappointed when they stand on the shores of the Humboldt or the Carson and find that a "river" in Nevada is a sickly rivulet which is just the counterpart of the Erie Canal in all respects save that the canal is twice as long and four times as deep. One of the pleasantest and most invigorating exercises one can contrive is to run and jump across the Humboldt River till he is overheated, and then drink it dry.

On the fifteenth day we completed our march of two hundred miles and entered Unionville, Humboldt County, in the midst of a driving snowstorm. Unionville consisted of eleven cabins and a liberty pole. Six of the cabins were strung along one side of a deep canyon, and the other five faced them. The rest of the landscape was made up of bleak mountain walls that rose so high into the sky from both sides of the canyon that the village was left, as it were, far down in the bottom of a crevice. It was always daylight on the mountaintops a long time before the darkness lifted and revealed Unionville.

We built a small, rude cabin in the side of the crevice and roofed it with canvas, leaving a corner open to serve as a chimney, through which the cattle used to tumble occasionally, at night, and mash our furniture and interrupt our sleep. It was very cold weather and fuel was scarce. Indians brought brush and bushes several miles on their backs; and when we could catch a laden Indian it was well—and when we could not (which was the rule, not the exception), we shivered and bore it.

I confess, without shame, that I expected to find masses of silver lying all about the ground. I expected to see it glittering in the sun on the mountain summits. I said nothing about this, for some instinct told me that I might possibly have an exaggerated idea about it, and so if I betrayed my thought I might bring derision upon myself. Yet I was as perfectly satisfied in my own mind as I could be of anything, that I was going to gather up, in a day or two, or at furthest a week or two, silver enough to make me satisfactorily wealthy—and so my fancy was already busy with plans for spending this money. The first opportunity that offered, I sauntered carelessly away from the cabin, keeping an eye on the other boys, and stopping and contemplating the sky when they seemed to be observing me; but as soon as the coast was manifestly clear, I fled away as guiltily as a thief might have done and never halted till I was far beyond sight and call. Then I began my search with a feverish excitement that was brimful of expectation—almost of certainty. I crawled about the ground, seizing and examining bits of stone, blowing the dust from them or rubbing them on my clothes, and then peering at them with anxious hope. Presently I found a bright fragment and my heart bounded! I hid behind a boulder and polished it and scrutinized it with a nervous eagerness and a delight that was more pronounced than absolute certainty itself could have afforded. The more I examined the fragment, the more I was convinced that I had found the door to fortune. I marked the spot and carried away my specimen. Up and down the rugged mountainside I searched, with always increasing interest and always augmenting gratitude that I had come to Humboldt and come in time. Of all the experiences of my life, this secret search among the hidden treasures of silver-land was the nearest to unmarred ecstasy. It was a delirious revel. By and by, in the bed of a shallow rivulet, I found a deposit of shining yellow scales, and my breath almost forsook me! A gold mine, and in my simplicity I had been content with vulgar silver! I was so excited that I half believed my overwrought imagination was deceiving me. Then a fear came upon me that people might be observing me and would guess my secret. Moved by this thought, I made a circuit of the place, and ascended a knoll to reconnoiter. Solitude. No creature was near. Then I returned to my mine, fortifying myself against possible disappointment, but my fears were groundless—the shining scales were still there. I set about scooping them up, and for an hour I toiled down the windings of the stream and robbed its bed. But at last the descending sun warned me to give up the quest, and I turned home laden with wealth. As I walked along I could not help smiling at the thought of my being so excited over a fragment of silver when a nobler metal was almost under my nose. In this little time the former had so fallen in my estimation that once or twice I was on the point of throwing it away.

The boys were as hungry as usual, but I could eat nothing. Neither could I talk. I was full of dreams and far away. Their conversation interrupted the flow of my fancy somewhat, and annoyed me a little, too. I despised the sordid and commonplace things they talked about. But as they proceeded, it began to amuse me. It grew to be rare fun to hear them planning their poor little economies and sighing over possible privations and distresses when a gold mine, all our own, lay within sight of the cabin and I could point it out at any moment. Smothered hilarity began to oppress me, presently. It was hard to resist the impulse to burst out with exultation and reveal everything; but I did resist. I said within myself that I would filter the great news through my lips calmly and be serene as a summer morning while I watched its effect in the faces. I said:

"Where have you all been?"

"Prospecting."

"What did you find?"

"Nothing."

"Nothing? What do you think of the country?"

"Can't tell, yet," said Mr. Ballou, who was an old gold miner, and had likewise had considerable experience among the silver mines.

"Well, haven't you formed any sort of opinion?"

"Yes, a sort of a one. It's fair enough here, maybe, but overrated. Seven-thousand-dollar ledges are scarce, though. That Sheba may be rich enough, but we don't own it; and besides, the rock is so full of base metals that all the science in the world can't work it. We'll not starve, here, but we'll not get rich, I'm afraid."

"So you think the prospect is pretty poor?"

"No name for it!"

"Well, we'd better go back, hadn't we?"

"Oh, not yet—of course not. We'll try a riffle, first."

"Suppose now—this is merely a supposition, you know—suppose you could find a ledge that would yield, say, a hundred and fifty dollars a ton—would that satisfy you?"

"Try us once!" from the whole party.

"Or suppose—merely a supposition, of course—suppose you were to find a ledge that would yield two thousand dollars a ton—would *that* satisfy you?"

"Here—what do you mean? What are you coming at? Is there some mystery behind all this?"

"Never mind. I am not saying anything. You know perfectly well there are no rich mines here—of course you do. Because you have been around and examined for yourselves. Anybody would know that, that had been around. But just for the sake of argument, suppose—in a kind of general way—suppose some person were to tell you that two-thousand-dollar ledges were simply contemptible—contemptible, understand—and that right yonder in sight of this very cabin there were piles of pure gold and pure silver—oceans of it—enough to make you all rich in twenty-four hours! Come!"

"I should say he was as crazy as a loon!" said old Ballou, but wild with excitement, nevertheless.

"Gentlemen," said I, "I don't say anything—*I* haven't been around, you know, and of course don't know anything—but all I ask of you is to cast your eye on *that*, for instance, and tell me what you think of it!" and I tossed my treasure before them.

There was an eager scramble for it, and a closing of heads together over it under the candlelight. Then old Ballou said:

"Think of it? I think it is nothing but a lot of granite rubbish and nasty glittering mica that isn't worth ten cents an acre."

So vanished my dream. So melted my wealth away. So toppled my airy castle to the earth and left me stricken and forlorn.

Moralizing, I observed, then, that "all that glitters is not gold."

Mr. Ballou said I could go further than that, and lay it up among my treasures of knowledge, that *nothing* that glitters is gold. So I learned then, once for all, that gold in its native state is but dull, unornamental stuff, and that only the lowborn metals excite the admiration of the ignorant with an ostentatious glitter. However, like the rest of the world, I still go on underrating men of gold and glorifying men of mica. Commonplace human nature cannot rise above that.

# The Story of the Old Ram

Every now and then, in these days, the boys used to tell me I ought to get one Jim Blaine to tell me the stirring story of his grandfather's old ram—but they always added that I must not mention the matter unless Jim was drunk at the time—just comfortably and sociably drunk. They kept this up until my curiosity was on the rack to hear the story. I got to haunting Blaine; but it was of no use, the boys always found fault with his condition; he was often moderately but never satisfactorily drunk. I never watched a man's condition with such absorbing interest, such anxious solicitude; I never pined to see a man uncompromisingly drunk before. At last, one evening I hurried to his cabin, for I learned that this time his situation was such that even the most fastidious could find no fault with it—he was tranquilly, serenely, symmetrically drunk—not a hiccup to mar his voice, not a cloud upon his brain thick enough to obscure his memory. As I entered, he was sitting upon an empty powder keg, with a clay pipe in one hand and the other raised to command silence. His face was round, red, and very serious; his throat was bare and his hair tumbled; in general appearance and costume he was a stalwart miner of the period. On the pine table stood a candle, and its dim light revealed "the boys" sitting here and there on bunks, candle-boxes, powder kegs, etc. They said:

"Sh—! Don't speak—he's going to commence."

I found a seat at once, and Blaine said:

"I don't reckon them times will ever come again. There never was a more bullier old ram than what he was. Grandfather fetched him from Illinois—got him of a man by the name of Yates—Bill Yates—maybe you might have heard of him; his father was a deacon—Baptist—and he was a rustler, too; a man had to get up ruther early to get the start of old Thankful Yates; it was him that put the Greens up to jining teams with my grandfather when he moved west. Seth Green was prob'ly the pick of the flock; he married a Wilkerson—Sarah Wilkerson—good cretur, she was—one of the likeliest heifers that was ever raised in old Stoddard, everybody said that knowed her. She could heft a bar'l of flour as easy I can flirt a flapjack. And spin? Don't mention it! Independent? Humph! When Sile Hawkins came a browsing around her, she let him know that for all his tin he couldn't trot in harness alongside of *her*. You see, Sile Hawkins was—no, it warn't Sile Hawkins, after all—it was a galoot by the name of Filkins—I disremember his first name; but he *was* a stump—come into pra'r meeting drunk, one night, hooraying for Nixon, becuz he thought it was a primary; and old Deacon Ferguson up and scooted him through the window and he lit on old Miss Jefferson's head, poor old filly. She was a good soul—had a glass eye and used to lend it to old Miss Wagner, that hadn't any, to receive company in; it warn't big enough, and when Miss Wagner warn't noticing, it would get twisted around in the socket, and look up, maybe, or out to one side, and every which way, while t'other one was looking as straight ahead as a spyglass. Grown people didn't mind it, but it most always made the children cry, it was so sort of scary. She tried packing it in raw cotton, but it wouldn't work, somehow—the cotton would get loose and stick out and look so kind of awful that the children couldn't stand it no way. She was always dropping it out, and turning her old deadlight on the company empty, and making them oncomfortable, becuz *she* never could tell when it hopped out, being blind on that side, you see. So somebody would have to hunch her and say, "Your game eye has fetched loose, Miss Wagner dear"—and then all of them would have to sit and wait till she jammed it in again—wrong side before, as a general thing, and green as a bird's egg, being a bashful cretur and easy sot back before company. But being wrong side before warn't much difference, anyway, becuz her own eye was sky-blue and the glass one was yaller on the front side, so whichever way she turned it it didn't match nohow. Old Miss Wagner was considerable on the borrow, she was. When she had a quilting, or a Dorcas S'iety[5] at her house she gen'ally borrowed Miss Higgins's wooden leg to stump around on; it was considerable shorter than her other pin, but much *she* minded that. She said she couldn't abide crutches when she had company, becuz they were so slow; said when she had company and things had to be done, she wanted to get up and hump herself. She was as bald as a jug, and so she used to borrow Miss Jacops's wig—Miss Jacops was the coffin peddler's wife—a ratty old buzzard, he was, that used to go roosting around where people was sick, waitin for 'em; and there that old rip would sit all day, in the shade, on a coffin that he judged would fit the can'idate; and if it was a slow customer and kind of uncertain, he'd fetch his rations and a blanket along and sleep in the coffin nights. He was anchored out that way, in frosty weather, for about three weeks, once, before old Robbins's place, waiting for him; and after that, for as much as two years, Jacops was not on speaking terms with the old man, on account of his disapp'inting him. He got one of his feet froze, and lost money, too, becuz old Robbins took a favorable turn and got well. The next time Robbins got sick, Jacops tried to make up with him, and varnished up the same old coffin and fetched it along; but old Robbins was too many for him;

[5] A Christian women's charitable organization.

he had him in, and 'peared to be powerful weak; he bought the coffin for ten dollars and Jacops was to pay it back and twenty-five more besides if Robbins didn't like the coffin after he'd tried it. And then Robbins died, and at the funeral he bursted off the lid and riz up in his shroud and told the parson to let up on the performances, becuz he could *not* stand such a coffin as that. You see he had been in a trance once before, when he was young, and he took the chances of another, cal'lating that if he made the trip it was money in his pocket, and if he missed fire he couldn't lose a cent. And by George he sued Jacops for the rhino and got jedgment; and he set up the coffin in his back parlor and said he 'lowed to take his time, now. It was always an aggravation to Jacops, the way that miserable old thing acted. He moved back to Indiany pretty soon—went to Wellsville—Wellsville was the place the Hogadorns was from. Mighty fine family. Old Maryland stock. Old Squire Hogadorn could carry more mixed licker, and cuss better than most any man I ever see. His second wife was the widder Billings—she that was Becky Martin; her dam was Deacon Dunlap's first wife. Her oldest child, Maria, married a missionary and died in grace—et up by the savages. They et *him*, too, poor feller—biled him. It warn't the custom, so they say, but they explained to friends of his'n that went down there to bring away his things, that they'd tried missionaries every other way and never could get any good out of 'em—and so it annoyed all his relations to find out that that man's life was fooled away just out of a dern'd experiment, so to speak. But mind you, there ain't anything ever reely lost; everything that people can't understand and don't see the reason of does good if you only hold on and give it a fair shake; Prov'dence don't fire no blank ca'tridges, boys. That there missionary's substance, unbeknowns to himself, actu'ly converted every last one of them heathens that took a chance at the barbacue. Nothing ever fetched them but that. Don't tell *me* it was an accident that he was biled. There ain't no such thing as an accident. When my uncle Lem was leaning up agin a scaffolding once, sick, or drunk, or suthin, an

Irishman with a hod full of bricks fell on him out of the third story and broke the old man's back in two places. People said it was an accident. Much accident there was about that. He didn't know what he was there for, but he was there for a good object. If he hadn't been there the Irishman would have been killed. Nobody can ever make me believe anything different from that. Uncle Lem's dog was there. Why didn't the Irishman fall on the dog? Becuz the dog would a seen him a coming and stood from under. That's the reason the dog warn't appinted. A dog can't be depended on to carry out a special providence. Mark my words it was a put-up thing. Accidents don't happen, boys. Uncle Lem's dog—I wish you could a seen that dog. He was a reglar shepherd—or ruther he was part bull and part shepherd—splendid animal; belonged to Parson Hagar before Uncle Lem got him. Parson Hagar belonged to the Western Reserve Hagars; prime family; his mother was a Watson; one of his sisters married a Wheeler; they settled in Morgan County, and he got nipped by the machinery in a carpet factory and went through in less than a quarter of a minute; his widder bought the piece of carpet that had his remains wove in, and people come a hundred mile to 'tend the funeral. There was fourteen yards in the piece. She wouldn't let them roll him up, but planted him just so—full length. The church was middling small where they preached the funeral, and they had to let one end of the coffin stick out the window. They didn't bury him—they planted one end, and let him stand up, same as a monument. And they nailed a sign on it and put—put on—put on it—sacred to—the m-e-m-o-r-y—of fourteen y-a-r-d-s—of three-ply car - - - pet—containing all that was—m-o-r-t-a-l—of—of—W-i-l-l-i-a-m—W-h-e—"

Jim Blaine had been growing gradually drowsy and drowsier—his head nodded, once, twice, three times—dropped peacefully upon his breast, and he fell tranquilly asleep. The tears were running down the boys' cheeks—they were suffocating with suppressed laughter—and had been from the start, though I had never noticed it. I perceived that I was "sold." I learned then that

Jim Blaine's peculiarity was that whenever he reached a certain stage of intoxication, no human power could keep him from setting out, with impressive unction, to tell about a wonderful adventure which he had once had with his grandfather's old ram—and the mention of the ram in the first sentence was as far as any man had ever heard him get, concerning it. He always maundered off, interminably, from one thing to another, till his whiskey got the best of him and he fell asleep. What the thing was that happened to him and his grandfather's old ram is a dark mystery to this day, for nobody has ever yet found out.

# Part Three

## *The Pacific*

*The Sandwich Islands remain my ideal of the perfect thing in the matter of tropical islands. I would add another story to Mauna Loa's 16,000 feet if I could, and make it particularly bold and steep and craggy and forbidding and snowy; and I would make the volcano spout its lava-flows out of its summit instead of its sides; but aside from these non-essentials I have no corrections to suggest. I hope these will be attended to; I do not wish to have to speak of it again.*

from *Following the Equator*

# Conquering an Enemy

Ours was a reasonably comfortable ship, with the customary sea-going fare—plenty of good food furnished by the Diety and cooked by the devil. The discipline observable on board was perhaps as good as it is anywhere in the Pacific and Indian Oceans. The ship was not very well arranged for tropical service; but that is nothing, for this is the rule for ships that ply in the tropics. Shc had an over-supply of cockroaches, but this is also the rule with ships doing business in the summer seas—at least such as have been long in service.

Our young captain was a very handsome man, tall and perfectly formed, the very figure to show up a smart uniform's finest effects. He was a man of the best intentions, and was polite and courteous even to courtliness. There was a soft grace and finish about his manners which made whatever place he happened to be in seem for the moment a drawing-room. He avoided the smoking-room. He had no vices. He did not smoke or chew tobacco or take snuff; he did not swear, or use slang, or rude, or coarse, or indelicate language, or make puns, or tell anecdotes, or laugh intemperately, or raise his voice above the moderate pitch enjoined by the canons of good form. When he gave an order, his manner modified it into a request. After dinner he and his officers joined the ladies and gentlemen in the ladies' saloon, and shared in the singing and piano-playing, and helped turn the music. He had a sweet and sympathetic tenor voice, and used it with taste and effect. After the music he played whist there, always with the same partner and opponents, until the ladies' bedtime. The electric lights burned there as late as the ladies and their friends might desire, but they were not allowed to burn in the smoking-room after eleven. There were many laws on the ship's statute-book, of course; but, so far as I could see, this and one other were the only ones that were rigidly enforced. The captain explained that he enforced this one because his own cabin adjoined the smoking-room, and the smell of tobacco smoke made him sick. I did not see how our smoke could reach him, for the smoking-room and his cabin were on the upper deck, targets for all the winds that blew; and besides there was no crack of communication between them, no opening of any sort in the solid intervening bulkhead. Still, to a delicate stomach even imaginary smoke can convey damage.

* * *

The brightest passenger in the ship, and the most interesting and felicitous talker, was a young Canadian who was not able to let the whisky bottle alone. He was of a rich and powerful family, and could have had a distinguished career and abundance of effective help toward it if he could have conquered his appetite for drink; but he could not do it, so his great equipment of talent was of no use to him. He had often taken the pledge to drink no more, and was a good example of what that sort of unwisdom can do for a man—for a man with anything short of an iron will. The system is wrong in two ways: it does not strike at the root of the trouble, for one thing, and to make a *pledge* of any kind is to declare war against nature; for a pledge is a chain that is always clanking and reminding the wearer of it that he is not a free man.

I have said that the system does not strike at the root of the trouble, and I venture to repeat that. The root is not the *drinking*, but the *desire* to drink. These are very different things. The one merely requires will—and a great deal of it, both as to bulk and staying capacity—the other merely requires watchfulness—and for no long time. The desire of course precedes the act, and should have one's first attention; it can do but little good to refuse the act over and over again, always leaving the desire unmolested, unconquered; the desire will continue to assert itself, and will be almost sure to win in the long run. When the desire intrudes, it should be at once banished out of the mind. One should be on the watch for it all the time—otherwise it will get *in*. It must be taken in time and not allowed to get a lodgment. A desire constantly repulsed for a fortnight should die, then. That should cure the drinking-habit. The system of refusing the mere *act* of drinking, and leaving the *desire* in full force, is unintelligent war tactics, it seems to me.

I used to take pledges—and soon violate them. My will was not strong, and I could not help it. And then, to be tied in any way naturally irks an otherwise free person and makes him chafe in his bonds and want to get his liberty. But when I ceased from taking definite pledges, and merely resolved that I would kill an injurious desire, but leave myself free to resume the desire and habit whenever I should choose to do so, I had no more trouble. In five days I drove out the desire to smoke and was not obliged to keep watch after that; and I never experienced any strong desire to smoke again. At the end of a year and a quarter of idleness I began to write a book, and presently found that the pen was strangely reluctant to go. I tried a smoke to see if that would help me out of the difficulty. It did. I smoked eight or ten cigars and as many pipes for five months, finished the book, and did not smoke again until a year had gone by and another book had to be begun.

I can quit any of my nineteen injurious habits at any time, and without discomfort or inconvenience. I think that the Dr. Tanners and those others who go forty days without eating do it by resolutely keeping out the desire to eat, in the beginning; and that after a few hours the desire is discouraged and comes no more.

Once I tried my scheme in a large medical way. I had been confined to my bed several days with lumbago. My case refused to improve. Finally the doctor said:

"My remedies have no fair chance. Consider what they have to fight, besides the lumbago. You smoke extravagantly, don't you?"

"Yes."

"You take coffee immoderately?"

"Yes."

"And some tea?"

"Yes."

"You eat all kinds of things that are dissatisfied with each other's company?"

"Yes."

"You drink two hot Scotches every night?"

"Yes."

"Very well, there you can see what I have to contend against. We can't make progress the way the matter stands. You must make a reduction in these things; you must cut down on your consumption of them considerably for some days."

"I can't, doctor."

"Why can't you?"

"I lack the will-power. I can cut them off entirely, but I can't merely moderate them."

He said that that would answer, and said he would come around in twenty-four hours and begin work again. He was taken ill himself and could not come; but I did not need him. I cut off all those things for two days and nights; in fact, I cut off all kinds of food, too, and all drinks except water, and at the end of the forty-eight hours the lumbago was discouraged and left me. I was a well man; so I gave thanks and took to those delicacies again.

It seemed a valuable medical course, and I recommended it to a lady. She had run down and down and down, and had at last reached a point where medicines no longer had any helpful effect upon her. I said I knew I could put her upon her feet in a week. It brightened her up, it filled her with hope, and she said she would do everything I told her to do. So I said she must stop swearing and drinking and smoking and eating for four days, and then she would be all right again. And it would have happened just so, I know it; but she said she could not stop swearing and smoking and drinking, because she had never done these things. So there it was. She had neglected her habits, and hadn't any. Now that they would have come good, there were none in stock. She had nothing to fall back on. She was a sinking vessel, with no freight in her to throw overboard and lighten ship withal. Why, even one or two little bad habits could have saved her, but she was just a moral pauper. When she could have acquired them she was dissuaded by her parents, who were ignorant people though reared in the best society, and it was too late to begin now. It seemed such a pity; but there was no help for it. These things ought to be attended to while a person is young; otherwise, when age and disease come, there is nothing effectual to fight them with.

# The Sandwich Islands[6]

On a certain bright morning the Islands hove in sight, lying low on the lonely sea, and everybody climbed to the upper deck to look. After two thousand miles of watery solitude the vision was a welcome one. As we approached, the imposing promontory of Diamond Head rose up out of the ocean, its rugged front softened by the hazy distance, and presently the details of the land began to make themselves manifest; first the line of the beach; then the plumed coconut trees of the tropics; then cabins of the natives; then the white town of Honolulu, said to contain between twelve and fifteen thousand inhabitants, spread over a dead level; with streets from twenty to thirty feet wide, solid and level as a floor, most of then straight as a line and few as crooked as a corkscrew.

The further I traveled through the town the better I liked it. Every step revealed a new contrast—disclosed something I was

[6] The name given to the Hawaiian Islands by Captain Cook in honor of his patron, the Earl of Sandwich, First Lord of the Admiralty, who, during his younger days, was a bit of a rake. A member of the Hellfire Club, he was so devoted to the card table that he had his food brought to him between two slices of bread so that he could continue gambling without the distraction of cutlery.

unaccustomed to. In place of the grand mud-colored brown fronts of San Francisco, I saw dwellings built of straw, adobes, and cream-colored pebble-and-shell-conglomerated coral, cut into oblong blocks and laid in cement; also a great number of neat white cottages, with green window-shutters; in place of front yards like billiard-tables with iron fences around them, I saw these homes surrounded by ample yards, thickly clad with green grass, and shaded by tall trees, through whose dense foliage the sun could scarcely penetrate; in place of the customary geranium, calla lily, etc., languishing in dust and general debility, I saw luxurious banks and thickets of flowers, fresh as a meadow after a rain, and glowing with the richest dyes; in place of the dingy horrors of San Francisco's pleasure grove, the "Willows," I saw huge-bodied, wide-spreading forest trees, with strange names and stranger appearance—trees that cast a shadow like a thundercloud, and were able to stand alone without being tied to green poles; in place of goldfish, wiggling around in glass globes, assuming countless shades and degrees of distortion through the magnifying and diminishing qualities of their transparent prison-house, I saw cats—Tom cats, Mary Ann cats, long-tailed cats, bob-tailed cats, blind cats, one-eyed cats, wall-eyed cats, cross-eyed cats, gray cats, black cats, white cats, yellow cats, striped cats, spotted cats, tame cats, wild cats, singed cats, individual cats, groups of cats, platoons of cats, companies of cats, regiments of cats, armies of cats, multitudes of cats, millions of cats, and all of them sleek, fat, lazy, and sound asleep.

I looked on a multitude of people, some white, in white coats, vests, pantaloons, even white cloth shoes, made snowy with chalk duly laid on every morning; but the majority of the people were almost as dark as Negroes—women with comely features, fine black eyes, rounded forms, inclining to the voluptuous, clad in a single red or white garment that fell free and unconfined from shoulder to heel, long black hair falling loose, gypsy hats, encircled with wreaths of natural flowers of a brilliant carmine tint;

plenty of dark men in various costumes, and some with nothing on but a battered stovepipe hat tilted on the nose, and a very scanty breech-clout; certain smoke-dried children were clothed in nothing but sunshine—a very neat fitting and picturesque apparel indeed.

In place of roughs and rowdies staring and blackguarding on the corners, I saw long-haired, saddle-colored Sandwich Island maidens sitting on the ground in the shade of corner houses, gazing indolently at whatever or whoever happened along; instead of wretched cobblestone pavements, I walked on a firm foundation of coral, built up from the bottom of the sea by the absurd but persevering insect of that name, with a light layer of lava and cinders overlaying the coral, belched up out of fathomless perdition long ago through the seared and blackened crater that stands dead and harmless in the distance now; instead of cramped and crowded streetcars, I met dusky native women sweeping by, free as the wind, on fleet horses and astride, with gaudy riding-sashes streaming like banners behind them; instead of the combined stenches of Chinadom and Brannan Street slaughterhouses, I breathed the balmy fragrance of jessamine, oleander, and the Pride of India; in place of the hurry and bustle and noisy confusion of San Francisco, I moved in the midst of summer calm as tranquil as dawn in the Garden of Eden; in place of the Golden City's skirting sand-hills and the placid bay, I saw on one side a framework of tall, precipitous mountains close at hand, clad in refreshing green, and cleft by deep, cool, chasm-like valleys—and in front the grand sweep of the ocean: a brilliant, transparent green near the shore, bound and bordered by a long white line of foamy spray dashing against the reef, and further out the dead blue water of the deep sea, flecked with "white caps," and in the far horizon a single, lonely sail—a mere accent-mark to emphasize a slumberous calm and a solitude that were without sound or limit. When the sun sunk down—the one intruder from other realms and persistent in suggestions of them—it was tranced luxury to sit in the perfumed air and forget that there was any world but these enchanted islands.

It was such ecstasy to dream and dream—till you got a bite. A scorpion bite. Then the first duty was to get up out of the grass and kill the scorpion; and the next to bathe the bitten place with alcohol or brandy; and the next to resolve to keep out of the grass in the future. Then came an adjournment to the bedchamber and the pastime of writing up the day's journal with one hand and the destruction of mosquitoes with the other—a whole community of them at a slap. Then, observing an enemy approaching—a hairy tarantula on stilts—why not set the spittoon on him? It is done, and the projecting ends of his paws give a luminous idea of the magnitude of his reach. Then to bed and become a promenade for a centipede of forty-two legs on a side and every foot hot enough to burn a hole through a rawhide. More soaking with alcohol, and a resolution to examine the bed before entering it, in future. Then wait, and suffer, till all the mosquitoes in the neighborhood have crawled in under the bar, then slip out quietly, and shut them in and sleep peacefully on the floor till morning. Meantime it is comforting to curse the tropics in occasional wakeful intervals.

We had an abundance of fruit in Honolulu, of course. Oranges, pineapples, bananas, strawberries, lemons, limes, mangoes, guavas, melons, and a rare and curious luxury called the chirimoya, which is deliciousness itself. Then there is the tamarind. I thought tamarinds were made to eat, but that was probably not the idea. I ate several, and it seemed to me that they were rather sour that year. They pursed up my lips, till they resembled the stem-end of a tomato, and I had to take my sustenance through a quill for twenty-four hours. They sharpened my teeth till I could have shaved with them, and gave them a "wire edge" that I was afraid would stay; but a citizen said, "No, it will come off when the enamel does"—which was comforting, at any rate. I found, afterward, that only strangers eat tamarinds—but they only eat them once.

* * *

In my diary of our third day in Honolulu, I find this:

> I am probably the most sensitive man in Hawaii tonight—especially about sitting down in the presence of my betters. I have ridden fifteen or twenty miles on horseback since 5 P.M., and to tell the honest truth, I have a delicacy about sitting down at all.

An excursion to Diamond Head and the King's Coconut Grove was planned today—time 4:30 P.M.—the party to consist of half a dozen gentlemen and three ladies. They all started at the appointed hour except myself. I was at the government prison (with Captain Fish and another whale-ship skipper, Captain Phillips), and got so interested in its examination that I did not notice how quickly the time was passing. Somebody remarked that it was twenty minutes past five o'clock, and that woke me up. It was a fortunate circumstance that Captain Phillips was along with his "turnout," as he calls a top-buggy that Captain Cook brought here in 1778, and a horse that was here when Captain Cook came. Captain Phillips takes a just pride in his driving and in the speed of his horse, and to his passion for displaying them I owe that we were only sixteen minutes in coming from the prison to the American Hotel—a distance which has been estimated to be over half a mile. But it took some fearful driving. The captain's whip came down fast, and the blows started so much dust out of the horse's hide that during the last half of the journey we rode through an impenetrable fog, and ran by a pocket-compass in the hands of Captain Fish, a whaler of twenty-six years' experience, who sat there through the perilous voyage as self-possessed as if he had been on the euchre-deck of his own ship, and calmly said, "Port your helm—port," from time to time, and "Hold her a little free—steady—so-o," and "Luff—hard down to starboard!" and never once lost his presence of mind or betrayed the least anxiety by voice or manner. When we came to anchor at last, and Captain Phillips looked at his watch and said, "Sixteen minutes—I told you it was in her! That's over three miles an hour!" I could see he felt entitled to a compliment, and so I said I had never seen lightning go like that horse. And I never had.

The landlord of the American said the party had been gone nearly an hour, but that he could give me my choice of several horses that could overtake them. I said, never mind—I preferred a safe horse to a fast one—I would like to have an excessively gentle horse—a horse with no spirit whatever—a lame one, if he had such a thing. Inside of five minutes I was mounted, and perfectly satisfied with my outfit. I had no time to label him "This is a horse," and so if the public took him for a sheep I cannot help it. I was satisfied, and that was the main thing. I could see that he had as many fine points as any man's horse, and so I hung my hat on one of them, behind the saddle, and swabbed the perspiration from my face and started. I named him after this island, "Oahu" (pronounced O-waw-hee). The first gate he came to he started in; I had neither whip nor spur, and so I simply argued the case with him. He resisted argument, but ultimately yielded to insult and abuse. He backed out of that gate and steered for another one on the other side of the street. I triumphed by my former process. Within the next six hundred yards he crossed the street fourteen times and attempted thirteen gates, and in the meantime the tropical sun was beating down and threatening to cave the top of my head in, and I was literally dripping with perspiration. He abandoned the gate business after that and went along peaceably enough, but absorbed in meditation. I noticed this latter circumstance, and it soon began to fill me with apprehension. I said to myself, this creature is planning some new outrage, some fresh deviltry or other—no other horse ever thought over a subject so profoundly as this one is doing just for nothing. The more this thing preyed upon my mind the more uneasy I became, until the suspense became almost unbearable, and I dismounted to see if there was anything wild in his eye—for I had heard that the eye of this noblest of our domestic animals is very expressive. I cannot describe what a load of anxiety was lifted from my mind when I found that he was only asleep. I woke him up and started him into a faster walk, and then the villainy of his nature came out again. He tried to climb over a stone wall, five or six feet high. I saw that I must apply force to this horse, and that I might as well begin first as last. I plucked a stout switch from a tamarind tree, and the moment he saw it, he surrendered. He broke into a convulsive sort of canter, which had three short steps in it and one long one, and reminded me alternately of the clattering shake of the great earthquake and the sweeping plunging of the *Ajax* in a storm.

And now there can be no fitter occasion than the present to pronounce a left-handed blessing upon the man who invented the American saddle. There is no seat to speak of about it—one might as well sit in a shovel—and the stirrups are nothing but an ornamental nuisance. If I were to write down here all the abuse I expended on those stirrups, it would make a large book, even without pictures. Sometimes I got one foot so far through that the stirrup partook the nature of an anklet; sometimes both feet were through, and I was handcuffed by the legs; and sometimes my feet got clear out and left the stirrups wildly dangling about my shins. Even when I was in proper position and carefully balanced upon the balls of my feet, there was no comfort in it, on account of my nervous dread that they were going to slip one way or the other in a moment. But the subject is too exasperating to write about.

A mile and a half from town, I came to a grove of tall coconut trees, with clean, branchless stems reaching straight up sixty or seventy feet and topped with a spray of green foliage sheltering clusters of coconuts—not more picturesque than a forest of colossal parasols, with bunches of magnified grapes under them, would be. I once heard a grouty Northern invalid say that a coconut tree might be poetical, possibly it was; but it looked like a feather-duster struck by lightning. I think that describes it better than a picture—and yet, without any question, there is something fascinating about a coconut tree—and graceful, too.

About a dozen cottages, some frame and the others of native grass, nestled sleepily in the shade here and there. The grass cabins are of a grayish color, are shaped much like our own cottages, only with higher and steeper roofs, usually, and are made of some kind of weed strongly bound together in bundles. The roofs are very thick, and so are the walls; the latter have square holes in them for windows. At a little distance these cabins have a furry appearance, as if they might be made of bearskins. They are very cool and pleasant inside. The King's flag was flying from the roof of one of the cottages, and His Majesty was probably within. He owns the whole concern thereabouts, and passes his time there frequently on sultry days "laying off." The spot is called "The King's Grove."

Nearby is an interesting ruin—the meager remains of an ancient temple—a place where human sacrifices were offered up in those old bygone days when the simple child of nature, yielding momentarily to sin when sorely tempted, acknowledged his error when calm reflection had shown it to him, and came forward with noble frankness and offered up his grandmother as an atoning sacrifice—in those old days when the luckless sinner could keep on cleansing his conscience and achieving periodical happiness as long as his relations held out; long, long before the missionaries braved a thousand privations to come and make them permanently miserable by telling them how beautiful and how blissful a place heaven is, and how nearly impossible it is to get there; and showed the poor native how dreary a place perdition is and what unnecessarily liberal facilities there are for going to it; showed him how, in his ignorance, he had gone and fooled away all his kinsfolk to no purpose; showed him what rapture it is to work all day long for fifty cents to buy food for the next day with, as compared with fishing for pastime and lolling in the shade through eternal summer, and eating of the bounty that nobody labored to provide but Nature. How sad it is to think of the multitudes who have gone to their graves in this beautiful island and never knew there was a hell.

* * *

In the breezy morning we went ashore and visited the ruined temple of the last god Lono. The high chief cook of this temple—the priest who presided over it and roasted the human sacrifices—was uncle to Obookia, and at one time that youth was an apprentice priest under him. Obookia was a young native of fine mind, who, together with three other native boys, was taken to New England by the captain of a whale-ship during the reign of Kemehameha I, and they were the means of attracting the attention of the religious world to their country. This resulted in the sending of missionaries there. And this Obookia was the very same sensitive savage who sat down on the church steps and wept because his people did not have the Bible. That incident has been very elaborately painted in many a charming Sunday-school book—aye, and told so plaintively and so tenderly that I have cried over it in Sunday-school myself, on general principles, although at a time when I did not know much and could not understand why the people of the Sandwich Islands needed to worry so much about it as long as they did not know there was a Bible at all.

* * *

Quite a broad tract of land near the temple, extending from the sea to the mountaintop, was sacred to the god Lono in olden times—so sacred that if a common native set his sacrilegious foot upon it, it was judicious for him to make his will, because his time had come. He might go around it by water, but he could not cross it. It was well sprinkled with pagan temples and stocked with awkward, homely idols carved out of logs of wood. There was a temple devoted to prayers for rain—and with fine sagacity it was placed at a point so well up on the mountainside that if you prayed there twenty-four times a day for rain you would be likely to get it every time. You would seldom get to your Amen before you would have to hoist your umbrella.

And there was a large temple near at hand which was built in a single night, in the midst of storm and thunder and rain, by the ghastly hands of dead men! Tradition says that by the weird glare of the lightning a noiseless multitude of phantoms were seen at their strange labor far up the mountainside at dead of night—flitting hither and thither and bearing great lava-blocks clasped in their nerveless fingers—appearing and disappearing as the pallid luster fell upon their forms and faded away again. Even to this day, it is said, the natives hold this dread structure in awe and reverence, and will not pass by it in the night.

At noon I observed a bevy of nude native young ladies bathing in the sea, and went and sat down on their clothes to keep them from being stolen. I begged them to come out, for the sea was rising and I was satisfied that they were running some risk. But they were not afraid, and presently went on with their sport. They were finished swimmers and divers, and enjoyed themselves to the last degree. They swam races, splashed and ducked and tumbled each other about, and filled the air with their laughter. It is said that the first thing an Islander learns is how to swim; learning to walk, being a matter of smaller consequence, comes afterward. One hears tales of native men and women swimming ashore from vessels many miles at sea—more miles, indeed, than I dare vouch for or even mention. And they tell of a native diver who went down in thirty-or forty-foot waters and brought up an anvil! I think he swallowed the anvil afterward, if my memory serves me. However, I will not urge this point.

I have spoken several times of the god Lono—I may as well furnish two or three sentences concerning him.

The idol the natives worshipped for him was a slender, unornamented staff twelve feet long. Tradition says he was a favorite god on the island of Hawaii—a great king who had been deified for meritorious services—just as our own fashion of rewarding heroes, with the difference that we would have made him a postmaster instead of a god, no doubt. In an angry moment he slew his wife, a goddess named Kaikilani Aiii. Remorse of conscience drove him mad, and tradition presents us with the singular spectacle of a god traveling "on the shoulder," for in his gnawing grief he wandered about from place to place boxing and wrestling with all whom he met. Of course, this pastime soon lost its novelty, inasmuch as it must necessarily have been the case that when so powerful a deity sent a frail human opponent "to grass" he never came back any more. Therefore, he instituted games called *makahiki*, and ordered that they should be held in his honor, and then sailed for foreign lands on a three-cornered raft, stating that he would return someday—and that was the last of Lono. He was never seen any more; his raft got swamped, perhaps. But the people always expected his return, and thus they were easily led to accept Captain Cook as the restored god.

Some of the old natives believed that Cook was Lono to the day of their death; but many did not, for they could not understand how he could die if he was a god.

* * *

We rode horseback all around the island of Hawaii (the crooked road making the distance two hundred miles), and enjoyed the journey very much. We were more than a week making the trip, because our Kanaka horses would not go by a house or hut without stopping—whip and spur could not alter their minds about it, and so we finally found that it economized time to let them have their way. Upon inquiry the mystery was explained; the natives are such thoroughgoing gossips that they never pass a house without stopping to swap news, and consequently their horses learn to regard that sort of thing as an essential part of the whole duty of man, and his salvation not to be compassed without it. However, at a former crisis of my life I had once taken an aristocratic young lady out driving, behind a horse that had just retired from a long and honorable career as the moving impulse of a milk-wagon, and so this present experience awoke a reminiscent sadness in me in place of the exasperation more natural to the occasion. I remembered how helpless I was that day, and how humiliated; how ashamed I was of having intimated to the girl that I had always owned the horse and was accustomed to grandeur; how hard I tried to appear easy, and even vivacious, under suffering that was consuming my vitals; how placidly and maliciously the girl smiled, and kept on smiling, while my hot blushes baked themselves into a permanent blood-pudding in my face; how the horse ambled from one side of the street to the other and waited complacently before every third house two minutes and a quarter while I belabored his back and reviled him in my heart; how I tried to keep him from turning corners, and failed; how I moved heaven and earth to get him out of town, and did not succeed; how he traversed the entire settlement and delivered imaginary milk at a hundred and sixty-two different domiciles, and how he finally brought up at a dairy depot and refused to budge further, thus rounding and completing the revealment of what the plebian service of his life had been; how, in eloquent silence, I walked the girl home, and how, when I took leave of her, her parting remark scorched my soul and appeared to blister me all over; she said that my horse was a fine, capable animal, and I must have taken great comfort in him in my time—but that if I would take along some milk-tickets next time, and appear to deliver them at the various halting-places, it might expedite his movements a little. There was a coolness between us after that.

# Underway for the Lands Downunder

Sailed from Honolulu. From diary:

> *Sept. 2.* Flocks of flying fish—slim, shapely, graceful, and intensely white. With the sun on them they look like a flight of silver fruit-knives. They are able to fly a hundred yards.
>
> *Sept. 3.* In 9° 50′ north latitude at breakfast. Approaching the equator on a long slant. Those of us who have never seen the equator are a good deal excited. I think I would rather see it than any other thing in the world. . . .
>
> *Sept. 5.* Closing in on the equator this noon. A sailor explained to a young girl that the ship's speed is poor because we are climbing up the bulge toward the center of the globe; but that when we should once get over, at the equator, and start downhill, we should fly. When she asked him the other day what the foreyard was, he said it was the front yard, the open area in the front end of the ship. That man

has a good deal of learning stored up, and the girl is likely to get it all.

*Afternoon*. Crossed the equator. In the distance it looked like a blue ribbon stretched across the ocean. Several passengers kodak'd it.

* * *

*Wednesday, Sept. 11*. In this world we often make mistakes of judgment. We do not, as a rule, get out of them sound and whole, but sometimes we do. At dinner yesterday evening—present, a mixture of Scotch, English, American, Canadian, and Australasian folk—a discussion broke out about the pronunciation of certain Scottish words. This was private ground, and the non-Scotch nationalities, with one exception, discreetly kept still. But I am not discreet, and I took a hand. I didn't know anything about the subject, but I took a hand just to have something to do. At that moment the word in dispute was the word *three*. One Scotchman was claiming that the peasantry of Scotland pronounced it *three*, his adversaries claimed that they didn't—that they pronounced it *thraw*. The solitary Scot was having a sultry time of it, so I thought I would enrich him with my help. In my position I was necessarily quite impartial, and was equally as well and as ill equipped to fight on the one side as on the other. So I spoke up and said the peasantry pronounced the word *three*, not *thraw*. It was an error of judgment. There was a moment of astonished and ominous silence, then weather ensued. The storm rose and spread in a surprising way, and I was snowed under in a very few minutes. It was a bad defeat for me—a kind of Waterloo. It promised to remain so, and I wished I had had better sense than to enter upon such a forlorn enterprise. But just then I had a saving thought—at least a thought that offered a chance. While the storm was still raging, I made up a Scotch couplet, and then spoke up and said:

"Very well, don't say any more. I confess defeat. I thought I knew, but I see my mistake. I was deceived by one of your Scotch poets."

"A *Scotch* poet! Oh, come! Name him."

"*Robert Burns.*"

It is wonderful, the power of that name. The men looked doubtful—but paralyzed, all the same. They were quite silent for a moment; then one of them said—with the reverence in his voice which is always present in a Scotchman's tone when he utters the name:

"Does Robbie Burns say—*what* does he say?"

"This is what he says:

> There were nae bairns but only three—
> Ane at the breast, twa at the knee."

It ended the discussion. There was no man there profane enough, disloyal enough, to say any word against a thing which Robert Burns had settled. I shall always honor that great name for the salvation it brought me in this time of my sore need.

It is my belief that nearly any invented quotation, played with confidence, stands a good chance to deceive. There are people who think that honesty is always the best policy. This is a superstition; there are times when the appearance of it is worth six of it.

# Squatters

All English-speaking colonies are made up of lavishly hospitable people, and New South Wales and its capital are like the rest in this. The English-speaking colony of the United States of America is always called lavishly hospitable by the English traveler. As to the other English-speaking colonies throughout the world from Canada all around, I know by experience that the description fits them. I will not go more particularly into this matter, for I find that when writers try to distribute their gratitude here and there and yonder by detail, they run across difficulties and do some ungraceful stumbling.

* * *

Sydney has a population of four hundred thousand. When a stranger from America steps ashore there, the first thing that strikes him is that the place is eight or nine times as large as he was expecting it to be; and the next things that strikes him is that it is an English city with American trimmings. Later on, in Melbourne, he will find the American trimmings still more in evidence; there, even the architecture will often suggest America; a photograph of its stateliest business street might be passed upon him for a picture of the finest street in a large American city. I was told that most of the fine residences were the city residences of squatters. The name seemed out of focus somehow. When the explanation came, it offered a new instance of the curious changes which words, as well as animals, undergo through change of habitat and climate. With us, when you speak of a squatter you are always supposed to be speaking of a poor man, but in Australia when you speak of a squatter you are supposed to be speaking of a millionaire; in America the word indicates the possessor of a few acres and a doubtful title, in Australia it indicates a man whose land front is as long as a railroad, and whose title has been perfected in one way or another; in America the word indicates a man who owns a dozen head of livestock, in Australia a man who owns anywhere from fifty thousand up to a half a million head; in America the word indicates a man who is obscure and not important, in Australia a man who is prominent and of the first importance; in America you take off your hat to no squatter, in Australia you do; in America if your uncle is a squatter you keep it dark, in Australia you advertise it; in America if your friend is a squatter nothing comes of it, but with a squatter for your friend in Australia you may sup with kings if there are any around.

In Australia it takes about two acres and a half of pastureland (some people say twice as many) to support a sheep; and when a squatter has half a million sheep his private domain is about as large as Rhode Island, to speak in general terms. His annual wool crop may be worth a quarter or a half million dollars.

He will live in a palace in Melbourne or Sydney or some other of the large cities, and make occasional trips to his sheep-kingdom several hundred miles away in the great plains to look after his battalions of riders and shepherds and other hands. He has a commodious dwelling out there, and if he approves of you he will invite you to spend a week in it, and will make you at home and comfortable, and let you see the great industry in all its details, and feed you and slake you and smoke you with the best that money can buy.

On at least one of these vast estates there is a considerable town, with all the various businesses and occupations that go to make an important town; and the town and the land it stands upon are the property of the squatters. I have seen that town, and it is not unlikely that there are other squatter-owned towns in Australia. . . .

The Australians did not seem to me to differ noticeably from Americans, either in dress, carriage, ways, pronunciation, inflections, or general appearance. There were fleeting and subtle suggestions of their English origin, but these were not pronounced enough, as a rule, to catch one's attention. The people have easy and cordial manners from the beginning—from the moment that the introduction is completed. This is American. To put it another way, it is English friendliness with the English shyness and self-consciousness left out.

Now and then—but this is rare—ones hears such words as *piper* for paper, *lydy* for lady, and *tyble* for table fall from lips whence one would not expect such pronunciations to come. There is a superstition prevalent in Sydney that this pronunciation is an Australianism, but people who have been "home"—as the native reverently and lovingly calls England—know better. It is "costermonger." All over Australasia this pronunciation is nearly as common among servants as it is in London among the uneducated and partially educated of all sorts and conditions of people. That mislaid *y* is rather striking when a person gets enough of it into a short sentence to enable it to show up. In a hotel in Sydney the chambermaid said one morning:

[7] The "lydy" in question was Mrs. Clemens.

"The tyble is set, and here is the piper; and if the lydy is ready I'll tell the wyter to bring up the breakfast."[7]

I have made passing mention, a moment ago, of the native Australasian's custom of speaking of England as "home." It was always pretty to hear it, and often it was said in an unconsciously caressing way that made it touching; in a way which transmuted a sentiment into an embodiment, and made one seem to see Australasia as a young girl stroking mother England's old gray head.

In the Australasian's home the table-talk is vivacious and unembarrassed; it is without stiffness and restraint. This does not remind one of England so much as it does of America. But Australasia is strictly democratic, and reserves and restraints are things that are bred by differences of rank.

English and colonial audiences are phenomenally alert and responsive. Where masses of people are gathered together in England, caste is submerged, and with it the English reserve; equality exists for the moment, and every individual is free; so free from any consciousness of fetters, indeed, that the Englishman's habit of watching himself and guarding himself against any injudicious exposure of his feelings is forgotten, and falls into abeyance—and to such a degree, indeed, that he will bravely applaud all by himself if he wants to—an exhibition of daring which is unusual elsewhere in the world.

But it is hard to move a new English acquaintance when he is by himself, or when the company present is small, and new to him. He is on guard then, and his natural reserve is to the fore. This has given him the false reputation of being without humor and without the appreciation of humor. Americans are not Englishmen, and American humor is not English humor; but both the American and his humor had their origin in England, and have merely undergone changes brought about by changed conditions and a new environment. About the best humorous speeches I have yet heard were a couple that were made in Australia at club suppers—one of them by an Englishman, the other by an Australian.

* * *

One of these old gentlemen told me some things of interest afterward; things about the aboriginals mainly. He thought them intelligent—remarkably so in some directions—and he said that along with their unpleasant qualities they had some exceedingly good ones . . . He instanced their invention of the boomerang and the "weet-weet" as evidences of their brightness; and as another evidence of it he said he had never seen a white man who had the cleverness to learn to do the miracles with those two toys that the aboriginals achieved. He said that even the smartest whites had been obliged to confess that they could not learn the trick of the boomerang in perfection; that it had possibilities which they could not master. The white man could not control its motions, could not make it obey him; but the aboriginal could. He told me some wonderful things—some almost incredible things—which he had seen the blacks do with the boomerang and the weet-weet. They have been confirmed to me since by other early settlers and by trustworthy books.

It is contended—and may be said to be conceded—that the boomerang was known to certain savage tribes in Europe in Roman times. In support of this, Virgil and two other Roman poets are quoted. It is also contended that it was known to the ancient Egyptians.

One of two things is then apparent: either some one with a boomerang arrived in Australia in the days of antiquity before European knowledge of the thing had been lost, or the Australian aboriginal re-invented it. It will take some time to find out which of these two propositions is the fact. But there is no hurry.

# A Christmas Pudding

Before I saw Australia I had never heard of the "weet-weet" at all. I met but few men who had seen it thrown—at least I met but few who mentioned having seen it thrown. Roughly described, it is a fat wooden cigar with its butt-end fastened to a flexible twig. The whole thing is only a couple of feet long, and weighs less than two ounces. This feather—so to call it—is not thrown through the air, but is flung with an underhanded throw and made to strike the ground a little way in front of the thrower; then it glances and makes a long skip; glances again, skips again, and again and again, like the flat stone which a boy sends skating over the water. The water is smooth, and the stone has a good chance; so a strong man may make it travel fifty or seventy-five yards; but the weet-weet has no such good chance, for it strikes sand, grass, and earth in its course. Yet an expert aboriginal has sent it a measured distance of *two hundred and twenty yards*. It would have gone even further but it encountered rank ferns and underwood on its passage and they damaged its speed. Two hundred and twenty yards; and so weightless a toy—a mouse on the end of a bit of wire, in effect; and not sailing through the accommodating air, but encountering grass and sand and stuff at every jump. It looks wholly impossible; but Mr. Brough Smyth saw the feat and did the measuring, and set down the facts in his book about aboriginal life, which he wrote by command of the Victoria Government.

What is the secret of the feat? No one explains. It cannot be physical strength, for that could not drive such a feather-weight any distance. It must be art. But no one explains what the art of it is; nor how it gets around that law of nature which says you shall not throw any two-ounce thing two hundred and twenty yards, either through the air or bumping along the ground.

* * *

There must have been a large distribution of acuteness among those naked, skinny aboriginals, or they couldn't have been such unapproachable trackers and boomerangers and weet-weeters. It must have been race-aversion that put upon them a good deal of the low-rate intellectual reputation which they bear and have borne this long time in the world's estimate of them.

They were lazy—always lazy. Perhaps that was their trouble. It is a killing defect. Surely they could have invented and built a competent house, but they didn't. And they could have invented and developed the agricultural arts, but they didn't. They went naked and houseless, and lived on fish and grubs and worms and wild fruits, and were just plain savages, for all their smartness.

With a country as big as the United States to live and multiply in, and with no epidemic diseases among them till the white man came with those and his other appliances of civilization, it is quite probable that there was never a day in his history when he could muster one hundred thousand of his race in all Australia. He diligently and deliberately kept population down by infanticide—largely; but mainly by certain other methods. He did not need to practice these artificialities any more after the white man came.

The white man knew ways of keeping down population which were worth several of his. The white man knew ways of reducing a native population eighty percent in twenty years. The native had never seen anything as fine as that before.

* * *

The early whites were not used to savages. They could not understand the primary law of savage life: that if a man do you a wrong, his whole tribe is responsible—each individual of it—and you may take your change out of any individual of it, without bothering to seek out the guilty one. When a white killed an aboriginal, the tribe applied the ancient law, and killed the first white they came across. To the whites this was a monstrous thing. Extermination seemed to be the proper medicine for such creatures as this. They did not kill all the blacks, but they promptly killed enough of them to make their own persons safe. From the dawn of civilization down to this day the white man has always used that very precaution. Mrs. Campbell Praed lived in Queensland, as a child, in the early days, and in her *Sketches of Australian Life* we get informing pictures of the early struggles of the white and the black to reform each other.

Speaking of the pioneer days in the mighty wilderness of Queensland, Mrs. Praed says:

> At first the natives retreated before the whites; and, except that they every now and then speared a beast in one of the herds, gave little cause for uneasiness. But, as the number of squatters increased, each one taking up miles of country and bringing two or three men in his train, so that shepherds' huts and stockmen's camps lay far apart, and defenseless in the midst of hostile tribes, the Blacks' depredations became more frequent and murder was no unusual event.

> The loneliness of the Australian bush can hardly be painted in words. Here extends mile after mile of primeval forest. . . . All wild, vast, and desolate. . . .

That is the theater for the drama. When you comprehend one or two other details, you will perceive how well suited for trouble it was, and how loudly it invited it. The cattlemen's stations were scattered over that profound wilderness miles and miles apart—at each station half a dozen persons. There was a plenty of cattle; the black natives were always ill-nourished and hungry. The land belonged to *them*. The whites had not bought it, and couldn't buy it; for the tribes had no chiefs, nobody in authority, nobody competent to sell and convey; and the tribes themselves had no comprehension of the idea of transferable ownership of land. The ousted owners were despised by the white interlopers, and this opinion was not hidden under a bushel. More promising materials for a tragedy could not have been collated. Let Mrs. Praed speak:

> At Nie Nie station, one dark night, the unsuspecting hut-keeper, having, as he believed, secured himself against assault, was lying wrapped in his blankets sleeping profoundly. The Blacks crept stealthily down the chimney and battered in his skull while he slept.

One could guess the whole drama from that little text. The curtain was up. It would not fall until the mastership of one party or the other was determined—and permanently:

> There was treachery on both sides. The Blacks killed the Whites when they found them defenseless, and the Whites slew the Blacks in wholesale and promiscuous fashion. . . . They were regarded as little above the level of brutes, and in some cases *were destroyed like vermin*.

> Here is an instance. A squatter, whose station was surrounded by Blacks, whom he suspected to be hostile and from whom he feared an attack, parleyed with them from

> his house door. He told them it was Christmas-time—a time at which all men, white and black, feasted; that there were flour, sugar-plums, good things in plenty in the store, and that he would make for them a pudding as they had never dreamed of—a great pudding of which all might eat and be filled. The Blacks listened and were lost. The pudding was made and distributed. Next morning there was howling in the camp, for it had been sweetened with sugar and arsenic.

The white man's spirit was right, but his method was wrong. His spirit was the spirit which the civilized white has always exhibited toward the savage, but the use of poison was a departure from custom. True, it was merely a technical departure, not a real one; still, it was a departure, and therefore a mistake, in my opinion. It was better, kinder, swifter, and much more humane than a number of the methods which have been sanctified by custom, but that does not justify its employment. That is, it does not wholly justify it. Its unusual nature makes it stand out and attract an amount of attention which it is not entitled to. It takes hold upon morbid imaginations and they work it up into a sort of exhibition of cruelty, and this smirches the good name of our civilization, whereas one of the old harsher methods would have had no such effect because usage has made those methods familiar to us and innocent. . . . In many countries we have taken the savage's land from him, and made him our slave, and lashed him every day, and broken his pride, and made death his only friend, and overworked him till he dropped in his tracks; and this we do not [mind] because custom has inured us to it; yet a quick death by poison is loving-kindness [compared] to it. . . .

Mrs. Praed says of the poisoner, "That squatter deserves to have his name handed down to the contempt of posterity."

I am sorry to hear her say that. I myself blame him for one thing, and severely, but I stop there. I blame him for the indiscretion of introducing a novelty which was calculated to attract attention to our civilization. There was no occasion to do that. It was his duty, and it is every loyal man's duty, to protect that heritage in every way he can; and the best way to do that is to attract attention elsewhere. The squatter's judgment was bad—that is plain; but his heart was right. He is almost the only pioneering representative of civilization in history who has risen above the prejudices of his caste and his heredity and tried to introduce the element of mercy into the superior race's dealings with the savage. His name is lost, and it is a pity; for it deserves to be handed down to posterity with homage and reverence. . . .

There are many humorous things in the world; among them the white man's notion that he is less savage than the other savages.

# Part Four

## *India*

*I could easily learn to prefer an elephant to any other vehicle, partly because of that immunity from collisions, and partly because of the fine view one has from up there, and partly because of the dignity one feels in that high place, and partly because one can look in at the windows and see what is going on privately among the family.*

from *Following the Equator*

# Only One

There is only one India! It is the only country that has a monopoly of grand and imposing specialties. When another country has a remarkable thing, it cannot have it all to itself—some other country has a duplicate. But India—that is different. Its marvels are its own; the patents cannot be infringed; imitations are not possible. And think of the size of them, the majesty of them, the weird and outlandish character of most of them!

There is the Plague, the Black Death: India invented it; India is the cradle of that mighty birth.

The Car of Juggernaut was India's invention.

So was the Suttee; and within the time of men still living eight hundred widows willingly, and, in fact, rejoicingly, burned themselves to death on the bodies of their dead husbands in a single year. Eight hundred would do it this year if the British Government would let them.

Famine is India's specialty. Elsewhere famines are inconsequential incidents—in India they are devastating cataclysms; in one case they annihilate hundreds; in the other, millions.

India has two million gods, and worships them all. In religion all other countries are paupers; India is the only millionaire.

With her everything is on a giant scale—even her poverty; no other country can show anything to compare with it. And she has been used to wealth on so vast a scale that she has to shorten to single words the expressions describing great sums. She describes one hundred thousand with one word—a *lakh*; she describes ten millions with one word—a *crore*.

In the bowels of the granite mountains she has patiently carved out dozens of vast temples, and made them glorious with sculptured colonnades and stately groups of statuary, and has adorned the eternal walls with noble paintings. She has built fortresses of such magnitude that the show-strongholds of the rest of the world are but modest little things by comparison; palaces that are wonders for rarity of materials, delicacy and beauty of workmanship, and for cost; and one tomb which men go around the globe to see. It takes eighty nations, speaking eighty languages, to people her. . . .

On top of all this she is the mother and home of that wonder of wonders—*caste*—and of that mystery of mysteries, the satanic brotherhood of the Thugs.[8]

India had the start of the whole world in the beginning of things. She had the first civilization; she had the first accumulation of material wealth; she was populous with deep thinkers and subtle intellects; she had mines, and woods, and a fruitful soil. It would seem as if she should have kept the lead, and should be today not the meek dependent of an alien master, but mistress of the world, and delivering law and command to every tribe and nation in it. But, in truth, there was never any possibility of such supremacy for her. If there had been but one India and one language—but there were eighty of them! Where there are eighty nations and several hundred governments, fighting and quarreling must be the common business of life; unity of purpose and policy are impossible; out of such elements

[8] A secretive religious cult dedicated to ritual murder of travelers.

supremacy in the world cannot come. Even caste itself could have had the defeating effect of a multiplicity of tongues, no doubt; for it separates a people into layers, and layers, and still other layers, that have no community of feeling with each other; and in such a condition of things as that, patriotism can have no healthy growth.

It was this division of the country into so many states and nations that made Thuggee possible and prosperous. It is difficult to realize the situation. But perhaps one may approximate it by imagining the states of our Union peopled by separate nations, speaking separate languages, with guards and custom-houses strung along all frontiers, plenty of interruptions for travelers and traders, interpreters able to handle all the languages very rare or non existent, and a few wars always going on here and there and yonder as a further embarrassment to commerce and excursioning. It would make inter-communication in a measure ungeneral. India had eighty languages, and more custom-houses than cats. No clever man with the instinct of a highway robber could fail to notice what a chance for business was here offered. India was full of clever men with the highwayman instinct, and so, quite naturally, the brotherhood of the Thugs came into being to meet the long-felt want.

How long ago that was nobody knows—centuries, it is supposed. One of the chiefest wonders connected with it was the success with which it kept its secret. The English trader did business in India two hundred years and more before he ever heard of it; and yet it was assassinating its thousands all around him every year, the whole time.

* * *

It is a curious people. With them, all life seems to be sacred, except human life. Even the life of vermin is sacred, and must not be taken. The good Jain[9] wipes off a seat before using it, lest he cause

[9] A follower of Jainism, an ancient Indian religion emphasizing the perfectability of man through asceticism and non violence to all living creatures.

the death of some valueless insect by sitting down on it. It grieves him to have to drink water, because the provisions in his stomach may not agree with the microbes. Yet India has invented Thuggery and the Suttee. India is a hard country to understand.

# Bombay

*Bombay*! A bewitching place, a bewildering place, an enchanting place—the Arabian Nights come again! It is a vast city; contains about a million inhabitants. Natives, they are, with a slight sprinkling of white people—not enough to have the slightest modifying effect upon the massed dark complexion of the public. It is winter here, yet the weather is the divine weather of June, and the foliage is the fresh and heavenly foliage of June. There is a rank of noble great shade trees across the way from the hotel, and under them sit groups of picturesque natives of both sexes; and the juggler in his turban is there with his snakes and his magic; and all day long the cabs and the multitudinous varieties of costumes flock by. It does not seem as if one could ever get tired of watching this moving show, this shining and shifting spectacle. In the great bazaar the pack and jam of natives was marvelous, the sea of rich-colored turbans and draperies an inspiring sight, and the quaint and showy Indian architecture was just the right setting for it. Toward sunset another show; this is the drive around the seashore to Malabar Point, where Lord Sandhurst, the Governor of the Bombay Presidency, lives. Parsee palaces all along the first part of the drive; and past them all the world is driving; the private carriages of wealthy Englishmen and natives of rank are manned by a driver and three footmen in stunning oriental liveries—two of these turbaned statues standing up behind, as fine as monuments. Sometimes even the public carriages have this superabundant crew, slightly modified—one to drive, one to sit by and see it done, and one to stand up behind and yell—yell when there is anybody in the way, and for practice when there isn't. It all helps to keep up the liveliness and augment the general sense of swiftness and energy and confusion and pow-wow.

In the region of Scandal Point—felicitous name—where there are handy rocks to sit on and a noble view of the sea on the one hand, and on the other the passing and repassing whirl and tumult of gay carriages, are great groups of comfortably off Parsee women—perfect flower-beds of brilliant color, a fascinating spectacle. Tramp, tramp, tramping along the road, in singles, couples, groups, and gangs, you have the working-man and the working-woman—but not clothed like ours. Usually the man is a nobly-built great athlete, with not a rag on but his loin-handkerchief; his color is a deep dark brown, his skin satin, his rounded muscles knobbing it as if it had eggs under it. Usually the woman is a slender and shapely creature, as erect as a lightning-rod, and she has but one thing on—a bright-colored piece of stuff which is wound about her head and her body down nearly halfway to her knees, and which clings like her own skin. Her legs and feet are bare, and so are her arms, except for her fanciful bunches of loose silver rings on her ankles and on her arms. She had jewelry bunched on the side of her nose also, and showy cluster-rings on her toes. When she undresses for bed she takes off her jewelry, I suppose. If she took off anything more she would catch cold. As a rule, she has a large shiny brass water-jar of graceful shape on her head, and one of her naked arms curves up and the hand holds it there. She is so straight, so erect, and she steps with such style, and such easy grace and dignity; and her curved arm and her brazen jar are such a help to the picture—indeed, our working-women cannot begin with her as a road-decoration.

It is all color, bewitching color, enchanting color—everywhere—all around—all the way around the curving great opaline bay clear to Government House, where the turbaned big native *chuprassies*[10] stand grouped in state at the door in their robes of fiery red, and do most properly and stunningly finish up the splendid show and make it theatrically complete. I wish I were a *chuprassy*.

This is indeed India; *the* land of dreams and romance, of fabulous wealth and fabulous poverty, of splendor and rags, of palaces and hovels, of famine and pestilence, of genii and giants and Aladdin lamps, of tigers and elephants, the cobra and the jungle, the country of a hundred nations amd a hundred tongues, of a thousand religions and two million gods, cradle of the human race, birthplace of human speech, mother of history, grandmother of legend, great-grandmother of tradition, whose yesterdays bear date with the mouldering antiquities of the rest of the nations—the one sole country under the sun that is endowed with an imperishable interest for alien prince and alien peasant, for lettered and ignorant, wise and fool, rich and poor, bond and free, the one land that *all* men desire to see, and having seen it once, by even a glimpse, would not give that glimpse for the shows of all the rest of the globe combined. . .

Our rooms were high up, on the front. A white man—he was a burly German—went up with us, and brought three natives along to see to arranging things. About fourteen others followed in procession, with the hand-baggage; each carried an article—and only one; a bag, in some cases, in other cases, less. One strong native carried my overcoat, another a parasol, another a box of cigars, another a novel, and the last man in the procession had no load but a

[10] A servant or messenger employed by the government.

fan. It was all done with earnestness and sincerity; there was not a smile in the procession from the head of it to the tail of it. Each man waited patiently, tranquilly, in no sort of hurry, till one of us found time to give him a copper, then he bent his head reverently, touched his forehead with his fingers, and went his way. They seemed a soft and gentle race, and there was something both winning and touching about their demeanor.

There was a vast glazed door which opened upon the balcony. It needed closing, or cleaning, or something, and a native got down on his knees and went to work at it. He seemed to be doing it well enough, but perhaps he wasn't, for the burly German put on a look that betrayed dissatisfaction, then without *explaining* what was wrong, gave the native a brisk cuff on the jaw and *then* told him where the defect was. It seemed such a shame to do that before us all. The native took it with meekness, saying nothing, and not showing in his face or manner any resentment. I had not seen the like of this for fifty years. It carried me back to my boyhood, and flashed upon me the forgotten fact that this was the *usual* way of explaining one's desires to a slave. I was able to remember that the method seemed right and natural to me in those days, I being born to it and unaware that elsewhere there were other methods; but I was also able to remember that those unresented cuffings made me sorry for the victim and ashamed for the punisher. My father was a refined and kindly gentleman, very grave, rather austere, of rigid probity, a sternly just and upright man, albeit he attended no church and never spoke of religious matters, and had no part nor lot in the pious joys of his Presbyterian family, nor ever seemed to suffer from this deprivation. He laid his hand upon me in punishment only twice in his life, and then not heavily; once for telling him a lie—which surprised me, and showed me how unsuspicious he was, for that was not my maiden effort. He punished me those two times only, and never any other member of the family at all; yet every now and then he cuffed our harmless slave-boy, Lewis, for trifling little blunders and awkwardnesses. My father had passed his life among the slaves from his cradle up, and his cuffings proceeded from the custom of the time, not from his nature. When I was ten years old I saw a man fling a lump of iron-ore at a slave-man in anger, for merely doing something awkwardly—as if that were a crime. It bounded from the man's skull, and the man fell and never spoke again. He was dead in an hour. I knew the man had a right to kill his slave if he wanted to, and yet it seemed a pitiful thing and somehow wrong, though why wrong I was not deep enough to explain if I had been asked to do it. Nobody in the village approved of that murder, but of course no one said much about it.

It is curious—this space-annihilating power of thought. For just one second, all that goes to make the *me* in me was in a Missourian village, on the other side of the globe, vividly seeing again these forgotten pictures of fifty years ago, and wholly unconscious of all things but just those; and in the next second I was back in Bombay, and that kneeling native's smitten cheek was not done tingling yet! Back to boyhood—fifty years; back to age again, another fifty; and a flight equal to the circumference of the globe—all in two seconds by the watch!

Some natives—I don't remember how many—went into my bedroom, now, and put things to rights and arranged the mosquito-bar, and I went to bed to nurse my cough. It was about nine in the evening. What a state of things! For three hours the yelling and shouting of the natives in the hall continued, along with the velvety patter of their swift bare feet—what a racket it was! They were yelling orders and messages down three flights. Why, in the matter of noise it amounted to a riot, an insurrection, a revolution. And then there were other noises mixed up with these and at intervals tremendously accenting them—roofs falling in, I judged, or windows smashing, persons being murdered, crows squawking, and deriding, and cursing, canaries screeching, monkeys jabbering, macaws blaspheming, and every now and then fiendish bursts of laughter and explosions of dynamite. By midnight I had suffered all the different kinds of shocks there are, and knew that

I could never more be disturbed by them, either isolated or in combination. Then came peace—stillness deep and solemn—and lasted till five.

Then it all broke loose again. And who restarted it? The Bird of Birds—the Indian crow. I came to know him well, by and by, and be infatuated with him. I suppose he is the hardest lot that wears feathers. Yes, and the cheerfulest, and the best satisfied with himself. He never arrived at what he is by any careless process, or any sudden one; he is a work of art, and "art is long"; he is the product of immemorial ages, and of deep calculation; one can't make a bird like that in a day. He has been reincarnated more times than Shiva; and he has kept a sample of each incarnation, and fused it into his constitution. In the course of his evolutionary promotions, his sublime march toward ultimate perfection, he has been a gambler, a low comedian, a dissolute priest, a fussy woman, a blackguard, a scoffer, a liar, a thief, a spy, an informer, a trading politician, a swindler, a professional hypocrite, a patriot for cash, a reformer, a lecturer, a lawyer, a conspirator, a rebel, a royalist, a democrat, a practicer and propagator of irreverence, a meddler, an intruder, a busybody, an infidel, and a wallower in sin for the mere love of it. The strange result, the incredible result, of this patient accumulation of all damnable traits is that he does not know what care is, he does not know what sorrow is, he does not know what remorse is; his life is one long thundering ecstasy of happiness, and he will go to his death untroubled, knowing that he will soon turn up again as an author or something, and be even more intolerably capable and comfortable than ever he was before.

In his straddling wide forward-step, and his springy sidewise series of hops, and his impudent air, and his cunning way of canting his head to one side upon occasion, he reminds one of the American blackbird. But the sharp resemblances stop there. He is much bigger than the blackbird; and he lacks the blackbird's trim and slender and beautiful build and shapely beak; and of course his sober garb of gray and rusty black is a poor and humble thing compared with the splendid luster of the blackbird's metallic sables and shifting and flashing bronze glories. The blackbird is a perfect gentleman, in deportment and attire, and is not noisy, I believe, except when holding religious services and political conventions in a tree; but this Indian sham Quaker is just a rowdy, and is always noisy when awake—always chaffing, scolding, scoffing, laughing, ripping, and cursing, and carrying on about something or other. I never saw such a bird for delivering opinions. Nothing escapes him; he notices everything that happens, and brings out his opinion about it, particularly if it is a matter that is none of his business. And it is never a mild opinion, but always violent—violent and profane—the presence of ladies does not affect him. His opinions are not the outcome of reflection, for he never thinks about anything, but heaves out the opinion that is on top of his mind, and which is often an opinion about some quite different thing and does not fit the case. But that is his way; his main idea is to get out an opinion, and if he stopped to think he would lose chances.

I suppose he has no enemies among men. The whites and Mohammedans never seem to molest him; and the Hindus, because of their religion, never take the life of any creature, but spare even the snakes and tigers and fleas and rats. If I sat at one end of the balcony, the crows would gather on the railing at the other end and talk about me, and edge closer, little by little, till I could almost reach them; and they would sit there, in the most unabashed way, and talk about my clothes, and my hair, and my complexion, and probable character and vocation and politics, and how I came to be in India, and what I had been doing, and how many days I had got for it, and how I happened to go unhanged so long, and when would it probably come off, and might there be more of my sort where I came from, and when would *they* be hanged—and so on, and so on, until I could no longer endure the embarrassment of it; then I would shoo them away, and they would circle around in the air a little while, laughing and deriding and mocking, and presently settle on the rail and do it all over again.

They were very sociable when there was anything to eat—oppressively so. With a little encouragement they would come in and light on the table and help me eat my breakfast; and once when I was in the other room and they found themselves alone, they carried off everything they could lift; and they were particular to choose things which they could make no use of after they got them. In India their number is beyond estimate, and their noise is in proportion. I suppose they cost the country more than the government does; yet that is not a light matter. Still, they pay; their company pays; it would sadden the land to take their cheerful voice out of it.

# Pilgrims

Then we struck into the hot plain and found the road crowded with pilgrims of both sexes, for one of the great religious fairs of India was being held . . . at the juncture of the sacred rivers, the Ganges and the Jumna. Three sacred rivers, I should have said, for there is a subterranean one. Nobody has seen it, but that doesn't signify. The fact that it is there is enough. These pilgrims had come from all over India; some of them had been months on the way, plodding patiently along in the heat and dust, worn, poor, hungry, but supported and sustained by an unwavering faith and belief; they were supremely happy and content, now; their full and sufficient reward was at hand; they were going to be cleansed from every vestige of sin and corruption by these holy waters which make utterly pure whatsoever thing they touch, even the dead and rotten. It is wonderful, the power of a faith like that, that can make multitudes upon multitudes of the old and weak and the young and frail enter without hesitation or complaint upon such incredible journeys and endure the resultant miseries without repining. It is done in love, or it is done in fear; I do not know which it is. No matter what the impulse is, the act born of it is beyond imagination—marvelous to our kind of people, the cold whites. There are choice great natures among us that could exhibit the equivalent of this prodigious self-sacrifice, but the rest of us know that we should not be equal to anything approaching it. Still, we all talk self-sacrifice, and this makes me hope that we are large enough to honor it in the Hindu.

Two millions of natives arrive at this fair every year. How many start, and die on the road, from age and fatigue and disease and scanty nourishment, and how many die on the return, from the same causes, no one knows; but the tale is great, one may say enormous. Every twelfth year is held to be a year of particular grace; a greatly augmented volume of pilgrims results then. The twelfth year has held this distinction since the remotest times, it is said. It is said also that there is to be but one more twelfth year—for the Ganges. After that, that holiest of all sacred rivers will cease to be holy, and will be abandoned by the pilgrim for many centuries; how many, the wise men have not stated. At the end of that interval it will become holy again. Meantime, the data will be arranged by those people who have charge of all such matters, the great chief Brahmans. It will be like shutting down a mint. At a first glance it looks most unbrahmanically uncommercial, but I am not disturbed, being soothed and tranquilized by their reputation. "Brer fox he lay low," as Uncle Remus says; and at the judicious time he will spring something on the Indian public which will show that he was not financially asleep when he took the Ganges out of the market.

Great numbers of the natives along the roads were bringing away holy water from the rivers. They would carry it far and wide in India and sell it. . . .

The Fort is a huge old structure, and has had a large experience in religions. In its great court stands a monolith which was placed there more than two thousand years ago to preach Buddhism by its pious inscription; the Fort was built three centuries ago by a Mohammedan emperor—a resanctification of the place in the interest of *that* religion. There is a Hindu temple, too, with subterranean ramifications stock with shrines and idols; and now the Fort belongs to the English, it contains a Christian church. Insured in all the companies.

From the lofty ramparts one has a fine view of the sacred rivers. They join at that point—the pale-blue Jumna, apparently clean and clear, and the muddy Ganges, dull yellow and not clean. On a long curved spit between the rivers, towns of tents were visible, with a multitude of fluttering pennons, and a mighty swarm of pilgrims. It was a troublesome place to get down to, and not a quiet place when you arrived; but it was interesting. There was a world of activity and turmoil and noise, partly religious, partly commercial; for the Mohammedans were there to curse and sell, and the Hindus to buy and pray. It was a fair as well as a religious festival. Crowds were bathing, praying, and drinking the purifying waters, and many sick pilgrims had come long journeys in palanquins to be healed of their maladies by a bath; or if that might not be, then to die on the blessed banks and so make sure of heaven. There were fakirs in plenty, with their bodies dusted over with ashes and their long hair caked together with cow-dung; for the cow is holy and so is the rest of it; so holy that the good Hindu peasant frescoes the walls of his hut with this refuse, and also constructs ornamental figures out of it for the gracing of his dirt floor. There were seated families, fearfully and wonderfully painted, who by attitude and grouping represented the families of certain great gods. There was a holy man who sat naked by the day and by the week on a cluster of iron spikes, and did not seem to mind it; and another holy man who stood all day holding his withered arms motionless aloft, and was said to have been doing it for years. All of these performers have a cloth on the ground beside them for the reception of contributions, and even the poorest of the people give a trifle and hope that the sacrifice will be blessed to him. At last came a procession of naked holy people marching by and chanting, and I wrenched myself away.

# Benares

The journey to Benares was all in daylight, and occupied but a few hours. It was admirably dusty. The dust settled upon you in a thick ashy layer and turned you into a fakir, with nothing lacking to the role but the cow-manure and the sense of holiness. There was a change of cars about mid-afternoon at Moghul-serai—if that was the name—and a wait of two hours there for the Benares train. We could have found a carriage and driven to the sacred city, but we should have lost the wait. In other countries a long wait at a station is a dull thing and tedious, but one has no right to have that feeling in India. You have the monster crowd of bejeweled natives, the stir, the bustle, the confusion, the shifting splendors of the costumes—dear me, the delight of it, the charm of it are beyond speech. The two-hour wait was over too soon. Among other satisfying things to look at was a minor native prince from the backwoods somewhere, with his guard of honor, a ragged but wonderfully gaudy gang of fifty dark barbarians armed with rusty flint-lock muskets. The general show came so near to exhausting variety that one would have said that no addition to it could be conspicuous, but when this

Falstaff and his motleys marched through it, one saw that that seeming impossibility had happened.

We got away by and by, and soon reached the outer edge of Benares; then there was another wait; but, as usual, with something to look at. There was a cluster of little canvas-boxes—palanquins. A canvas-box is not much of a sight—when empty; but when there is a lady in it, it is an object of interest. These boxes were grouped apart, in the full blaze of the terrible sun, during the three-quarters of an hour that we tarried there. They contained zenana[11] ladies. They had to sit up; there was not room enough to stretch out. They probably did not mind it. They are used to the close captivity of their dwellings all their lives; when they go on a journey they are carried to the train in these boxes; in the train they have to be secluded from inspection. Many people pity them, and I always did myself and never charged anything; but it is doubtful this compassion is valued. While we were in India some good-hearted Europeans in one of the cities proposed to restrict a large park to the use of zenana ladies, so that they could go there and in assured privacy go about unveiled and enjoy the sunshine and air as they had never enjoyed them before. The good intentions back of the proposition were recognized, and sincere thanks returned for it, but the proposition itself met with a prompt declination at the hands of those who were authorized to speak for the zenana ladies. Apparently, the idea was shocking to the ladies—indeed, it was quite manifestly shocking. Was that proposition the equivalent of inviting European ladies to assemble scantily and scandalously clothed in the seclusion of a private park? It seemed to be about that.

Without doubt modesty is nothing less than a holy feeling; and without doubt the person whose rule of modesty has been transgressed feels the same sort of wound that he would feel if something made holy to him by his religion had suffered a desecration. I say "rule

[11] A practice originated by the Moslems and adopted by some Hindus of keeping the women in a household segregated and sequestered.

of modesty" because there are about a million rules in the world, and this makes a million standards to be looked out for. [There was] the case of some high-caste veiled ladies who were profoundly scandalized when some English young ladies passed by with faces bare to the world; so scandalized that they spoke out with strong indignation and wondered that people could be so shameless as to expose their persons like that. And yet the legs of the objectors were naked to mid-thigh. Both parties were clean-minded and irreproachably modest, while abiding by their separate rules, but they couldn't have traded rules for a change without suffering considerable discomfort. All human rules are more or less idiotic, I suppose. It is best so, no doubt. The way it is now, the asylums can hold the sane people, but if we tried to shut up the insane we should run out of building materials.

You have a long drive through the outskirts of Benares before you get to the hotel. And all the aspects are melancholy. It is a vision of dusty sterility, decaying temples, crumbling tombs, broken mud walls, shabby huts. The whole region seems to ache with age and penury. It must take ten thousand years of want to produce such an aspect. We were still outside of the great native city when we reached the hotel. It was a quiet and homelike house, inviting, and manifestly comfortable. But we liked its annex better, and went thither. It was a mile away, perhaps, and stood in the midst of a large compound, and was built bungalow fashion, everything on the ground floor, and a veranda all around. They have doors in India, but I don't know why. They don't fasten, and they stand open, as a rule, with a curtain hanging in the door-space to keep out the glare of the sun. Still, there is plenty of privacy, for no white person will come in without notice, of course. The native men servants will, but they don't seem to count. They glide in, barefoot and noiseless, and are in the midst before one knows it. At first this is a shock, and sometimes it is an embarrassment; but one has to get used to it, and does.

There was one tree in the compound, and a monkey lived in it. At first I was strongly interested in the tree, for I was told that it was the renowned *peepul*—the tree in whose shadow you cannot tell a lie. This one failed to stand the test, and I went away from it disappointed. There was a softly creaking well close by, and a couple of oxen drew water from it by the hour, superintended by two natives dressed in the usual "turban and pocket handkerchief." The tree and the well were the only scenery, and so the compound was a soothing and lonesome and satisfying place; and very restful after so many activities.

* * *

Benares was not a disappointment. It justified its reputation as a curiosity. It is on high ground and overhangs a great curve of the Ganges. It is a vast mass of building, compactly crusting a hill, and is cloven in all directions by an intricate confusion of cracks which stand for streets. Tall, slim minarets and beflagged temple-spires rise out of it and give it picturesqueness, viewed from the river. The city is as busy as an anthill, and the hurly-burly of human life swarming along the web of narrow streets reminds one of the ants. The sacred cow swarms along, too, and goes whither she pleases, and takes toll of the grain-shops, and is very much in the way, and is a good deal of a nuisance, since she must not be molested.

Benares is older than history, older than tradition, older even than legend, and looks twice as old as all of them put together. From a Hindu statement . . . I find the site of the town was the beginning-place of the Creation. It was merely an upright "lingam,"[12] at first, no larger than a stovepipe, and stood in the midst of a shoreless ocean. This was the work of the god Vishnu. Later he spread the lingam out till its surface was ten miles across. Still it was not large enough for the business; therefore he

[12] A phallus, symbol of Shiva.

presently built the globe around it. Benares is thus the center of the earth. This is considered an advantage.

It has had a tumultuous history, both materially and spiritually. It started Brahmanically, many years ago; then by and by Buddha came in recent times twenty-five hundred years ago, and after that it was Buddhist during many centuries—twelve, perhaps—but the Brahmans got the upper hand again, then, and have held it ever since. It is unspeakably sacred in Hindu eyes, and is as unsanitary as it is sacred, and smells like the rind of the dorian[13]. It is the headquarters of the Brahman faith, and one-eighth of the population are priests of that church. But it is not an overstock, for they have all India as a prey. All India flocks thither on pilgrimage, and pours its savings into the pockets of the priests in a generous stream, which never fails. A priest with a good stand on the shore of the Ganges is much better off than the sweeper of the best crossing in London. A good stand is worth a world of money. The holy proprietor of it sits under his grand spectacular umbrella and blesses people all his life, and collects his commission, and grows fat and rich; and the stand passes from father to son, down and down and down through the ages, and remains a permanent and lucrative estate in the family.

* * *

I should have been glad to acquire some sort of idea of Hindu theology, but the difficulties were too great, the matter was too intricate. Even the mere A B C of it is baffling. There is a trinity—Brahma, Shiva, and Vishnu—independent powers, apparently, though one cannot feel quite sure of that, because in one of the temples there is an image where an attempt has been made to concentrate the three in one person. The three have other names and plenty of them, and this makes confusion in one's mind. The three have wives and the

[13] A fruit whose rind gives off an atrocious odor.

wives have several names, and this increases the confusion. There are children, and the children have many names, and thus the confusion goes on and on. It is not worthwhile to try to get any grip upon the cloud of minor gods; there are too many of them.

It is even a justifiable economy to leave Brahma, the chiefest god of all, out of your studies, for he seems to cut no great figure in India. The vast bulk of the national worship is lavished upon Shiva and Vishnu and their families. Shiva's symbol—the "lingam" with which Vishnu began the Creation—is worshipped by everybody, apparently. It is the commonest object in Benares. It is on view everywhere, it is garlanded with flowers, offerings are made to it, it suffers no neglect. Commonly it is an upright stone, shaped like a thimble—sometimes like an elongated thimble. This priapus-worship, then, is older than history. . . .

In Benares there are many Mohammedan mosques. There are Hindu temples without number—these quaintly shaped and elaborately sculpted little stone jugs crowd all the lanes. The Ganges itself and every individual drop of water in it are temples. Religion, then, is the *business* of Benares. . . . Other industries count for nothing as compared with the vast and all-absorbing rush and drive and boom of the town's specialty. Benares is the sacredest of sacred cities. The moment you step across the sharply defined line which separates it from the rest of the globe, you stand upon ineffably and unspeakably holy ground. . . .

Yes, the city of Benares is in effect just a big church, a religious hive, whose every cell is a temple, a shrine, or a mosque and whose every conceivable earthly and heavenly good is procurable under one roof, so to speak a sort of Army and Navy Stores, theologically stocked.

# The Taj Mahal

In Agra and its neighborhood, and afterward at Delhi, we saw forts, mosques, and tombs, which were built in the great days of the Mohammedan emperors, and which are marvels of cost, magnitude, and richness of materials and ornamentation, creations of surpassing grandeur, wonders which do indeed make the like things in the rest of the world seem tame and inconsequential by comparison. I am not purposing to describe them. By good fortune I had not read much about them, and therefore was able to get a natural and rational focus upon them, with the result that they thrilled, blessed, and exalted me. But if I had previously overheated my imagination by drinking too much pestilential literary hot Scotch, I should have suffered disappointment and sorrow.

I mean to speak of only one of these world-renowned buildings, the Taj Mahal, the most celebrated construction in the earth. I had read a great deal too much about it. I saw it in the daytime, I saw it in the moonlight, I saw it near at hand, I saw it from a distance; and I knew all the time, that of its kind it was *the* wonder of the world, with no competitor now and no possible future competitor; and yet, it was not *my* Taj. My Taj had been built by excitable literary people; it was solidly lodged in my head, and I could not blast it out. . . . These descriptions do really state the truth—as nearly as the limitations of language will allow. But language is a treacherous thing, a most unsure vehicle, and it can seldom arrange descriptive words in such a way that they will not inflate the facts—by help of the reader's imagination, which is always ready to take a hand, and work for nothing, and do the bulk of it at that.

* * *

I had to visit Niagara fifteen times before I succeeded in getting my imaginary Falls gaged to the actuality and could begin to sanely and wholesomely wonder at them for what they were, not what I had expected them to be. When I first approached them it was with my face lifted toward the sky, for I thought I was going to see an Atlantic Ocean pouring down thence, over cloud-vexed Himalayan heights, a sea-green wall of water sixty miles front and six miles high, and so, when the toy reality came suddenly into view—that beruffled little wet apron hanging out to dry—the shock was too much for me, and I fell with a dull thud.

Yet slowly, surely, steadily, in the course of my fifteen visits, the proportions adjusted themselves to the facts, and I came to realize that a waterfall a hundred and sixty-five feet high and a quarter of a mile wide was an impressive thing. It was not a dipperful to my vanished great vision, but it would answer.

I know that I ought to do with the Taj as I was obliged to do with Niagara—see it fifteen times, and let my mind gradually get rid of the Taj built in it by the describers, by help of my imagination, and substitute for it the Taj of fact. It would be noble and fine, then, and a marvel; not the marvel which it replaced, but still a marvel, and fine enough. I am a careless reader, I suppose—an *impressionist* reader; an impressionist reader of what is *not* an impressionist picture; a reader who overlooks the informing details or masses their sum improperly, and gets only a large, splashy, general effect—an effect which is not correct, and which is not warranted by the particulars placed before me—particulars which I did not examine, and whose meanings I did not cautiously and carefully estimate. It is an effect which is thirty-five of forty times finer than the reality, and is therefore a great deal better and more valuable than the reality; and so, I ought never to hunt up the reality, but stay miles away from it, and thus preserve undamaged my own mighty Niagara tumbling out of the vault of heaven, and my own ineffable Taj, built of tinted mists upon jeweled arches of rainbows supported by colonnades of moonlight. It is a mistake for a person with an unregulated imagination to go and look at an illustrious world's wonder.

I suppose that many, many years ago I gathered the idea that the Taj's place in the achievements of man was exactly the place of the ice-storm in the achievements of Nature; that the Taj represented man's supremest possibility in the creation of grace and beauty and exquisiteness and splendor, just as the ice-storm represents Nature's supremest possibility in the combination of those same qualities. I do not know how long ago that idea was bred in me, but I know that I cannot remember back to a time when the thought of either of these symbols of gracious and unapproachable perfection did not at once suggest the other. If I thought of the ice-storm, the Taj rose before me divinely beautiful; if I thought of the Taj, with its encrustings and inlayings of jewels, the vision of the ice-storm rose. And so, to me, all these years, the Taj has had no rival among the temples and palaces of men, none that even remotely approached it—it was man's architectural ice-storm.

. . . [T]he other night I was talking with some Scotch and English friends, and I mentioned the ice-storm, using it as a figure—a figure which failed, for none of them had heard of the ice-storm. One gentleman, who was very familiar with American literature, said he had never seen it mentioned in any book. That is strange. And I, myself, was not able to say that I had seen it mentioned in a book; and yet the autumn foliage, with all other American scenery, has received full and competent attention.

The oversight is strange, for in America the ice-storm is an event. And it is not an event which one is careless about. When it comes, the news flies from room to room in the house; there are bangings on the doors, and shoutings, "The ice-storm! The ice-storm!" and even the laziest sleepers throw off the covers and join the rush for the windows. The ice-storm occurs in midwinter, and usually its enchantments are wrought in the silence and the darkness of the night. A fine drizzling rain falls hour after hour upon the naked twigs and branches of the trees, and as it falls it freezes. In time the trunk and every branch and twig are encased in hard pure ice, so that the tree looks like a skeleton tree made all of glass—glass that is crystal-clear. All along the underside of every branch and twig is a comb of little icicles—the frozen drip. Sometimes these pendants do not quite amount to icicles, but are round beads—frozen tears.

The weather clears, toward dawn, and leaves a brisk, pure atmosphere and a sky without a shred of cloud in it—and everything is still; there is not a breath of wind. The dawn breaks and spreads, the news of the storm goes about the house, and the little and the big, in wraps and blankets, flock to the window and press together there, and gaze intently out upon the great white ghost in the grounds, and nobody says a word, nobody stirs. All are waiting; they know what is coming, and they are waiting—waiting for the miracle. The minutes drift on and on and on, with not a sound but the ticking of the clock; at last the sun fires a sudden sheaf of rays into the ghostly tree and turns it into a white splendor of glittering diamonds. Everybody catches his breath, and feels a swelling in his throat and a moisture in his eyes—but waits again; for he knows what is coming; there is more yet. The sun climbs higher, and still higher, flooding the tree from its loftiest spread of branches to its lowest, turning it to a glory of white fire; then in a moment, without warning, comes the great miracle, the supreme miracle, the miracle without its fellow in the earth; a gust of wind sets every branch and twig to swaying, and in an instant turns the whole white tree into a spouting and spraying explosion of flashing gems of every conceivable color; and there it stands and sways this way and that, flash! flash! flash! a dancing and glancing world of rubies, emeralds, diamonds, sapphires, the most radiant spectacle, the most blinding spectacle, the divinest, the most exquisite, the most intoxicating vision of fire and color and intolerable and unimaginable splendor that ever any eye has rested upon in this world, or will ever rest upon outside the gates of heaven.

By all my senses, all my faculties, I know that the ice-storm is Nature's supremest achievement in the domain of the superb and the beautiful; and by my reason, at least, I know that the Taj is man's ice-storm.

In the ice-storm every one of the myriad ice-beads pendent from twig and branch is an individual gem, and changes color with every motion caused by the wind; each tree carries a million, and a forest-front exhibits the splendors of the single tree multiplied by a thousand.

It occurs to me now that I have never seen the ice-storm put upon canvas, and have not heard that any painter has tried to do it. I wonder why that is. Is it that paint cannot counterfeit the intense blaze of a sun-flooded jewel? There should be, and must be, a reason, and a good one, why the most enchanting sight that Nature has created has been neglected by the brush.

Often, the surest way to convey misinformation is to tell the strict truth. The describers of the Taj have used the word *gem* in its strictest sense—its scientific sense. In that sense it is a mild word, and promises but little to the eye—nothing bright, nothing brilliant, nothing sparkling, nothing splendid in the way of color. It *accurately* describes the sober and unobtrusive gem-work of the Taj; that is, to the very highly educated one person in a thousand; but it most falsely describes it to the 999. But the 999 are the people who ought to be especially taken care of, and to them it does not mean quiet-colored designs wrought in carnelians, or agates, or such things; they know the word in its wide and ordinary sense only, and so to them it means diamonds and rubies and opals and their kindred, and the moment their eyes fall upon it in print they see a vision of glorious colors clothed in fire.

These describers are writing for the "general," and so, in order to make sure of being understood, they ought to use words in their ordinary sense, or else explain. The word *fountain* means one thing in Syria, where there is but a handful of people; it means quite another thing in North America, where there are seventy-five million. If I were describing some Syrian scenery and should exclaim, "Within the narrow space of a quarter of a mile square I saw, in the glory of the flooding moonlight, two hundred noble fountains—imagine the spectacle!" the North American would have a vision of clustering columns of water soaring aloft, bending over in graceful arches, bursting in beaded spray and raining white fire in the moonlight—and he would be deceived. But the Syrian would not be deceived; he would merely see two hundred fresh-water springs—two hundred drowsing puddles, as level and unpretentious and unexcited as so many door-mats, and even with the help of moonlight he would not lose his grip in the presence of the exhibition. My word "fountain" would be correct; it would speak the strict truth; and it would convey the strict truth to a handful of Syrians, and the strictest misinformation to the North American millions. With their gems—and gems—and more gems—and gems again—and still other gems—the describers of the Taj are within their legal but not their moral rights; they are dealing in the strictest scientific truth; and in doing it they succeed to admiration in telling "what ain't so."

# Underway Again

We are far abroad upon the smooth waters of the Indian Ocean, now; it is shady and pleasant and peaceful under the vast spread of the awnings, and life is perfect again—ideal.

The difference between a river and a sea is that the river looks fluid, the sea solid—usually looks as if you could step out and walk on it.

The captain has this peculiarity—he cannot tell the truth in a plausible way. In this he is the very opposite of the austere Scot who sits midway of the table; *he* cannot tell a lie in an *un*plausible way. When the captain finishes a statement the passengers glance at each other privately, as who should say, "Do you believe that?" When the Scot finishes one, the look says, "How strange and interesting." The whole secret is the manner and method of the two men. The captain is a little shy and diffident, and he states the simplest fact as if he were a little afraid of it, while the Scot delivers himself of the most abandoned lie with such an air of stern veracity that one is forced to believe it although one knows it isn't so. For instance, the Scot told about a pet flying-fish he once owned, that lived in a little fountain in his conservatory, and supported itself by catching birds and frogs and rats in the neighboring fields. It was plain that no one at the table doubted this statement.

By and by, in the course of some talk about custom-house annoyances, the captain brought out the following simple everyday incident, but through his infirmity of style managed to tell it in such a way that it got no credence. He said:

"I went ashore in Naples one voyage when I was in that trade, and stood around helping my passengers, for I could speak a little Italian. Two or three times, at intervals, the officer asked me if I had anything dutiable about me, and seemed more and more put out and disappointed every time I told him no. Finally, a passenger whom I had helped through asked me to come out and take something. I thanked him, but excused myself, saying I had taken a whisky just before I came ashore.

"It was a fatal admission. The officer at once made me pay sixpence import duty on the whisky—just from ship to shore, you see; and he fined me five pounds for not declaring the goods, another five pounds for falsely denying that I had anything dutiable about me, also five pounds for concealing the goods, and fifty pounds for smuggling, which is the maximum penalty for unlawfully bringing in goods under the value of sevenpence ha'penny. Altogether, sixty-five pounds sixpence for a little thing like that."

The Scot is always believed, yet he never tells anything but lies; whereas the captain is never believed, although he never tells a lie, so far as I can judge. If he should say his uncle was a male person, he would probably say it in such a way that nobody would believe it; at the same time the Scot could claim that he had a female uncle and not stir a doubt in anybody's mind. My own luck has been curious all my literary life; I never could tell a lie that anybody would doubt, nor a truth that anybody would believe.

* * *

The sea is a Mediterranean blue; and I believe that that is about the divinest color known to nature.

It is strange and fine—Nature's lavish generosities to her creatures. At least to all of them except man. For those that fly she has provided a home that is nobly spacious—a home which is forty miles deep and envelopes the whole globe, and has not an obstruction in it. For those that swim she has provided a more than imperial domain—a domain which is miles deep and covers four-fifths of the globe. But as for man, she has cut him off with the mere odds and ends of the creation. She has given him the thin skin, the meager skin which is stretched over the remaining one-fifth—the naked bones stick up through it in most places. On the one-half of this domain he can raise snow, ice, sand, rocks, and nothing else. So the valuable part of his inheritance really consists of but a single fifth of the family estate; and out of it he has to grub hard to get enough to keep him alive and provide kings and soldiers and powder to extend the blessings of civilization with. Yet man, in his simplicity and complacency and inability to cipher, thinks Nature regards him as the important member of the family—in fact, her favorite. Surely, it must occur to even his dull head, sometimes, that she has a curious way of showing it.

The captain has been telling how, in one of his Arctic voyages, it was so cold that the mate's shadow froze fast to the deck and had to be ripped loose by main strength. And even then he got only about two-thirds of it back. Nobody said anything, and the captain went away. I think he is becoming disheartened. . . .

[T]here is another word of praise due to this ship's library: it contains no copy of the *Vicar of Wakefield*, that strange menagerie of complacent hypocrites and idiots, of theatrical cheap-john heroes and heroines, who are always showing off, of bad people who are not interesting, and good people who are fatiguing. A singular book. Not a sincere line in it, and not a character that invites respect; a book which is one long waste-pipe discharge of goody-goody puerilities and dreary moralities; a book which is full of pathos which revolts, and humor which grieves the heart. . . .

Jane Austen's books, too, are absent from this library. Just that one omission alone would make a fairly good library out of a library that hadn't a book in it.

* * *

I do not know how a day could be more reposeful: no motion; a level blue sea; nothing in sight from horizon to horizon; the speed of the ship furnishes a cooling breeze; there is no mail to read and answer; no newspapers to excite you; no telegrams to fret you or fright you—the world is far, far away; it has ceased to exist for you—seemed a fading dream, along in the first days; has dissolved to an unreality now; it is gone from your mind with all its businesses and ambitions, its prosperities and disasters, its exultations and despairs, its joys and griefs and cares and worries. They are no concern of yours any more; they have gone out of your life; they are a storm which has passed and left a deep calm behind. The people group themselves about the decks in their snowy-white linen, and read, smoke, sew, play cards, talk, nap, and so on. In other ships the passengers are always ciphering about when they are going to arrive; out in these seas it is rare, very rare, to hear that subject broached. In other ships there is always an eager rush to the bulletin board at noon to find out what the "run" has been; in these seas the bulletin seems to attract no interest; I have seen no one visit it; in thirteen days I have visited it only once. Then I happened to notice the figures of the day's run. On that day there happened to be talk, at dinner, about the speed of modern ships. I was the only passenger present who knew this ship's gait. Necessarily, the Atlantic custom of betting on the ship's run is not a custom here—nobody ever mentions it.

I myself am wholly indifferent as to when we are going to "get in"; if anyone else feels interested in the matter he has not indicated it in my hearing. If I had my way we should never get in at all. This sort of sea-life is charged with an indestructible charm. There is no weariness, no fatigue, no worry, no responsibility, no work, no depression of spirits. There is nothing like this serenity, this comfort, this peace, this deep contentment, to be found anywhere on land. If I had my way I would sail on forever and never go to live on the solid ground again.

# Part Five

## *The Middle East*

*One of our most inveterate relic-hunters had his hammer with him and tried to break a fragment off the upright Needle and could not do it; he tried the prostrate one and failed; he borrowed a heavy sledge hammer from a mason and failed again. He tried Pompey's pillar, and this baffled him. Scattered all about the mighty monolith were sphinxes of noble countenance, carved out of Egyptian granite as hard as blue steel, and whose shapely features the wear of five thousand years had failed to mark or mar. The relic-hunter battered at these persistently and sweated profusely over his work. He might as well have attempted to deface the moon. They regarded him serenely with the stately smile they had worn so long, and which seemed to say: "Peck away, poor insect; we were not made to fear such as you; in tenscore dragging ages we have seen more of your kind than there are sands at your feet—have they left a blemish upon us?"*

from *The Innocents Abroad*

* * *

*The people who go into ecstasies over St. Sophia must sure get them out of the guidebook (where every church is spoken of as being "considered by good judges to be the most marvelous structure, in many respects, that the world has ever seen"). Or else they are those old connoisseurs from the wilds of New Jersey who laboriously learn the difference between a fresco and a fireplug and from that day forward feel privileged to void their critical bathos on painting, sculpture, and architecture forevermore.*

from *The Innocents Abroad*

# Egypt

When we reached the pier we found an army of Egyptian boys with donkeys no larger than themselves, waiting for passengers—for donkeys are the omnibuses of Egypt. We preferred to walk, but we could not have our own way. The boys crowded about us, clamored around us, and slewed their donkeys exactly across our path, no matter which way we turned. They were good-natured rascals, and so were the donkeys. We mounted, and the boys ran behind us and kept the donkeys in a furious gallop. . . . I believe I would rather ride a donkey than any beast in the world. He goes briskly, he puts on no airs, he is docile, though opinionated. Satan himself could not scare him, and he is convenient—very convenient. When you are tired of riding you can rest your feet on the ground and let him gallop from under you.

* * *

The donkeys were all good, all handsome, all strong and in good condition, all fast and all willing to prove it. They were the best we had found anywhere, and the most recherché. I do not know what "recherché" is, but that is what these donkeys were anyhow. Some were of a soft mouse color, and the others were white, black, and varicolored. Some were close-shaven all over, except that a tuft like a paintbrush was left on the end of the tail. Others were so shaven in fanciful landscape garden patterns as to mark their bodies with curving lines, which were bounded on one side by hair and on the other by the close plush left by the shears. They had all been newly barbered and were exceedingly stylish. Several of the white ones were barred like zebras with rainbow stripes of blue and red and yellow paint. These were indescribably gorgeous. . . . The donkey boys were lively young Egyptian rascals who could follow a donkey and keep him in a canter half a day without tiring. We had plenty of spectators when we mounted, for the hotel was full of English people bound overland to India and officers getting ready for the African campaign against the Abysinnian King Theodorus.[14] We were not a very large party, but as we charged through the streets of the great metropolis we made noise for five hundred and displayed activity and created excitement in proportion. Nobody can steer a donkey, and some collided with camels, dervishes, effendies, asses, beggars, and everything else that offered to the donkeys a reasonable chance for a collision. When we turned into the broad avenue that leads out of the city toward Old Cairo, there was plenty of room. The walls of stately date palms that fenced the gardens and bordered the way threw their shadows down and made the air cool and bracing. We rose to the spirit of the time and the race became a wild rout, a stampede, a terrific panic. I wish to live to enjoy it again.

Somewhere along this route we had a few startling exhibitions of Oriental simplicity. A girl apparently thirteen years of age came along the great thoroughfare dressed like Eve before the fall. We would have called her thirteen at home; but here girls who look

[14] An insane monarch who imprisoned all the Europeans in his country and made extravagant demands for their release. The British sent an army instead, whereupon Theodorus killed himself.

thirteen are often not more than nine in reality. Occasionally we saw stark-naked men of superb build, bathing and making no attempt at concealment. However, an hour's acquaintance with this cheerful custom reconciled the pilgrims to it, and then it ceased to occasion remark. Thus easily do the most startling novelties grow tame and spiritless to these sight-surfeited wanderers.

Arrived at Old Cairo, the camp followers took up the donkeys and tumbled them bodily aboard a small boat with a lateen sail, and we followed and got underway. The deck was closely packed with donkeys and men; the two sailors had to climb over and under and through the wedged mass to work the sails, and the steersman had to crowd four or five donkeys out of the way when he wished to swing his tiller and put his helm hard-down. But what were their troubles to us? We had nothing to do; nothing to do but enjoy the trip; nothing to do but shove the donkeys off our corns and look at the charming scenery of the Nile.

On the island at our right was the machine they call the Nilometer, a stone column whose business it is to mark the rise of the river and prophesy whether it will reach only thirty-two feet and produce a famine, or whether it will properly flood the land at forty and produce plenty, or whether it will rise to forty-three and bring death and destruction to flocks and crops—but how it does all this they could not explain to us so that we could understand. On the same island is still shown the spot where Pharaoh's daughter found Moses in the bulrushes. Near the spot we sailed from, the Holy Family dwelt when they sojourned in Egypt till Herod should complete his slaughter of the innocents. The same tree they rested under when they first arrived was there a short time ago, but the Viceroy of Egypt sent it to the Empress Eugenie lately. He was just in time, otherwise our pilgrims would have had it.

The Nile at this point is muddy, swift, and turbid, and does not lack a great deal of being as wide as the Mississippi.

We scrambled up the steep bank at the shabby town of Ghizeh, mounted the donkeys again, and scampered away. For four or five miles the route lay along a high embankment which they say is to be the bed of a railway the Sultan means to build for no other reason than when the Empress of the French comes to visit him she can go to the pyramids in comfort. This is true Oriental hospitality. I am very glad it is our privilege to have donkeys instead of cars.

At the distance of a few miles the pyramids rising above the palms looked very clean-cut, very grand and imposing, and very soft and filmy as well. They swam in a rich haze that took from them all suggestions of unfeeling stone and made them seem only the airy nothings of a dream—structures which might blossom into tiers of vague arches or ornate colonnades maybe, and change and change again into all graceful forms of architecture, while we looked, and then melt deliciously away and blend with the tremulous atmosphere.

At the end of the levee we left the mules and went in a sailboat across an arm of the Nile or an overflow, and landed where the sands of the great Sahara left their embankment, as straight as a wall, along the verge of the alluvial plain of the river. A laborious walk in the flaming sun brought us to the foot of the great pyramid of Cheops. It was a fairy vision no longer. It was a corrugated, unsightly mountain of stone. Each of its monstrous sides was a wide stairway which rose upward, step above step, narrowing as it went, till it tapered to a point far aloft in the air. Insect men and women—pilgrims from the *Quaker City*—were creeping about its dizzy perches, and one little black swarm were waving postage stamps from the airy summit—handkerchiefs will be understood.

Of course we were besieged by a rabble of muscular Egyptians and Arabs who wanted the contract of dragging us to the top—all tourists are. Of course you could not hear your own voice for the din that was around you. Of course the sheikhs said *they* were the only responsible parties, that all contracts must be made with them, all moneys paid over to them, and none extracted from us by any but themselves alone. Of course they contracted that the varlets who dragged us up should not mention baksheesh[15] once. For such is the usual routine. Of course we contracted with them, paid them, were delivered into the hands of the draggers, dragged up the pyramids, and harried and bedeviled for baksheesh from the foundation clear to the summit. We paid it, too, for we were purposely spread very far apart over the vast side of the pyramid. There was no help near if we called, and the Herculeses who dragged us had a way of asking sweetly and flatteringly for baksheesh, which was seductive, and of looking fierce and threatening to throw us down the precipice, which was persuasive and convincing.

Each step being full as high as a dinner table; there being very, very many of the steps; an Arab having hold of each of our arms and springing upward from step to step and snatching us with him, forcing us to lift our feet as high as our breasts every time, and to do it rapidly and keep it up till we were ready to faint—who shall say it is not lively, exhilarating, lacerating, muscle-straining, bone-wrenching and perfectly excruciating and exhausting pastime climbing the pyramids? I beseeched the varlets not to twist *all* my joints asunder; I iterated, reiterated, even *swore* to them that I did not wish to beat anybody to the top; did all I could to convince them that if I got there the last of all, I would feel blessed among men and grateful to them forever; I begged them, prayed them, pleaded with them to let me stop and rest a moment—only one little moment—and they only answered with some more frightful springs, and an unenlisted volunteer behind opened a bombardment of determined boosts with his head which threatened to batter my whole political economy to wreck and ruin.

Twice, for one minute, they let me rest while they extorted baksheesh, and then continued their maniac flight up the pyramid. It was nothing to them that I, a stranger, must be sacrificed upon the altar of their unholy ambition. But in the midst of sorrow, joy

[15] Gratuities.

blooms. Even in this dark hour I had a sweet consolation. For I knew that except these Mohammedans repented, they would go straight to perdition someday. And *they* never repent—they never forsake their paganism. This thought calmed me, cheered me, and I sank down, limp and exhausted, upon the summit, but happy, *so* happy and serene within.

On the one hand, a mighty sea of yellow sand stretched away toward the ends of the earth, solemn, silent, shorn of vegetation, its solitude uncheered by any forms of creature life; on the other, the Eden of Egypt was spread below us—a broad green floor, cloven by the sinuous river, dotted with villages, its vast distances measured and marked by the diminishing stature of receding clusters of palms. It lay asleep in an enchanted atmosphere. There was no sound, no motion. Above the date plumes in the middle distance swelled a domed and pinnacled mass, glimmering through a tinted, exquisite mist; away toward the horizon a dozen shapely pyramids watched over ruined Memphis; and at our feet the bland impassible sphinx looked out upon the picture from her throne in the sands as placidly and pensively as she had looked upon its like full fifty lagging centuries ago.

We suffered torture no pen can describe from the hungry appeals for baksheesh that gleamed from Arab eyes and poured incessantly from Arab lips. Why try to call up the traditions of vanished Egyptian grandeur; why try to fancy Egypt following dead Rameses to his tomb in the pyramid or the long multitude of Israel departing over the desert yonder? Why try to think at all? The thing was impossible. One must bring his meditations cut and dried, or else cut and dry them afterward.

The traditional Arab proposed, in the traditional way, to run down Cheops, cross the eighth of a mile of sand intervening between it and the tall pyramid of Cephron, ascend to Cephron's summit and return to us on the top of Cheops—all in nine minutes by the watch, and the whole service to be rendered for a single dollar. In the first flush of irritation I said let the Arab and his exploits go to the mischief. But stay. The upper third of Cephron was coated with dressed marble smooth as glass. A blessed thought entered my brain. He must infallibly break his neck. Close the contract with dispatch, I said, and let him go. He started. We watched. He went bounding down the vast broadside, spring after spring, like an ibex. He grew smaller and smaller till he became a bobbing pygmy, away down toward the bottom—then disappeared. We turned and peered over the other side—forty seconds—eighty seconds—a hundred—happiness, he is dead already!—two minutes—and a quarter. "There he goes!" Too true—it was too true. He was very small now. Gradually, but surely, he overcame the level ground. He began to spring and climb again. Up, up, up—at last he reached the smooth coating—now for it. But he clung to it with toes and fingers, like a fly. He crawled this way and that—away to the right, slanting upward—away to the left, still slanting upward—and stood at last, a black peg on the summit, and waved his pygmy scarf. Then he crept downward to the raw steps again, then picked up his agile heels and flew. We lost him presently. But presently again we saw him under us, mounting with undiminished energy. Shortly he bounded into our midst with a gallant war whoop. Time: eight minutes, forty-one seconds. He had won. His bones were intact. It was a failure. I reflected. I said to myself, "He is tired and must grow dizzy. I will risk another dollar on him."

He started again. Made the trip again. Slipped on the smooth coating—I almost had him. But an infamous crevice saved him. He was with us once more—perfectly sound. Time: eight minutes, forty-six seconds.

I said to Dan, "Lend me a dollar—I can beat this game yet."

Worse and worse. He won again. Time: eight minutes, forty-eight seconds. I was out of all patience now. I was desperate. Money was no longer of any consequence. I said,"Sirrah, I will give you a hundred dollars to jump off this pyramid head first. If you do not like the terms, name your bet. I scorn to stand on expenses now. I will stay right here and risk money on you as long as Dan has got a cent."

I was in a fair way to win now, for it was a dazzling opportunity for an Arab. He pondered a moment, and would have done it, I think, but his mother arrived then and interfered. Her tears moved me—I never can look upon the tears of woman with indifference—and I said I would give her a hundred to jump off, too.

But it was a failure. The Arabs are too high-priced in Egypt. They put on airs unbecoming to such savages.

* * *

Each side of the pyramid of Cheops is about as long as the Capitol at Washington or the Sultan's new palace on the Bosporus, and is longer than the greatest depth of St. Peter's at Rome—which is to say that each side of Cheops extends seven hundred and some-odd feet. It is about seventy-five feet higher than the cross on St. Peter's. The first time I ever went down the Mississippi, I thought the highest bluff on the river between St. Louis and New Orleans—it was near Selma, Missouri—was probably the highest mountain in the world. It was four hundred and thirteen feet high. It still looms in my memory with undiminished grandeur. I can still see the trees and bushes growing smaller and smaller as I followed them up its huge slant with my eye till they became a feathery fringe on the distant summit. This symmetrical pyramid of Cheops—this solid mountain of stone reared by the patient hands of men—this mighty tomb of a forgotten monarch—dwarfs my cherished mountain. For it is four hundred and eighty feet high. In still earlier years than those I have been recalling, Holliday's Hill, in our town, was to me the noblest work of God. It appeared to pierce the skies. It was nearly three hundred feet high. In those days I pondered the subject much, but I never could understand why it did not swathe its summit with never-failing clouds and crown its majestic brow with ever lasting snows. I had heard that such was the custom of great mountains in other parts of the world. I remembered how I worked with another boy, at odd afternoons stolen from study and paid for with stripes, to undermine and start from its bed an immense boulder that rested upon the edge of that hilltop; I remembered how, one Saturday afternoon, we gave three hours of honest effort to the task, and saw at last that our reward was at hand; I remembered how we sat down then and wiped the perspiration away, and waited to let a picnic party get out of the way in the road below—and then we started the boulder. It was splendid. It went crashing down the hillside, tearing up saplings, mowing bushes down like grass, ripping and crushing and smashing everything in its path—eternally splintered and scattered a woodpile at the foot of the hill, and then sprang from the high bank clear over a dray in the road—the Negro glanced up once and dodged—and the next second it made infinitesimal mincemeat of a frame cooper shop, and the coopers swarmed out like bees. Then we said it was perfectly magnificent and left. Because the coopers were starting up the hill to inquire.

Still, that mountain, prodigious as it was, was nothing to the pyramid of Cheops. I could conjure up no comparison that would convey to my mind a satisfactory comprehension of the magnitude of a pile of monstrous stones that covered thirteen acres of ground and stretched upward four hundred and eighty tiresome feet, and so I gave it up and walked down to the sphinx.

After years of waiting it was before me at last. The great face was so sad, so earnest, so longing, so patient. There was a dignity not of earth in its mien, and in its countenance a benignity such as never anything human wore. It was stone, but it seemed sentient. If ever image of stone thought, it was thinking. It was looking toward the verge of the landscape, yet looking *at* nothing—nothing but distance and vacancy. It was looking over and beyond everything of the present and far into the past. It was gazing out over the ocean of Time—over lines of century waves which, further and further receding, closed nearer and nearer together, and blended at last into one unbroken tide, away toward the horizon of remote antiquity. It was thinking of the wars of departed ages; of the empires it had seen created and destroyed; of the nations whose birth it had witnessed, whose progress it had watched, whose annihilation it had noted; of the joy and sorrow, the life and death, the grandeur and decay, of five thousand slow revolving years. It was the type of an attribute of man—of a faculty of his heart and brain. It was MEMORY—RETROSPECTION—wrought into visible, tangible form. All who know what pathos there is in memories of days that are accomplished and faces that have vanished—albeit only a trifling score of years gone by—will have some appreciation of the pathos that dwells in these grave eyes that look so steadfastly back upon the things they knew before History was born—before Tradition had being—things that were and forms that moved in a vague era which even Poetry and Romance scarce know of—and passed one by one away and left the stony dreamer solitary in the midst of a strange new age and uncomprehended scenes.

The sphinx is grand in its loneliness; it is imposing in its magnitude; it is impressive in the mystery that hangs over its story. And there is that in the overshadowing majesty of this eternal figure of stone, with its accusing memory of the deeds of all ages, which reveals to one something of what he shall feel when he shall stand at last in the awful presence of God.

There are some things which, for the credit of America, should be left unsaid perhaps; but these very things happen sometimes to be the very things which, for the real benefit of Americans, ought to have prominent notice. While we stood looking, a wart or an excrescence of some kind appeared on the jaw of the sphinx. We heard the familiar clink of a hammer and understood the case at once. One of our well-meaning reptiles—I mean the relic-hunters—had crawled up there and was trying to break a "specimen" from the face of this the most majestic creation the hand of man has wrought. But the great image contemplated the dead ages as calmly as ever, unconscious of the small insect that was fretting at its jaw. Egyptian granite that has defied the storms and earthquakes of all time has nothing to fear from the tack hammers of ignorant excursionists—highwaymen—like this specimen. He failed in his enterprise. We sent a sheikh to arrest him if he had the authority, or to warn him, if he had not, that by the laws of Egypt the crime he was attempting to commit was punishable with imprisonment or the bastinado.[16] Then he desisted and went away.

The sphinx: a hundred and twenty-five feet long, sixty feet high, and a hundred and two feet around the head, if I remember rightly—carved out of one solid block of stone harder than any iron. The block must have been as large as the Fifth Avenue Hotel before the usual waste (by the necessities of sculpture) of a fourth or a half of the original mass was begun. I only set down these figures and these remarks to suggest the prodigious labor the carving of it so elegantly, so symmetrically, so faultlessly, must have cost. This species of stone is so hard that figures cut in it remain sharp and unmarred after exposure to the weather for two or three thousand years. Now, did it take a hundred years of patient toil to carve the sphinx? It seems probable.

* * *

We were glad to have seen the land which was the mother of civilization—which taught Greece her letters, and through Greece Rome, and through Rome the world; the land which could have humanized and civilized the hapless children of Israel, but allowed them to depart out of her borders little better than savages. We were glad to have seen that land which had an enlightened religion with future eternal rewards and punishment in it, while even Israel's religion contained no promise of a hereafter. We were glad to have seen that land which had glass three thousand years before England had it, and could paint upon it as none of us can paint now; that land which knew, three thousand years ago, well-nigh all of medicine and surgery which science has *discovered* lately; which

[16] Flogging with a stick or cudgel.

had all those curious surgical instruments which science has *invented* recently; which had in high excellence a thousand luxuries and necessities of an advanced civilization which we have gradually contrived and accumulated in modern times and claimed as things that were new under the sun; that had paper untold centuries before we dreamt of it—and waterfalls[17] before our women thought of them; that had a perfect system of common schools so long before we boasted of our achievements in that direction that it seems forever and forever ago; that so embalmed the dead that flesh was made almost immortal—which we cannot do; that built temples which mock at destroying time and smile grimly upon our lauded little prodigies of architecture; that old land that knew all which we know now, perchance, and more; that walked in the broad highway of civilization in the gray dawn of creation, ages and ages before we were born; that left the impress of exalted, cultivated Mind upon the eternal front of the sphinx to confound all scoffers who, when all her other proofs had passed away, might seek to persuade the world that imperial Egypt, in the days of her high renown, had groped in darkness.

[17] A hairstyle consisting of long, loose waves.

# A Caravan to Damascus

As might have been expected, a notion got abroad in Syria and Egypt that the whole population of the province of America (the Turks consider us a trifling little province in some unvisited corner of the world) were coming to the Holy Land—and so, when we got to Beirut yesterday, we found the place full of dragomen[18] and their outfits. We had all intended to go by diligence to Damascus, and switch off to Baalbek as we went along—because we expected to rejoin the ship, go to Mount Carmel, and take to the woods from there. However, when our own private party of eight found it was possible, and proper enough, to make the "long trip," we adopted that program. . . .

Well, out of our eight, three were selected to attend to all business connected with the expedition. The rest of us had nothing to do but look at the beautiful city of Beirut, with its bright, new houses nestled among a wilderness of green shrubbery spread abroad over an upland that sloped gently down to the sea; and also at the mountains of Lebanon that environ it; and likewise to bathe

[18] A dragoman is an outfitter, interpreter, and general factotum.

in the transparent blue water that rolled its billows about the ship (we did not know that there were sharks there). . . .

At the appointed time our business committee reported and said all things were in readiness—that we were to start today, with horses, pack animals, and tents, and go to Baalbek, Damascus, the Sea of Tiberias, and thence southward by way of the scene of Jacob's Dream and other notable Bible localities to Jerusalem—from thence probably to the Dead Sea, but possibly not—and then strike for the ocean and rejoin the ship three or four weeks hence at Joppa; terms, five dollars a day apiece, in gold, and everything to be furnished by the dragoman. They said we would live as well as at a hotel. I had read something like that before, and did not shame my judgment by believing a word of it. I said nothing, however, but packed up a blanket and a shawl to sleep in, pipes and tobacco, two or three woolen shirts, a portfolio, a guidebook, and a Bible. I also took along a towel and a cake of soap, to inspire respect in the Arabs, who would take me for a king in disguise.

We were to select our horses at 3 P.M. At that hour Abraham, the dragoman, marshaled them before us. With all solemnity I set it down here that those horses were the hardest lot I ever did come across, and their accoutrements were in exquisite keeping with their style. One brute had an eye out; another had his tail sawed off close, like a rabbit, and was proud of it; another had a bony ridge running from his neck to his tail, like one of those ruined aqueducts one sees about Rome, and had a neck on him like a bowsprit; they all limped and had sore backs, and likewise raw places and old scales scattered about their persons like brass nails in a hair trunk; their gaits were marvelous to contemplate and replete with variety—underway the procession looked like a fleet in a storm. It was fearful. . . .

I said nothing. The display was exactly according to the guidebook, and were we not traveling by the guidebook? I selected a certain horse because I thought I saw him shy, and I thought a horse that had spirit enough to shy was not to be despised.

At six o'clock P.M. we came to a halt here on the breezy summit of a shapely mountain overlooking the sea, and the handsome valley where dwelt some of those enterprising Phoenicians of ancient times we read so much about; all around us are what were once the dominions of Hiram, King of Tyre, who furnished timber from the cedars from these Lebanon hills to build portions of King Solomon's Temple with.

Shortly after six our pack train arrived. I had not seen it before, and a good right I had to be astonished. We had nineteen serving men and twenty-six pack mules! It was a perfect caravan. It looked like one, too, as it wound among the rocks. I wondered what in the very mischief we wanted with such a vast turnout as that, for eight men. I wondered awhile, but soon I began to long for a tin plate and some bacon and beans. I had camped out many and many a time before and knew just what was coming. I went off, without waiting for serving men, and unsaddled my horse, and washed such portions of his ribs and spine as projected through his hide, and when I came back, behold, five stately circus tents were up—tents that were brilliant within with blue and gold and crimson and all manner of splendid adornment! I was speechless. Then they brought eight little iron bedsteads and set them up in the tents; they put a soft mattress and pillows and good blankets and two snow-white sheets on each bed. Next they rigged a table about the center pole and on it placed pewter pitchers, basins, soap, and the whitest of towels—one set for each man; they pointed to pockets in the tent and said we could put our small trifles in them for convenience, and if we needed pins or such things, they were sticking everywhere. Then came the finishing touch—they spread carpets on the floor! I simply said, "If you call this camping out, all right—but it isn't the style *I* am used to; my little baggage that I brought along is at a discount."

It grew dark, and they put candles on the tables—candles set in bright, new, brazen candlesticks. And soon the bell—a genuine, simon-pure bell—rang, and we were invited to "the saloon." I had thought before that we had a tent or so too many, but now here was one, at least, provided for; it was to be used for nothing but an eating saloon. Like the others, it was high enough for a family of giraffes to live in, and was very handsome and clean and bright-colored within. It was a gem of a place. A table for eight and eight canvas chairs; a tablecloth and napkins whose whiteness and whose fineness laughed to scorn the things we were used to in the great excursion steamer; knives and forks, soup plates, dinner plates—everything in the handsomest kind of style. It was wonderful! And they call *this* camping out. Those stately fellows in baggy trousers and turbaned fezzes brought in a dinner which consisted of roast mutton, roast chicken, roast goose, potatoes, bread, tea, pudding, apples, and delicious grapes; the viands were better cooked than any we had eaten for weeks, and the table made a finer appearance, with its large German silver candlesticks and other finery, than any table we had sat down to for a good while, and yet that polite dragoman, Abraham, came bowing in and apologizing for the whole affair, on account of the unavoidable confusion of getting underway for a very long trip, and promising to do a great deal better in the future!

It is midnight now, and we break camp at six in the morning.

They call this camping out. At this rate it is a glorious privilege to be a pilgrim to the Holy Land.

* * *

We are camped near Temnin el Foka—a name which the boys have simplified a good deal for the sake of convenience in spelling. They call it Jacksonville. It sounds a little strangely, here in the valley of Lebanon, but it has the merit of being easier to remember than the Arabic name.

*Come Like Spirits, So Depart*

The night shall be filled with music,

And the cares that infest the day

Shall fold their tents like the Arabs,

And as silently steal away.[19]

I slept very soundly last night, yet when the dragoman's bell rang at half-past five this morning and the cry went abroad of "Ten minutes to dress for breakfast!" I heard both. It surprised me, for I have not heard the breakfast gong in the ship for a month, and whenever we have had occasion to fire a salute at daylight, I have only found it out in the course of conversation afterward. However, camping out, even though it be in a gorgeous tent, makes one fresh and lively in the morning—especially if the air you are breathing is the cool, fresh air of the mountains.

I was dressed within the ten minutes and came out. The saloon tent had been stripped of its sides and had nothing left but its roof; so when we sat down to table we could look out over a noble panorama of mountain, sea, and hazy valley. And sitting thus, the sun rose slowly up and suffused the picture with a world of rich coloring.

Hot mutton chops, fried chicken, omelets, fried potatoes, and coffee—all excellent. This was the bill of fare. It was sauced with a savage appetite purchased by hard riding the day before and refreshing sleep in a pure atmosphere. As I called for a second cup of coffee I glanced over my shoulder, and behold, our white village was gone—the splendid tents had vanished like magic! It was wonderful how quickly those Arabs had "folded their tents"; and it was wonderful also how quickly they had gathered the thousand odds and ends of the camp together and disappeared with them.

By half-past six we were underway, and all the Syrian world seemed to be underway also. The road was filled with mule trains and long processions of camels. This reminds me that we have been trying for some time to think what a camel looks like, and now we have made it out. When he is down on all his knees, flat on his breast to receive his load, he looks something like a goose swimming, and when he is upright he looks like an ostrich with an extra set of legs.

[19] From *The Day Is Done*—Longfellow.

Camels are not beautiful, and their long underlip gives them an exceedingly "gallus"[20] expression. They have immense, flat, forked cushions of feet, that make a track in the dust like a pie with a slice cut out of it. They are not particular about their diet. They would eat a tombstone if they could bite it. A thistle grows about here which has needles on it that would pierce through leather, I think; if one touches you, you can find relief in nothing but profanity. The camels eat these. They show by their actions that they enjoy them. I suppose it would be a real treat to a camel to have a keg of nails for supper.

While I am speaking of animals I will mention that I have a horse now by the name of "Jericho." He is a mare. I have seen remarkable horses before, but none so remarkable as this. I wanted a horse that could shy, and this one fills the bill. I had an idea that shying indicated spirit. If I was correct, I have got the most spirited horse on earth. He shies at everything he comes across, with the utmost impartiality. He appears to have a mortal dread of telegraph poles especially; and it is fortunate that these are on both sides of the road, because as it is now, I never fall off twice in succession on the same side. If I fell on the same side always, it would get to be monotonous after a while. This creature has scared at everything he has seen today except a haystack. He walked up to that with an intrepidity and a recklessness that were astonishing. And it would fill anyone with admiration to see how he preserves his self-possession in the presence of a barley sack. This daredevil bravery will be the death of this horse someday.

He is not particularly fast, but I think he will get me through the Holy Land. He has only one fault. His tail has been chopped off, or else he has sat down on it too hard some time or other, and he has to fight the flies with his heels. This is all very well, but when he tries to kick a fly off the top of his head with his hindfoot, it is too much variety. He is going to get himself into trouble that way someday. He reaches around and bites my legs too. I do not care particularly about that, only I do not like to see a horse too sociable.

[20] Excuse the slang—no other word will describe it.—M.T.

I think the owner of this prize had a wrong opinion about him. He had an idea that he was one of those fiery, untamed steeds, but he is not of that character. I know the Arab had this idea, because when he brought the horse out for inspection in Beirut, he kept jerking at the bridle and shouting in Arabic, "Ho! Will you? Do you want to run away, you ferocious beast, and break your neck?" when all the time the horse was not doing anything in the world, and only looked like he wanted to lean up against something and think. Whenever he is not shying at things or reaching after a fly, he wants to do that yet. How it would surprise his owner to know this.

* * *

Back yonder, an hour's journey from here, we passed through an Arab village of stone dry-goods boxes (they look like that) where Noah's tomb lies under lock and key. (Noah built the ark.) Over these old hills and valleys the ark that contained all that was left of a vanished world once floated.

I make no apologies for detailing the above information. It will be news to some of my readers, at any rate.

Noah's tomb is built of stone and is covered with a long stone building. Baksheesh let us in. The building had to be long, because the grave of the honored old navigator is two hundred and ten feet long itself! It is only about four feet high, though. He must have cast a shadow like a lightning rod. The proof that this is the genuine spot where Noah was buried can only be doubted by uncommonly incredulous people. The evidence is pretty straight. Shem, the son of Noah, was present at the burial, and showed the place to his descendents, who transmitted the knowledge to their descendents, and the lineal descendents of these introduced themselves to us today. It was pleasant to make the acquaintance of members of so respectable a family. It was a thing to be proud of. It was the next thing to being acquainted with Noah himself.

Noah's memorable voyage will always possess a living interest for me henceforward.

* * *

Properly, with the sorry relics we bestrode, it was a three days' journey to Damascus. It was necessary that we should do it in less than two. It was necessary because our three pilgrims would not travel on the Sabbath day. We were all perfectly willing to keep the Sabbath day, but there are times when to keep the *letter* of a sacred law whose spirit is righteous becomes a sin, and this was a case in point. We pleaded for the tired, ill-treated horses, and tried to show that their faithful service deserved kindness in return and their hard lot compassion. But when did ever self-righteousness know the sentiment of pity? What were a few long hours added to the hardships of some overtaxed brutes when weighed against the peril of those human souls? It was not the most promising party to travel with and hope to gain a higher veneration for religion through the example of its devotees. We said the Saviour, who pitied dumb beasts and taught that the ox must be rescued from the mire even on the Sabbath day, would not have counseled a forced march like this. We said the "long trip" was exhausting and therefore dangerous in the blistering heats of summer, even when the ordinary day's stages were traversed, and if we persisted in this hard march, some of us might be stricken down with the fevers of the country in consequence of it. Nothing could move the pilgrims. They *must* press on. Men might die, horses might die, but they must enter upon holy soil next week with no Sabbath-breaking stain upon them. Thus they were willing to commit a sin against the spirit of religious law in order that they might preserve the letter of it. It was not worthwhile to tell them "the letter kills." I am talking now about personal friends, men whom I like, men who are good citizens, who are honorable, upright, conscientious, but whose idea of the Saviour's religion seems to me distorted. They lecture our shortcomings unsparingly, and every night they call us together and read to us chapters from the Testament that are full of gentleness, of charity, and of tender mercy; and then all the next day they stick to their saddles clear up to the summits of these rugged mountains and clear down again. Apply the Testament's gentleness and charity and tender mercy to a toiling, worn and weary horse? Nonsense—these are for God's human creatures, not his dumb ones. What the pilgrims choose to do, respect for their almost sacred character demands that I should allow to pass—but I would so like to catch any other member of the party riding his horse up one of these exhausting hills once!

We have given the pilgrims a good many examples that might benefit them, but it is virtue thrown away. They have never heard a cross word out of our lips toward each other—but *they* have quarreled once or twice. We love to hear them at it after they have been lecturing us. The very first thing they did, coming ashore at Beirut, was to quarrel in the boat. I have said I like them, and I do like them—but every time they read me a scorcher of a lecture I mean to talk back in print.

Not content with doubling the legitimate stages, they switched off the main road and went away out of the way to visit an absurd fountain called Figia, because Baalam's ass had drank there once. So we journeyed on, through the terrible hills and deserts and roasting sun, and then far into the night, seeking the honored pool of Baalam's ass, the patron saint of all pilgrims like us. I find no entry but this in my notebook:

> Rode today altogether thirteen hours, through deserts partly, and partly over barren, unsightly hills, and latterly through wild, rocky scenery, and camped at about eleven o'clock at night on the banks of a limpid stream, near a Syrian village. Do not know its name—do not wish to know it—want to go to bed. Two horses lame (mine and Jack's) and the others worn out. Jack and I walked three or four miles over the hills and led the horses. Fun—but of a mild type.

Twelve or thirteen hours in the saddle, even in a Christian land and a Christian climate, and on a good horse, is a tiresome journey; but in an oven like Syria, in a ragged spoon of a saddle that slips fore and aft, and "thort-ships," and every way, and on a horse that is tired and lame and yet must be whipped and spurred with hardly a moment's cessation all day long, till the blood comes from his side, and your conscience hurts every time you strike if you are half a man—it is a journey to be remembered in bitterness of spirit and execrated with emphasis for a liberal division of a man's lifetime.

*  *  *

The last twenty-four hours we stayed in Damascus I lay prostrate with a violent attack of cholera or cholera morbus, and therefore had a good chance and a good excuse to lie there on that wide divan and take an honest rest. I had nothing to do but listen to the pattering of the fountains and take medicine and throw it up again. It was dangerous recreation, but it was pleasanter than traveling in Syria. I had plenty of snow from Mount Hermon, and as it would not stay in my stomach, there was nothing to interfere with my eating it—there was always room for more. I enjoyed myself very well. Syrian travel has its interesting features, like travel in any other part of the world, and yet to break your leg or have the cholera adds a welcome variety to it.

We left Damascus at noon and rode across the plain a couple of hours, and then the party stopped awhile in the shade of some fig trees to give me a chance to rest. It was the hottest day we had seen yet—the sun flames shot down like the shafts of fire that stream out before a blowpipe; the rays seemed to fall in a steady deluge on the head and pass downward like rain from a roof. I imagined I could distinguish between the floods of rays—I thought I could tell when each flood struck my head, when it reached my shoulders, and when the next one came. It was terrible. All the desert glared so fiercely that my eyes were swimming in tears all the time. The boys had white umbrellas heavily lined with dark green. They were a priceless blessing. I thanked fortune that I had one, too, notwithstanding it was packed up with the baggage and was ten miles ahead. It is madness to travel in Syria without an umbrella. They told me in Beirut (those people who always gorge you with advice) that it was madness to travel in Syria without an umbrella. It was on this account that I got one.

But, honestly, I think an umbrella is a nuisance anywhere when its business is to keep the sun off. No Arab wears a brim to his fez or uses an umbrella or anything to shade his eyes or his face, and he always looks comfortable and proper in the sun. But of all the ridiculous sights I ever have seen, our party of eight is the most so—they do cut such an outlandish figure. They travel single file; they all wear the endless white rag of Constantinople wrapped round and round their hats and dangling down their backs; they all wear thick green spectacles, with side glasses to them; they all hold white umbrellas, lined with green, over their heads; without exception their stirrups are too short—they are the very worst gang of horsemen on earth; their animals to a horse trot fearfully hard—and when they get strung out one after the other, glaring straight ahead and breathless, bouncing high and out of turn, all along the line, knees well up and stiff, elbows flapping like a rooster's that is going to crow, and the long file of umbrellas popping convulsively up and down—when one sees this outrageous picture exposed to the light of day, he is amazed that the gods don't get out their thunderbolts and destroy them off the face of the earth! I do—I wonder at it. I wouldn't let any such caravan go through a country of mine.

And when the sun drops below the horizon and the boys close their umbrellas and put them under their arms, it is only a variation of the picture, not a modification of its absurdity.

But maybe you cannot see the wild extravagance of my panorama. You could if you were here. Here you feel all the time just as if you were living about the year 1200 before Christ—or back to the patriarchs—or forward to the New Era. The scenery of the Bible is about you—the customs of the patriarchs are around you—the same people, in the same flowing robes and in sandals, cross your path—the same long trains of stately camels go and come—the same impressive religious solemnity and silence rest upon the desert and the mountains that were upon them in the remote ages of antiquity, and behold, intruding upon a scene like this, comes this fantastic mob of green-spectacled Yanks, with their flapping elbows and bobbing umbrellas! It is Daniel in the lion's den, with a green cotton umbrella under his arm, all over again.

My umbrella is with the baggage, and so are my green spectacles—and there they shall stay. I will not use them. I will show some respect for the eternal fitness of things. It will be bad enough to get sunstruck without looking ridiculous into the bargain. If I fall, let me fall bearing about me the semblance of a Christian at least.

* * *

[T]his last new horse I have got is trying to break his neck over the tent ropes, and I shall have to go out and anchor him. Jericho and I have parted company. The new horse is not much to boast of, I think. One of his hindlegs bends the wrong way, and the other is as straight and stiff as a tent pole. Most of his teeth are gone, and he is as blind as a bat. His nose has been broken at some time or other and is arched like a culvert now. His underlip hangs down like a camel's, and his ears are chopped off close to his head. I had some trouble at first to find a name for him, but I finally concluded to call him Baalbek, because he is such a magnificent ruin. I cannot keep from talking about my horses, because I have a very long and tedious journey before me, and they naturally occupy my thoughts about as much as matters of apparently much greater importance.

We satisfied our pilgrims by making those hard rides from Baalbek to Damascus, but Dan's horse and Jack's were so crippled we had to leave them behind and get fresh animals for them. The dragoman says that Jack's horse died. I swapped horses with Muhammad, the kingly-looking Egyptian who is our Ferguson's lieutenant. By Ferguson I mean our dragoman Abraham, of course. I did not take this horse on account of his personal appearance, but because I have not seen his back. I do not wish to see it. I have seen the backs of all the other horses and found most of them covered with dreadful saddle boils which I know have not been washed or doctored for years. The idea of riding all day long over such ghastly inquisitions of torture is sickening. My horse must be like the others, but I have at least the consolation of not knowing it to be so.

I hope that in future I may be spared any more sentimental praises of the Arab's idolatry of his horse. In boyhood I longed to be an Arab of the desert and have a beautiful mare, and call her Selim or Benjamin or Muhammad, and feed her with my own hands, and let her come into the tent, and teach her to caress me and look fondly upon me with her great tender eyes; and I wished that a stranger might come at such a time and offer me a hundred thousand dollars for her, so that I could do like the other Arabs—hesitate, yearn for the money, but, overcome by my love for my mare, at last say, "Part with thee, my beautiful one! Never with my life! Away, tempter, I scorn thy gold!" and then bound into the saddle and speed over the desert like the wind!

But I recall those aspirations. If these Arabs be like the other Arabs, their love for their beautiful mares is a fraud. These of my acquaintance have no love for their horses, no sentiment of pity for them, and no knowledge of how to treat them or care for them. The Syrian saddle blanket is a quilted mattress two or three inches thick. It is never removed from the horse, day or night. It gets full of dirt and hair, and becomes soaked with sweat. It is bound to breed sores. These pirates never think of washing a horse's back.

They do not shelter the horses in the tents, either; they must stay out and take the weather as it comes. Look at poor cropped and dilapidated "Baalbek," and weep for the sentiment that has been wasted upon the Selims of romance!

# Galilee

The celebrated Sea of Galilee is not so large a sea as Lake Tahoe[21] by a good deal—it is just about two-thirds as large. And when we come to speak of beauty, this sea is no more to be compared to Tahoe than a meridian of longitude is to a rainbow. The dim waters of this pool cannot suggest the limpid brilliancy of Tahoe; these low, shaven, yellow hillocks of rocks and sand, so devoid of perspective, cannot suggest the grand peaks that compass Tahoe like a wall, and whose ribbed and chasmed fronts are clad with stately pines that seem to grow small and smaller as they climb, till one might fancy them reduced to weeds and shrubs far upward, where they join the everlasting snows. Silence and solitude brood over Tahoe; and silence and solitude brood also over this

[21] I measure all lakes by Tahoe, partly because I am far more familiar with it than any other, and partly because I have such a high admiration for it and such a world of pleasant recollections of it that it is very nearly impossible for me to speak of lakes and not mention it.—M.T.

lake of Gennesaret.[22] But the solitude of one is as cheerful and fascinating as the solitude of the other is dismal and repellent.

In the early morning one watches the silent battle of dawn and darkness upon the waters of Tahoe with placid interest; but when the shadows sulk away and one by one the hidden beauties of the shore unfold themselves in the full splendor of noon; when the still surface is belted like a rainbow with broad bars of blue and green and white, half the distance from circumference to center; when, in the lazy summer afternoon, he lies in a boat, far out to where the dead blue of the deep water begins, and smokes the pipe of peace and idly winks at the distant crags and patches of snow from under his cap brim; when the boat drifts shoreward to the white water, and he lolls over the gunwale and gazes by the hour down through the crystal depths and notes the colors of the pebbles and reviews the finny armies gliding in procession a hundred feet below; when at night he sees moon and stars, mountain ridges feathered with pines, jutting white capes, bold promontories, grand sweeps of rugged scenery topped with bald, glimmering peaks, all magnificently pictured in the polished mirror of the lake in richest, softest detail, the tranquil interest that was born with the morning deepens and deepens, by sure degrees, till it culminates at last in resistless fascination!

It is solitude, for birds and squirrels on the shore and fishes in the water are all the creatures that are near to make it otherwise, but it is not the sort of solitude to make one dreary. Come to Galilee for that. If these unpeopled deserts, these rusty mounds of barrenness, that never, never, never do shake the glare from their harsh outlines, and fade and faint into vague perspective; that melancholy ruin of Capernaum; this stupid village of Tiberias, slumbering under its six funereal plumes of palms; yonder desolate declivity where the swine of the miracle ran down into the sea, and doubtless thought it was better to swallow a devil or two and get drowned into the bargain than have to live longer in such a place; this cloudless, blistering sky;

[22] Gennesaret was another name for the Sea of Galilee taken from the ancient city on its western shore. The word means "garden of riches." Twain would have appreciated the irony.

this solemn, sailless, tintless lake, reposing within its rim of yellow hills and low, steep banks, and looking just as expressionless and unpoetical (when we leave its sublime history out of the question) as any metropolitan reservoir in Christendom—if these things are not food for "Rock Me to Sleep, Mother," none exist, I think.

* * *

Nearly every book concerning Galilee and its lake describes the scenery as beautiful. No—not always so straightforward as that. Sometimes the *impression* intentionally conveyed is that it is beautiful, at the same time that the author is careful not to *say* that it is in plain Saxon. But a careful analysis of these descriptions will show that the materials of which they are formed are not individually beautiful and cannot be wrought into combinations that are beautiful. The veneration and affection which some of these men felt for the scenes they were speaking of heated their fancies and biased their judgment; but the pleasant falsities they wrote were full of honest sincerity, at any rate. Others wrote as they did because they feared it would be unpopular to write otherwise. Others were hypocrites and deliberately meant to deceive. Any of them would say in a moment, if asked, that it was *always* right and always *best* to tell the truth. They would say that, at any rate, if they did not perceive the drift of the question.

But why should not the truth be spoken of this region? Is the truth harmful? Has it ever needed to hide its face? God made the Sea of Galilee and its surroundings as they are. Is it the province of Mr. Grimes[23] to improve upon the work?

I am sure, from the tenor of books I have read, that many who have visited this land in years gone by were Presbyterians, and came seeking evidences in support of their particular creed; they found a Presbyterian Palestine, and they had already made up their minds to find no other, though possibly they did not know it, being

[23] A writer of overheated travel books about the Holy Land.

blinded by their zeal. Others were Baptists, seeking Baptist evidences and a Baptist Palestine. Others were Catholics, Methodists, Episcopalians, seeking evidences endorsing their several creeds and a Catholic, a Methodist, an Episcopalian Palestine. Honest as these men's intentions may have been, they were full of partialities and prejudices, they entered the country with their verdicts already prepared, and they could no more write dispassionately and impartially about it than they could about their own wives and children. Our pilgrims have brought *their* verdicts with them. They have shown it in their conversation ever since we left Beirut. I can almost tell, in set phrase, what they will say when they see Tabor, Nazareth, Jericho, and Jerusalem—*because I have the books they will "smouch" their ideas from.* These authors write pictures and frame rhapsodies, and lesser men follow and see with the author's eyes instead of their own, and speak with his tongue.

* * *

Pilgrims, sinners, and Arabs are all abed now, and the camp is still. Labor in loneliness is irksome. Since I made my last few notes, I have been sitting outside the tent for half an hour. Night is the time to see Galilee. Gennesaret under these lustrous stars has nothing repulsive about it. Gennesaret with the glittering reflections of the constellations flecking its surface almost makes me regret that I ever saw the rude glare of the day upon it. Its history and associations are its chiefest charm in any eyes, and the spells they weave are feeble in the searching light of the sun. Then we scarcely feel the fetters. Our thoughts wander constantly to the practical concerns of life and refuse to dwell upon things that seem vague and unreal. But when the day is done, even the most unimpressible must yield to the dreamy influences of this tranquil starlight. The old traditions of the place steal upon his memory and haunt his reveries, and then his fancy clothes all sights and sounds with the supernatural. In the lapping of the waves upon the beach he hears the dip of ghostly oars; in the secret noises of the night he hears spirit voices; in the soft sweep of the breeze, the rush of invisible wings. Phantom ships are on the sea, the dead of twenty centuries come forth from the tombs, and in the dirges of the night wind the songs of old forgotten ages find utterance again.

In the starlight Galilee has no boundaries but the broad compass of the heavens, and is a theater meet for great events, meet for the birth of a religion able to save the world, and meet for the stately Figure appointed to stand upon its stage and proclaim its high decrees. But in the sunlight one says: Is it for the deeds which were done and the words which were spoken in this little acre of rocks and sand eighteen centuries gone that the bells are ringing today in the remote islands of the sea and far and wide over continents that clasp the circumference of the huge globe?

One can comprehend it only when night has hidden all incongruities and created a theater proper for so grand a drama.

# Jerusalem

One naturally goes first to the Holy Sepulchre. It is right in the city, near the western gate; it and the place of the Crucifixion, and, in fact, every other place intimately connected with that tremendous event, are ingeniously massed together and covered by one roof—the dome of the Church of the Holy Sepulchre.

Entering the building, through midst of the usual assemblage of beggars, one sees on his left a few Turkish guards—for Christians of different sects will not only quarrel, but fight, also, in this sacred place if allowed to do it. Before you is a marble slab, which covers the Stone of Unction, whereon the Saviour's body was laid to prepare it for burial. It was found necessary to conceal the real stone in this way in order to save it from destruction. Pilgrims were too much given to chipping off pieces of it to carry home. Nearby is a circular railing which marks the spot where the Virgin stood when the Lord's body was anointed.

Entering the great Rotunda, we stand before the most sacred locality in Christendom—the grave of Jesus. It is in the center of the church, and immediately under the great dome. It is enclosed in a sort of little temple of yellow and white stone, of fanciful design. Within the little temple is a portion of the very stone which was rolled away from the door of the Sepulchre, and on which the angel was sitting when Mary came thither "at early dawn." Stooping low, we enter the vault—the Sepulchre itself. It is only about six feet by seven, and the stone couch on which the dead Saviour lay extends from end to end of the apartment and occupies half its width. It is covered with a marble slab which has been much worn by the lips of pilgrims. The slab serves as an altar now. Over it hang fifty gold and silver lamps, which are always kept burning, and the place is otherwise scandalized by trumpery, gewgaws, and tawdry ornamentation.

All sects of Christians (except Protestants) have chapels under the roof of the Church of the Holy Sepulchre, and each must keep to itself and not venture upon another's ground. It has been proven conclusively that they cannot worship together around the grave of the Saviour of the world in peace. The chapel of the Syrians is not handsome; that of the Copts is the humblest of them all. It is nothing but a dismal cavern, roughly hewn in the living rock of the Hill of Calvary. In one side of it two ancient tombs are hewn, which are claimed to be those in which Nicodemus and Joseph of Aramithea were buried.

As we moved among the great piers and pillars of another part of the church we came upon a party of black-robed, animal-looking Italian monks, with candles in their hands, who were chanting something in Latin and going through some kind of religious performance around a disk of white marble let into the floor. It was there that the risen Saviour appeared to Mary Magdalen in the likeness of a gardener. Nearby was a similar stone, shaped like a star—here the Magdalen herself stood at the same time. Monks were performing in this place also. They perform everywhere—all over the vast building and at all hours. Their candles are always flitting about in the gloom and making the dim old church more dismal than there is any necessity that it should be, even though it is a tomb.

We were shown the place where our Lord appeared to his mother after the Resurrection. Here also a marble slab marks the place where St. Helena, the mother of the Emperor Constantine, found the crosses about three hundred years after the Crucifixion. According to the legend, this great discovery elicited extravagant demonstrations of joy. But they were of short duration. The question intruded itself: "Which bore the blessed Saviour, and which the thieves?" To be in doubt in so mighty a matter as this—to be uncertain which one to adore—was a grievous misfortune. It turned the public joy to sorrow. But when lived there a holy priest who could not set so simple a trouble as this at rest? One of these soon hit upon a plan that would be a certain test. A noble lady lay very ill in Jerusalem. The wise priests ordered that the three crosses be taken to her bedside one at a time. It was done. When her eyes fell upon the first one, she uttered a scream that was heard beyond the Damascus Gate, and even upon the Mount of Olives, it was said, and then fell back in a deadly swoon. They recovered her and brought the second cross. Instantly she went into fearful convulsions, and it was with the greatest difficulty that six strong men could hold her. They were afraid now to bring in the third cross. They began to fear that possibly they had fallen upon the wrong crosses, and that the true Cross was not with this number at all. However, as the woman seemed likely to die with the convulsions that were tearing her, they concluded that the third could do no more than put her out of her misery with a happy dispatch. So they brought it, and behold, a miracle! The woman sprang from her bed, smiling and joyful, and perfectly restored to health. When we listen to evidence like this, we cannot but believe. We would be ashamed to doubt, and properly, too. Even the very part of Jerusalem where this all occurred is there yet. So there really is no room for doubt.

The priests tried to show us, through a small screen, a fragment of the genuine Pillar of Flagellation, to which Christ was bound when they scourged him. But we could not see it because it was dark inside the screen. However, a baton is kept there, which the pilgrim thrusts through a hole in the screen, and then he no longer doubts that the true Pillar of Flagellation is in there. He cannot have any excuse to doubt it, for he can feel it with the stick. He can feel it as distinctly as he could feel anything.

Not far from here was a niche where they used to preserve a piece of the true Cross, but it is gone now. This piece of the Cross was discovered in the sixteenth century. The Latin priests say it was stolen away, long ago, by priests of another sect. That seems a hard statement to make, but we know very well that it *was* stolen, because we have seen it ourselves in several of the cathedrals of Italy and France.

But the relic that touched us most was the plain old sword of that stout Crusader Godfrey of Bouillon—King Godfrey of Jerusalem. No blade in Christendom wields such enchantment as this—no blade of all that rust in the ancestral halls of Europe is able to invoke such visions of romance in the brain of him who looks upon it—none that can prate of such chivalric deeds or tell such brave tales of the warrior days of old. It stirs within a man every memory of the Holy Wars that has been sleeping in his brain for years, and peoples his thoughts with mail-clad images, with marching armies, with battles, and with sieges. It speaks to him of Baldwin, and Tancred, the princely Saladin, and great Richard of the Lion Heart. It was with just such blades as these that these splendid heroes of romance used to segregate a man, so to speak, and leave the half of him to fall one way and the other half the other.

* * *

They showed us where the great Godfrey and his brother Baldwin, the first Christian kings of Jerusalem, once lay buried by that sacred sepulchre they had fought so long and so valiantly to wrest from the hands of the infidel. But the niches that contained the ashes of these renowned Crusaders were empty. Even the coverings of their tombs were gone—destroyed by devout members of the Greek Church because Godfrey and Baldwin were Latin princes and had been reared in a Christian faith whose creed differed in some unimportant respects from their own.

We passed on and halted before the tomb of Melchizedek! You will remember Melchizedek, no doubt; he was the king who came out and levied a tribute on Abraham the time that he pursued Lot's captors to Dan, and took all their property from them. That was about four thousand years ago, and Melchizedek died shortly afterward. However, his tomb is in a good state of preservation.

When one enters the Church of the Holy Sepulchre, the Sepulchre itself is the first thing he desires to see, and really is almost the first thing he does see. The next thing he has a strong yearning to see is the spot where the Saviour was crucified. But this they exhibit last. It is the crowning glory of the place. One is grave and thoughtful when he stands in the little Tomb of the Saviour—he could not well be otherwise in such a place—but he has not the slightest possible belief that ever the Lord lay there, and so the interest he feels in the spot is very, very greatly marred by that reflection. He looks at the place where Mary stood, in another part of the church, and where John stood and Mary Magdalen; where the mob derided the Lord; where the angel sat; where the crown of thorns was found and the true Cross; where the risen Saviour appeared—he looks at all these places with interest but with the same conviction he felt in the case of the Sepulchre, that there is nothing genuine about them and that they are imaginary holy places created by the monks. But the place of the Crucifixion affects him differently. He fully believes that he is looking upon the very spot where the Saviour gave up his life. He remembers that Christ was very celebrated long before he came to Jerusalem; he knows that his fame was so great that crowds followed him all the time; he is aware that his entry into the city produced a stirring sensation, and that his reception was a kind of ovation; he cannot overlook the fact that when he was crucified there were very many in Jerusalem who believed that he was the true Son of God. To publicly execute such a personage was sufficient in itself to make the locality of the execution a memorable place for ages; added to this, the storm, the darkness, the earthquake, the rending of the veil of the temple, and the untimely waking of the dead were events calculated to fix the execution and the scene of it in the memory of even the most thoughtless witness. Fathers would tell their sons about the strange affair and point out the spot; the sons would transmit the story to their children, and thus a period of three hundred years would easily be spanned[24]—at which time Helena came and built a church upon Calvary to commemorate the death and burial of the Lord and preserve the sacred place in the memories of men; since that time there has always been a church there. It is not possible that there can be any mistake about the locality of the Crucifixion. Not half a dozen people knew where they buried the Saviour, perhaps, and a burial is not a startling event anyhow; therefore we can be pardoned for unbelief in the Sepulchre, but not in the place of the Crucifixion. Five hundred years hence there will be no vestige of Bunker Hill Monument left, but Americans will still know where the battle was fought and where Warren fell. The crucifixion of Christ was too notable an event in Jerusalem, and the Hill of Calvary made too celebrated by it, to be forgotten in the short space of three hundred years. I climbed the stairway in the church which brings one to the top of the small enclosed pinnacle of rock, and looked upon the place where the true Cross once stood, with a far more absorbing interest than I had ever felt in anything earthly before. I could not believe that the three holes in the top of the rock were the actual ones the crosses stood in, but I felt satisfied that those crosses had stood so near the place now occupied by them that the few feet of possible difference were a matter of no consequence.

[24] The thought is Mr. Grimes's, not mine, and is full of good sense. I borrowed it from his *Tent Life*.—M.T.

# Part Six

## *Italy*

*We were a little fatigued with sightseeing, and so we rattled through a good deal of the country by rail without caring to stop. I took a few notes. I find no mention of Bologna in my memorandum book, except that we arrived there in good season, but saw none of the sausages for which the place is so justly celebrated.*

from *The Innocents Abroad*

# Venice

The Venetian gondola is as free and graceful in its gliding movement as a serpent. It is twenty or thirty feet long, and is narrow and deep like a canoe; its sharp bow and stern sweep upward from the water like the horns of a crescent with the abruptness of the curve slightly modified.

The bow is ornamented with a steel comb with a battle-ax attachment which threatens to cut passing boats in two occasionally, but never does. The gondola is painted black because in the zenith of Venetian magnificence the gondolas became too gorgeous altogether, and the Senate decreed that all such display must cease, and a solemn, unembellished black be substituted. If the truth were known, it would doubtless appear that rich plebeians grew too prominent in their affectation of patrician show on the Grand Canal, and required a wholesome snubbing. Reverence for the hallowed Past and its traditions keeps the dismal fashion in force now that the compulsion exists no longer. So let it remain. It is the color of mourning. Venice mourns. The stern of the boat is decked over and the gondolier stands there. He uses a single oar—a long blade, of course, for he stands nearly erect. A wooden peg, a foot and a half high, with two slight crooks or curves in one side of it and one on the other, projects above the starboard gunwale. Against that peg the gondolier takes a purchase with his oar, changing it at intervals to the other side of the peg or dropping it into another of the crooks, as the steering of the craft may demand—and how in the world he can back and fill, shoot straight ahead, or flirt suddenly around a corner, and make the oar stay in those insignificant notches is a problem to me and a never-diminishing matter of interest. I am afraid I study the gondolier's marvelous skill more than I do the sculptured palaces we glide among. He cuts a corner so closely, now and then, or misses another gondola by such an imperceptible hairbreadth that I feel myself "scrooching," as the children say, just as one does when a buggy wheel grazes his elbow. But he makes all his calculations with the nicest precision, and goes darting in and out among a Broadway confusion of busy craft with the easy confidence of the educated hackman. He never makes a mistake.

Sometimes we go flying down the great canals at such a gait that we can get only the merest glimpses into front doors, and again, in obscure alleys in the suburbs, we put on a solemnity suited to the silence, the mildew, the stagnant waters, the clinging weeds, the deserted houses, and the general lifelessness of the place, and move to the spirit of grave meditation.

The gondolier *is* a picturesque rascal for all he wears no satin harness, no plumed bonnet, no silken tights. His attitude is stately; he is lithe and supple; all his movements are full of grace. When his long canoe and his fine figure, towering from its high perch on the stern, are cut against the evening sky, they make a picture that is very novel and striking to a foreign eye.

We sit in the cushioned carriage body of a cabin, with the curtains drawn, and smoke or read or look out upon the passing boats, the houses, the bridges, the people, and enjoy ourselves much more than we could in a buggy jolting over our cobblestone pavements at home. This is the gentlest, pleasantest locomotion we have ever known.

But it seems queer—ever so queer—to see a boat doing duty as a private carriage. We see businessmen come to the front door, step into a gondola instead of a streetcar, and go off downtown to the counting room.

* * *

We have been pretty much everywhere in our gondola. We have bought beads and photographs in the stores and wax matches in the Great Square of St. Mark. This last remark suggests a digression. Everybody goes to this vast square in the evening. The military bands play in the center of it and countless couples of ladies and gentlemen promenade up and down on either side, and platoons of them are constantly drifting away toward the old cathedral, and by the venerable column with the Winged Lion of St. Mark on its top, and out to where the boats lie moored; and other platoons are as constantly arriving from the gondolas and joining the great throng. Between the promenaders and the sidewalks are seated hundreds and hundreds of people at small tables, smoking and taking *granita* (a first cousin to ice cream); on the sidewalks are more employing themselves in the same way. The shops in the first floor of the tall rows of buildings that wall the three sides of the square are brilliantly lighted, the air is filled with music and merry voices, and altogether the scene is as bright and spirited and full of cheerfulness as any man could desire. We enjoy it thoroughly. Very many of the young women are exceedingly pretty and dress with rare good taste. We are gradually and laboriously learning the ill manners of staring them unflinchingly in the face—not because such conduct is agreeable to us, but because it is the custom of the country and they say the girls like it. We wish to learn all the curious, outlandish ways of all the different countries, so that we can "show off" and astonish people when we get home. We wish to excite the envy of our untraveled friends with our strange foreign fashions which we can't shake off. All our passengers are paying strict attention to this thing, with the end in view which I have mentioned. The gentle reader will never, never know what a consummate ass he can become until he goes abroad. I speak now, of course, in the supposition that the gentle reader has not been abroad, and therefore is not already a consummate ass. If the case be otherwise, I beg his pardon and extend to him the cordial hand of fellowship and call him brother. I shall always delight to meet an ass after my own heart when I have finished my travels.

On this subject let me remark that there are Americans abroad in Italy who have actually forgotten their mother tongue in three months—forgot it in France. They cannot even write their address in English in a hotel register. I append these evidences, which I copied verbatim from the register of a hotel in a certain Italian city:

> John P. Whitcomb, *Etats Unis.*
>
> Wm. L. Ainsworth, *travailleur* (he meant traveler, I suppose) *Etats Unis.*
>
> George P. Morton, *et fils, d'Amerique.*
>
> Lloyd B. Williams, *et trois amis, ville de* Boston, *Amerique.*
>
> J. Ellsworth Baker, *tout de suite de France, place de naissance Amerique, destination la Grand Bretagne.*

I love this sort of people. A lady passenger of ours tells of a fellow citizen of hers who spent eight weeks in Paris and then returned home and addressed his dearest old bosom friend Herbert as Mr. "Er-bare!" He apologized, though, and said, "'Pon my soul, it is aggravating, but I cahn't help it—I have got so used to speaking nothing but French, my dear Erbare—damme, there is goes again!—got so used to French pronunciation that I cahn't get rid of it—it is positively annoying, I assure you." This entertaining idiot, whose name was Gordon, allowed himself to be hailed three times in the street before he paid any attention, and then begged a thousand pardons and said he had grown so accustomed to hearing himself addressed as "M'sieu Gor-r-*dong*," with a roll to the r, that he had forgotten the legitimate sound of his name! He wore a rose in his buttonhole; he gave the French salutation—two flips of the hand in front of the face; he called Paris *Pairee* in ordinary English conversation; he carried envelopes bearing foreign postmarks protruding from his breast pocket; he cultivated a moustache and imperial, and did what else he could to suggest to the beholder his pet fancy that he resembled Louis Napoleon—and in a spirit of thankfulness which is entirely unaccountable, considering the slim foundation there was for it, he praised his Maker that he was *as* he was, and went on enjoying his little life just the same as if he really *had* been deliberately designed and erected by the great Architect of the Universe.

Think of our Whitcombs and our Ainsworths and our Williamses writing themselves down in dilapidated French in foreign hotel registers! We laugh at Englishmen, when we are home, for sticking so sturdily to their national ways and customs, but we look back upon it from abroad very forgivingly. It is not pleasant to see an American thrusting his nationality *obtrusively* in a foreign land, but, oh, it is pitiable to see him making of himself a thing that is neither male nor female, neither fish, flesh, nor fowl—a poor, miserable, hermaphrodite Frenchman!

* * *

Yes, I think we have seen all of Venice. We have seen, in these old churches, a profusion of costly and elaborate sepulchre ornamentation such as we never dreamt of before. We have stood in the dim religious light of these hoary sanctuaries, in the midst of long ranks of dusty monuments and effigies of the great dead of Venice, until we seemed drifting back, back, back, into the solemn past, and looking upon the scenes and mingling with the peoples of a remote antiquity. We have been in a half-waking sort of dream all the time. I do not know how else to describe the feeling. A part of our being has remained still in the nineteenth century, while another part of it has seemed in some unaccountable way walking among the phantoms of the tenth.

We have seen famous pictures until our eyes are weary with looking at them and refuse to find interest in them any longer. And what wonder, when there are twelve hundred pictures by Palma the Younger in Venice and fifteen hundred by Tintoretto? And behold there are Titians and the works of other artists in proportion. We have seen Titian's celebrated "Cain and Abel," his "David and Goliath," his "Abraham's Sacrifice." We have seen Tintoretto's monster picture, which is seventy-four feet long and I do not know how many feet high, and thought it a very commodious picture. We have seen pictures of martyrs enough and saints enough to regenerate the world. I ought not to confess it, but still, since one has no opportunity in America to acquire a critical judgment in art, and since I could not hope to become educated in it in Europe in a few short weeks, I may therefore as well acknowledge, with such apologies as may be due, that to me it seemed that when I had seen one of these martyrs I had seen them all. They all have a marked family resemblance to each other; they dress alike, in coarse monkish robes and sandals, they are all bald-headed, they all stand in about the same attitude, and without exception they are gazing heavenward with countenances which the Ainsworths, the Mortons, and the Williamses *et fils* inform me are full of "expression." To me there is nothing tangible about these imaginary portraits, nothing that I can grasp and take a living interest in. If great Titian had only been gifted with prophecy, and had skipped a martyr, and gone over to England and painted a portrait of Shakespeare, even as a youth, which we could all have confidence in now, the world down to the latest generations would have forgiven him the lost martyr in the rescued seer. I think posterity could have spared one more martyr for the sake of a great historical picture of Titian's time and painted by his brush—such as Columbus returning in chains from the discovery of a world, for instance. The old masters did paint some Venetian historical pictures, and these we did not tire of looking at, notwithstanding representations of the formal introduction of defunct doges to the Virgin Mary in regions beyond the clouds clashed rather harshly with the proprieties, it seemed to us.

But humble as we are, and unpretending, in the matter of art, our researches among the painted monks and martyrs have not been wholly in vain. We have striven hard to learn. We have had some success. We have mastered some things, possibly of trifling import in the eyes of the learned, but to us they give pleasure, and we take as much pride in our little acquirements as do others who have learned far more, and we love to display them full as well. When we see a monk going about with a lion and looking tranquilly up to heaven, we know that that is St. Mark. When we see a monk with a book and a pen, looking tranquilly up to heaven, trying to think of a word, we know that that is St. Matthew. When we see a monk sitting on a rock, looking tranquilly up to heaven, with a human skull beside him, and without other baggage, we know that that is St. Jerome. Because we know that he always went flying light in the matter of baggage. When we see a party looking tranquilly up to heaven, unconscious that his body is shot through and through with arrows, we know that that is St. Sebastian. When we see other monks looking tranquilly up to heaven, but having no trademark, we always ask who those parties are. We do this because we humbly wish to learn. We have seen thirteen thousand St. Jeromes, and twenty-two thousand St. Marks, and sixteen thousand St. Matthews, and sixty thousand St. Sebastians, and four millions of assorted monks, undesignated, and we feel encouraged to believe that when we have seen some more of these various pictures and had a larger experience, we shall begin to take an absorbing interest in them like our cultivated countrymen from *Amerique.*

Now it does give me real pain to speak in this almost unappreciative way of the old masters and their martyrs, because good friends of mine in the ship—friends who do thoroughly and conscientiously appreciate them and are in every way competent to discriminate between good pictures and inferior ones—have urged me for my own sake not to make public the fact that I lack this appreciation and this critical discrimination myself. I believe that what I have written and may still write about pictures will give them pain, and I am honestly sorry for it. I even promised that I would hide my uncouth sentiments in my own breast. But alas! I never could keep a promise. I do not blame myself for this weakness, because the fault must lie in my physical organization. It is likely that such a very liberal amount of space was given to the organ which enables me to *make* promises that the organ which should enable me to keep them was crowded out. But I grieve not. I like no halfway things. I had rather have one faculty nobly developed than two faculties of mere ordinary capacity. I certainly meant to keep that promise, but I find I cannot do it. It is impossible to travel through Italy without speaking of pictures, and can I see them through others' eyes?

If I did not so delight in the grand pictures that are spread before me every day of my life by that monarch of all the old masters, Nature, I should come to believe sometimes that I had in me no appreciation of the beautiful whatsoever.

# Milan

"Do you wis zo haut can be?"

This was what the guide asked when we were looking up at the bronze horses on the Arch of Peace. It meant, do you wish to go up there? I give it as a specimen of guide-English. These are the people that make life a burden to the tourist. Their tongues arc never still. They talk forever and forever, and that is the kind of billingsgate they use. Inspiration itself could hardly comprehend them. If they would only show you a masterpiece of art, or a venerable tomb, or a prison house, or a battlefield, hallowed by touching memories or historical reminiscences, or grand traditions, and then step aside and hold still for ten minutes and let you think, it would not be so bad. But they interrupt every dream, every pleasant train of thought, with their tiresome cackling. Sometimes when I have been standing before some cherished old idol of mine that I remembered years and years ago in pictures in the geography at school, I have thought I would give a whole world if the human parrot at my side would suddenly perish where he stood and leave me to gaze and ponder and worship.

No, we did not "wis zo haut can be." We wished to go to La Scala, the largest theater in the world, I think they call it. We did so. It was a large place. Seven separate and distinct masses of humanity—six great circles and a monster parquette.

We wished to go to the Ambrosian Library, and we did that also. We saw a manuscript of Vergil, with annotations in the handwriting of Petrarch, the gentleman who loved another man's Laura and lavished upon her all through life a love which was a clear waste of raw material. It was sound sentiment, but bad judgment. It brought both parties fame and created a fountain of commiseration for them in sentimental breasts that is running yet. But who says a word in behalf of poor Mr. Laura? (I do not know his other name.) Who glorifies him? Who bedews him with tears? Who writes poetry about him? Nobody. How do you suppose *he* liked the state of things that has given the world so much pleasure? How did he enjoy having another man following his wife everywhere and making her name a familiar word in every garlic-exterminating mouth in Italy with his sonnets to her preempted eyebrows? *They* got fame and sympathy—he got neither. This is a peculiarly felicitous instance of what is called poetical justice. It is all very fine, but it does not chime with my notions of right. It is too one-sided—too ungenerous. Let the world go on fretting about Laura and Petrarch if it will; but as for me, my tears and my lamentations shall be lavished upon the unsung defendant.

We saw also an autograph letter of Lucrezia Borgia, a lady for whom I have always entertained the highest respect, on account of her rare histrionic capabilities, her opulence in solid gold goblets made of gilded wood, her high distinction as an operatic screamer, and the facility with which she could order a sextuple funeral and get the corpses ready for it. We saw one single coarse yellow hair from Lucrezia's head, likewise. It awoke emotions, but we still live. In this same library we saw some drawings by Michelangelo (these Italians call him Mickelangelo) and Leonardo da Vinci. (They spell it Vinci and pronounce it Vinchy; foreigners always spell better than they pronounce.) We reserve our opinions of these sketches.

# Exasperating the Fergusons

Everybody knows the picture of the Coliseum; everybody recognizes at once that "looped and windowed" bandbox with a side bitten out. Being rather isolated, it shows to better advantage than any other of the monuments of ancient Rome. Even the beautiful Pantheon, whose pagan altars uphold the cross now, and whose Venus, tricked out in consecrated gimcracks, does reluctant duty as a Virgin Mary today, is built about with shabby houses and its stateliness sadly marred. But the monarch of all European ruins, the Coliseum, maintains that reserve and that royal seclusion which is proper to majesty. Weeds and flowers spring from its massy arches and its circling seats, and vines hang their fringes from its lofty walls. An impressive silence broods over the monstrous structure where such multitudes of men and women were wont to assemble in other days. The butterflies have taken the places of the queens of fashion and beauty of eighteen centuries ago, and the lizards sun themselves in the sacred seat of the emperor. More vividly than all the written histories, the Coliseum tells the story of Rome's grandeur and Rome's decay. It is the worthiest type of both that exists. Moving about the

Rome of today, we might find it hard to believe in her old magnificence and her millions of population; but with this stubborn evidence before us that she was obliged to have a theater with sitting room for eighty thousand persons and standing room for twenty thousand more, to accommodate such of her citizens as required amusement, we find belief less difficult. The Coliseum is over one thousand six hundred feet long, seven hundred and fifty wide, and one hundred and sixty-five high. Its shape is oval.

In America we make convicts useful at the same time that we punish them for their crimes. We farm them out and compel them to earn money for the State by making barrels and building roads. Thus we combine business with retribution, and all things are lovely. But in ancient Rome they combined religious duty with pleasure. Since it was necessary that the new sect called Christians should be exterminated, the people judged it wise to make this work profitable to the State at the same time, and entertaining to the public. In addition to the gladiatorial combats and other shows, they sometimes threw members of the hated sect into the arena of the Coliseum and turned wild beasts in upon them. It is estimated that seventy thousand Christians suffered martyrdom in this place. This has made the Coliseum holy ground in the eyes of the followers of the Saviour. And well it might; for if the chain that bound a saint and the footprints a saint has left upon a stone he chanced to stand upon be holy, surely the spot where a man gave up his life for his faith is holy.

Seventeen or eighteen centuries ago this Coliseum was *the* theater of Rome, and Rome was mistress of the world. Splendid pageants were exhibited here, in the presence of the emperor, the great ministers of State, the nobles, and vast audiences of citizens of smaller consequence. Gladiators fought with gladiators and at times with warrior prisoners from many a distant land. It was *the* theater of Rome—of the world—and the man of fashion who could not let fall in a casual and unintentional manner something about "my private box at the Coliseum" could not move in the first circles.

When the clothing-store merchant wished to consume the corner grocery man with envy, he bought secured seats in the front row and let the thing be known. When the irresistible dry-goods clerk wished to blight and destroy, according to his native instinct, he got himself up regardless of expense and took some other fellow's young lady to the Coliseum, and then accented the affront by cramming her with ice cream between the acts or by approaching the cage and stirring up the martyrs with his whalebone cane for her edification. The Roman swell was in his true element only when he stood up against a pillar and fingered his moustache unconscious of the ladies; when he viewed the bloody combats through an opera glass two inches long; when he excited the envy of provincials by criticisms which showed that he had been to the Coliseum many and many a time and was long over the novelty of it; when he turned with a yawn at last and said:

"*He* a star! Handles his sword like an apprentice brigand! He'll do for the country maybe, but he don't answer for the metropolis!"

Glad was the contraband that had a seat in the pit at the Saturday matinee, and happy the Roman street boy who ate his peanuts and guyed the gladiators from the dizzy gallery.

* * *

So far, so good. If any man has a right to feel proud of himself and satisfied, surely it is I. For I have written about the Coliseum and the gladiators, the martyrs and the lions, and yet have never once used the phrase "butchered to make a Roman holiday." I am the only free white man of mature age who has accomplished this since Byron originated the expression.

Butchered to make a Roman holiday sounds well for the first seventeen or eighteen hundred thousand times one sees it in print, but after that it begins to grow tiresome. I find it in all the books concerning Rome—and here latterly it reminds me of Judge Oliver. Oliver was a young lawyer, fresh from the schools, who had gone out to the deserts of Nevada to begin life. He found that country and our ways of life there, in those early days, different from life in New England or Paris. But he put on a woolen shirt and strapped a navy revolver to his person, took to the bacon and beans of the country, and determined to do in Nevada as Nevada did. Oliver accepted the situation so completely that although he must have sorrowed over many of his trials, he never complained—that is, he never complained but once. He, two others, and myself started to the new silver mines in Humboldt Mountains—he to be Probate Judge of Humboldt County and we to mine. The distance was two hundred miles. It was dead of winter. We bought a two-horse wagon and put eighteen hundred pounds of bacon, flour, beans, blasting powder, picks, and shovels in it; we bought two sorry-looking Mexican "plugs," with the hair turned the wrong way and more corners on their bodies than there are on the Mosque of Omar; we hitched up and started. It was a dreadful trip. But Oliver did not complain. The horses dragged the wagon two miles from town and then gave out. Then we three pushed the wagon seven miles, and Oliver moved ahead and pulled the horses after him by the bits. We complained, but Oliver did not. The ground was frozen, and it froze our backs while we slept; the wind swept across our faces and froze our noses. Oliver did not complain. Five days of pushing the wagon by day and freezing by night brought us to the bad part of the journey—the Forty-Mile Desert, or the Great American Desert, if you please. Still this mildest-mannered man that ever was had not complained. We started across at eight in the morning, pushing through sand that had no bottom; toiling all day long by the wrecks of a thousand wagons, the skeletons of ten thousand oxen; by wagon tires enough to hoop the Washington Monument to the top, and ox chains enough to girdle Long Island; by human graves; with our throats parched always with thirst; lips bleeding from the alkali dust; hungry, perspiring, and very, very weary—so weary that when we dropped in the sand every fifty yards to rest the horses, we could hardly keep from going to sleep—no complaints from Oliver; none the next morning at three o'clock, when we got across, tired to death. Awakened two or three nights afterward at midnight, in a narrow canyon, by the snow falling on our faces, and appalled at the imminent danger of being "snowed in," we harnessed up and pushed on till eight in the morning, passed the "Divide," and knew we were saved. No complaints. Fifteen days of hardship and fatigue brought us to the end of the two hundred miles, and the judge had not complained. We wondered if anything *could* exasperate him. We built a Humboldt house. It is done in this way. You dig a square in the steep base of the mountain and set up two uprights and top them with two joists. Then you stretch a great sheet of "cotton domestic" from the point where the joists join the hillside down over the joists to the ground; this makes the roof and the front of the mansion; the sides and back are the dirt walls your digging has left. A chimney is easily made by turning up one corner of the roof. Oliver was sitting alone in this dismal den one night, by a sagebrush fire, writing poetry; he was very fond of digging poetry out of himself—or blasting it out when it came hard. He heard an animal's footsteps close to the roof; a stone or two and some dirt came through and fell by him. He grew uneasy and said, "Hi! Clear out from there, can't you!"—from time to time. But by and by he fell asleep where he sat, and pretty soon a mule fell down the chimney! The fire flew in every direction, and Oliver went over backwards. About ten nights after that, he recovered confidence enough to go to writing poetry again. Again he dozed off to sleep, and again a mule fell down the chimney. This time about half of that side of the house came in with the mule. Struggling to get up, the mule kicked the candle out and smashed most of the kitchen furniture, and raised considerable dust. These violent awakenings must have been annoying to Oliver, but he never complained. He moved to a mansion on the opposite side of the canyon, because he had noticed the mules did not go there. One night about eight o'clock he was endeavoring to finish his poem, when a stone rolled in—then a hoof appeared below the canvas—then part of a cow—the after part. He leaned back in dread and shouted, "Hooy! Hooy! Get out of this!" And the cow struggled manfully—lost ground steadily—dirt and dust streamed down—and before Oliver could get well away, the entire cow crashed through onto the table and made a shapeless wreck of everything!

Then, for the first time in his life, I think, Oliver complained. He said:

*"This thing is growing monotonous!"*

Then he resigned his judgeship and left Humboldt County. "Butchered to make a Roman holiday" has grown monotonous to me.

In this connection I wish to say one word about Michelangelo Buonarroti. I used to worship the mighty genius of Michelangelo—that man who was great in poetry, painting, sculpture, architecture—great in everything he undertook. But I do not want Michelangelo for breakfast—for luncheon—for dinner—for tea—for supper—for between meals. I like a change occasionally. In Genoa he designed everything; in Milan he or his pupils designed everything; he designed the Lake of Como; in Padua, Verona, Venice, Bologna, who did we ever hear of from guides but Michelangelo? In Florence he painted everything, designed everything nearly, and what he did not design he used to sit on a favorite stone and look at, and they showed us the stone. In Pisa designed everything but the old shot tower, and they would have attributed that to him if it had not been so awfully out of the perpendicular. He designed the piers of Leghorn and the custom-house regulations of Civitavecchia. But here—here it is frightful. He designed St. Peter's; he designed the Pope; he designed the Pantheon, the uniform of the Pope's soldiers, the Tiber, the Vatican, the Coliseum, the Capitol, the Tarpeian Rock, the Barbarini Palace, St. John Lateran, the Campagna, the Appian Way, the Seven Hills, the Baths of Caracalla, the Claudian Aqueduct, the Cloaca Maxima—the eternal bore designed the Eternal City, and unless all men and books do lie, he painted everything in it!

Dan[25] said the other day to the guide, "Enough, enough, enough! Say no more! Lump the whole thing! Say that the Creator made Italy from designs by Michelangelo!"

I never felt so fervently thankful, so soothed, so tranquil, so filled with a blessed peace as I did yesterday when I learned that Michelangelo was dead.

But we have taken it out of this guide. He has marched us through miles of pictures and sculpture in the vast corridors of the Vatican, and through miles of pictures and sculpture in twenty other palaces; he has shown us the great picture in the Sistine Chapel, and frescoes enough to fresco the heavens—pretty much all done by Michelangelo. So with him we have played that game which has vanquished so many guides for us—imbecility and idiotic questions. These creatures never suspect—they have no idea of a sarcasm.

He shows us a figure and says: "Statoo brunzo." (Bronze statue.)

We look at it indifferently and the doctor asks: "By Michelangelo?"

"No—not know who."

Then he shows us the ancient Roman Forum. The doctor asks: "Michelangelo?"

A stare from the guide. "No—thousan' year before he is born."

Then an Egyptian obelisk. Again: "Michelangelo?"

"Oh, *mon dieu*, genteelmen! Zis is *two* thousan' years before he is born!"

He grows so tired of that unceasing question sometimes that he dreads to show us anything at all. The wretch has tried all the ways he can think of to make us comprehend that Michelangelo is only responsible for the creation of a *part* of the world, but somehow he has not succeeded yet. Relief for overtaxed eyes and brain from study and sightseeing is necessary or we shall become idiotic sure enough. Therefore this guide must continue to suffer. If he does not enjoy it, so much the worse for him. We do.

[25] Dan, along with "the doctor," are friends of M.T.'s from the *Quaker City*.

In this place I may as well jot down a chapter concerning those necessary nuisances, European guides. Many a man has wished in his heart he could do without his guide, but, knowing he could not, has wished he could get some amusement out of him as remuneration for the affliction of his society. We accomplished this latter matter, and if our experience can be made useful to others they are welcome to it.

Guides know about enough English to tangle everything up so that a man can make neither head nor tail of it. They know their story by heart—the history of every statue, painting, cathedral, or other wonder they show you. They know it and tell it as a parrot would—and if you interrupt and throw them off the track, they have to go back and begin over again. All their lives long they are employed in showing strange things to foreigners and listening to their bursts of admiration. It is human nature to take delight in exciting admiration. It is what prompts children to say "smart" things, and do absurd ones, and in other ways "show off" when company is present. It is what makes gossips turn out in rain and storm to go and be the first to tell a startling bit of news. Think, then, what a passion it becomes with a guide, whose privilege it is, every day, to show to strangers wonders that throw them into perfect ecstasies of admiration! He gets so that he could not by any possibility live in a soberer atmosphere. After we discovered this, we *never* went into ecstasies anymore—we never admired anything—we never showed any but impassible faces and stupid indifference in the presence of the sublimest wonders a guide had to display. We had found their weak point. We have made good use of it ever since. We have made some of those people savage at times, but we have never lost our own serenity.

The doctor asks the questions generally because he can keep his countenance, and look more like an inspired idiot, and throw more imbecility into the tone of his voice than any man that lives. It comes natural to him.

The guides in Genoa are delighted to secure an American party, because Americans so much wonder and deal so much in sentiment and emotion before any relic of Columbus. Our guide there fidgeted about as if he had swallowed a spring mattress. He was full of animation—full of impatience. He said:

"Come wis me, genteelmen! Come! I show you ze letter-writing by Christopher Colombo! Write it himself! Write it wis his own hand! Come!"

He took us to the municipal palace. After much impressive fumbling of keys and opening of locks, the stained and aged document was spread before us. The guide's eyes sparkled. He danced about us and tapped the parchment with his finger:

"What I tell you, genteelmen! Is it not so? See! Handwriting Christopher Colombo! Write it himself!"

We looked indifferent—unconcerned. The doctor examined the document very deliberately, during a painful pause. Then he said, without any show of interest:

"Ah—Ferguson[26]—what—what did you say was the name of the party who wrote this?"

"Christopher Colombo! Ze great Christopher Colombo!"

Another deliberate examination.

"Ah—did he write it himself or—or how?"

"He write it himself! Christopher Colombo! His own hand-writing, write by himself!"

Then the doctor laid the document down and said:

"Why, I have seen boys in America only fourteen years old that could write better than that."

"But zis is ze great Christo —— "

"I don't care who it is! It's the worst writing I ever saw. Now you mustn't think you can impose on us because we are strangers. We are not fools, by a good deal. If you have got any specimens of penmanship of real merit, trot them out! And if you haven't, drive on!"

[26] M.T.'s generic name for his various guides.

We drove on. The guide was considerably shaken up, but he made one more venture. He had something which he thought would overcome us. He said:

"Ah, genteelmen, you come wis me! I show you beautiful, oh, magnificent bust Christopher Colombo! Splendid, grand, magnificent!"

He brought us before the beautiful bust—for it *was* beautiful—and sprang back and struck an attitude:

"Ah, look, genteelmen! Beautiful, grand—bust Christopher Colombo! Beautiful bust, beautiful pedestal!"

The doctor put up his eyeglass—procured for such occasions:

"Ah—what did you say this gentleman's name was?"

"Christopher Colombo! Ze great Christopher Colombo!"

"Christopher Colombo—the great Christopher Colombo. Well, what did *he* do?"

"Discover America! Discover America, oh, ze devil!"

"Discover America. No—that statement will hardly wash. We are just from America ourselves. We heard nothing about it. Christopher Colombo—pleasant name—is—is he dead?"

"Oh, corpo di Baccho! Three hundred year!"

"What did he die of?"

"I do not know! I cannot tell."

"Smallpox, think?"

"I do not know, genteelmen! I do not know *what* he die of!"

"Measles, likely?"

"Maybe—maybe—I do *not* know—I think he die of somethings."

"Parents living?"

"Im-posseeble!"

"Ah—which is the bust and which is the pedestal?"

"Santa Maria! *Zis* ze bust! *Zis* ze pedestal!"

"Ah, I see, I see—happy combination—very happy combination indeed. Is—is this the first time this gentleman was ever on a bust?"[27]

[27] A spree.

That joke was lost on the foreigner—guides cannot master the subtleties of the American joke.

We have made it interesting for this Roman guide. Yesterday we spent three or four hours in the Vatican again, that wonderful world of curiosities. We came very near expressing interest sometimes—even admiration—it was very hard to keep from it. We succeeded, though. Nobody else ever did in the Vatican museums. The guide was bewildered—nonplussed. He walked his legs off nearly, hunting up extraordinary things, and exhausted all his ingenuity on us, but it was a failure; we never showed any interest in anything. He had reserved what he considered to be his greatest wonder till the last—a royal Egyptian mummy, the best preserved in the world, perhaps. He took us there. He felt so sure this time that some of his old enthusiasm came back to him:

"See, genteelmen! Mummy! Mummy!"

The eyeglass came up as calmly, as deliberately as ever.

"Ah—Ferguson—what did I understand you to say the gentleman's name was?"

"Name? He got no name! Mummy! 'Gyptian mummy!"

"Yes, yes. Born here?"

"No! *'Gyptian* mummy!"

"Ah, just so. Frenchman, I presume?"

"No! *Not* Frenchman, not Roman! Born in Egypta!"

"Born in Egypta. Never heard of Egypta before. Foreign locality, likely. Mummy—mummy. How calm he is—how selfpossessed. Is, ah—is he dead?"

"Oh, *sacre bleu*, been dead three thousan' year!"

The doctor turned on him savagely.

"Here, now, what do you mean by such conduct as this! Playing us for Chinamen because we are strangers and trying to learn! Trying to impose your vile secondhand carcasses on *us*! Thunder and lightning, I've a notion to—to—if you've got a nice *fresh* corpse, fetch him out! Or, by George, we'll brain you!"

We make it exceedingly interesting for this Frenchman. However, he has paid us back partly, without knowing it. He came to the hotel this morning to ask if we were up, and he endeavored as well as he could to describe us, so that the landlord would know which persons he meant. He finished with the casual remark that we were lunatics. The observation was so innocent and so honest that it amounted to a very good thing for a guide to say.

There is one remark (already mentioned) which never yet has failed to disgust these guides. We use it always when we can think of nothing else to say. After they have exhausted their enthusiasm pointing out to us and praising the beauties of some ancient bronze image or broken-legged statue, we look at it stupidly and in silence for five, ten, fifteen minutes—as long as we can hold out, in fact—and then ask:

"Is—is he dead?"

That conquers the serenest of them. It is not what they are looking for—especially a new guide. Our Roman Ferguson is the most patient, unsuspecting, long-suffering subject we have had yet. We shall be sorry to part with him. We have enjoyed his society very much. We trust he has enjoyed ours, but we are harassed with doubts.

* * *

There is one thing I am certain of, though. With all the Michelangelos, the Raphaels, the Guidos, and all the other old masters, the sublime history of Rome remains unpainted! They painted Virgins enough and popes enough and saintly scarecrows enough to people paradise almost, and these things are all they did paint. "Nero fiddling o'er burning Rome," the assassination of Caesar, the stirring spectacle of a hundred thousand people bending forward with rapt interest, in the Coliseum, to see two skillful gladiators hacking away each other's lives, a tiger springing on a kneeling martyr—these and a thousand other matters which we read of with a living interest must be sought for only in books, not among the rubbish left by the old masters—who are no more, I have the satisfaction of informing the public.

They did paint, and they did carve in marble, one historical scene, and one only (of any great historical consequence). And what was it and why did they choose it particularly? It was the Rape of the Sabines, and they chose it for the legs and busts.

I like to look at statues, however, and I like to look at pictures also—even of monks looking up in sacred ecstasy and monks looking down in meditation, and monks skirmishing for something to eat—and therefore I drop ill nature to thank the papal government for so jealously guarding and so industriously gathering up these things, and for permitting me, a stranger and not an entirely friendly one, to roam at will and unmolested among them, charging me nothing and only requiring that I shall behave myself simply as well I ought to behave in any other man's house. I thank the Holy Father right heartily, and I wish him long life and plenty of happiness.

The popes have long been the patrons and preservers of art, just as our new, practical republic is the encourager and upholder of mechanics. In their Vatican is stored up all that is curious and beautiful in art; in our Patent Office is hoarded all that is curious or useful in mechanics. When a man invents a new style of horse collar or discovers a new and superior method of telegraphing, our government issues a patent to him that is worth a fortune; when a man digs up an ancient statue in the Campagna, the Pope gives him a fortune in gold coin. We can make something of a guess at a man's character by the style of nose he carries on his face. The Vatican and the Patent Office are governmental noses, and they bear a deal of character about them.

The guide showed us a colossal statue of Jupiter in the Vatican, which he said looked so damaged and rusty—so like the god of the Vagabonds—because it had but recently been dug up in the Campagna. He asked how much we supposed this Jupiter was worth. I replied, with intelligent promptness, that he was probably worth about four dollars—maybe four and a half. "A hundred thousand dollars!" Ferguson said. Ferguson said, further, that the Pope permits no ancient work of this kind to leave his dominions. He appoints a commission to examine discoveries like this and report upon the value; then the Pope pays the discoverer one-half of that assessed value and takes the statue. He said this Jupiter was dug from a field which had just been bought for thirty-six thousand dollars, so the first crop was a good one for the new farmer. I do not know whether Ferguson always tells the truth or not, but I suppose he does. I know that an exorbitant export duty is exacted upon all pictures painted by the old masters, in order to discourage the sale of those in the private collections. I am satisfied also that genuine old masters hardly exist at all in America, because the cheapest and most insignificant of them are valued at the price of a fine farm. I proposed to buy a small trifle of a Raphael myself, but the price of it was eighty thousand dollars, the export duty would have made it considerably over a hundred, and so I studied on it awhile and concluded not to take it.

# Part Seven

## *Germany*

*I suppose there are two kinds of music—one kind which one feels, just as an oyster might, and another sort which requires a higher faculty, a faculty which must be assisted and developed by teaching. Yet if base music gives certain of us wings, why should we want any other? But we do. We want it because the higher and better like it. But we want it without giving the necessary time and trouble; so we climb into that upper tier, that dress circle, by a lie: we pretend we like it. I know several of that sort of people—and I propose to be one of them myself when I get home with my fine European education.*

from *A Tramp Abroad*

# An Evening of Suffering

One day we took the train and went down to Mannheim to see *King Lear* played in German. It was a mistake. We sat in our seats three whole hours and never understood anything but the thunder and lightning, and even that was reversed to suit German ideas, for the thunder came first and the lightning followed after.

The behavior of the audience was perfect. There were no rustlings or whisperings or other little disturbances. Each act was listened to in silence, and the applauding was done after the curtain was down. The doors opened at half-past four, the play began promptly at half-past five, and within two minutes afterward all who were coming were in their seats, and quiet reigned. A German gentleman in the train had said that a Shakespearian play was an appreciated treat in Germany and that we should find the house filled. It was true. All six tiers were filled, and remained so to the end—which suggested that it is not only balcony people who like Shakespeare in Germany, but those in the pit and the gallery too.

Another time we went to Mannheim and attended a shivaree—otherwise an opera—the one called *Lohengrin*. The banging and slamming and booming and crashing were something beyond belief. The racking and pitiless pain of it remains stored up in my memory alongside the memory of the time that I had my teeth fixed. There were circumstances which made it necessary for me to stay through the four hours to the end, and I stayed, but the recollection of that long, dragging, relentless season of suffering is indestructible. To have to endure it in silence, and sitting still, made it all the harder. I was in a railed compartment with eight or ten strangers of the two sexes, and this compelled repression; yet at times the pain was so exquisite that I could hardly keep the tears back. At those times, as the howlings and wailings and shriekings of the singers, and the ragings and roarings and explosions of the vast orchestra rose higher and higher and wilder and wilder and fiercer and fiercer, I could have cried if I had been alone. Those strangers would not have been surprised to see a man do such a thing who was being gradually skinned, but they would have marveled at it here and made remarks about it, no doubt, whereas there was nothing in the present case which was an advantage over being skinned. There was a wait of half an hour at the end of the first act, and I could have gone out and rested during that time, but I could not trust myself to do it, for I felt that I should desert and stay out. There was another wait of half an hour toward nine o'clock, but I had gone through so much by that time that I had no spirit left and so had no desire but to be let alone.

I do not wish to suggest that the rest of the people there were like me, for indeed they were not. Whether it was that they naturally liked that noise or whether it was that they had learned to like it by getting used to it, I did not at that time know, but they did like it—this was plain enough. While it was going on they sat and looked as rapt and grateful as cats do when one strokes their backs, and whenever the curtain fell they rose to their feet in one solid mighty multitude, and the air was snowed thick with waving handkerchiefs, and hurricanes of applause swept the place. This was not comprehensible to me. Of course, there were many people there who were not under compulsion to stay, yet the tiers were as full at the close of the play as they had been at the beginning. This showed that the people liked it.

It was a curious sort of play. In the matter of costumes and scenery it was fine and showy enough, but there was not much action. That is to say, there was not much really done, it was only talked about and always violently. It was what one might call a narrative play. Everybody had a narrative and a grievance and none were reasonable about it, but all in an offensive and ungovernable state. There was little of that sort of customary thing where the tenor and the soprano stand down by the footlights, warbling with blended voices, and keep holding out their arms toward each other and drawing them back and spreading both hands over first one breast and then the other with a shake and a pressure—no, it was every rioter for himself and no blending. Each sang his indictive narrative in turn, accompanied by the whole orchestra of sixty instruments, and when this had continued for some time and one was hoping they might come to an understanding and modify the noise, a great chorus composed entirely of maniacs would suddenly break forth, and then during two minutes and sometimes three I lived over again all that I had suffered the time the orphan asylum burned down.

We only had one brief little season of heaven and heaven's sweet ecstasy and peace during all this long and diligent and acrimonious reproduction of the other place. This was while a gorgeous procession of people marched around and around in the third act and sang the Wedding Chorus. To my untutored ear that was music—almost divine music. While my seared soul was steeped in the healing balm of those gracious sounds, it seemed to me that I could almost resuffer the torments which had gone before, in order to be so healed again. There is where the deep ingenuity of the operatic idea is betrayed. It deals so largely in pain that its scattered delights are prodigiously augmented by the contrasts. A pretty air in an opera is prettier there than it could be anywhere else, I suppose, just as an honest man in politics shines more than he would elsewhere.

I have since found out that there is nothing the Germans like so much as an opera. They like it not in a mild and moderate way but with their whole hearts. This is a legitimate result of habit and education. Our nation will like the opera too, by and by, no doubt. One in fifty of those who attend our operas likes it already, perhaps, but I think a good many of the other forty-nine go in order to learn to like it, and the rest in order to be able to talk knowingly about it. The latter usually hum the airs while they are being sung, so that their neighbors may perceive that they have been to operas before. The funerals of these do not occur often enough.

* * *

Three or four hours. That is a long time to sit in one place, whether one be conspicuous or not, yet some of Wagner's operas bang along for six whole hours on a stretch! But the people sit there and enjoy it all and wish it would last longer. A German lady in Munich told me that a person could not like Wagner's music at first but must go through the deliberate process of learning to like it—then he would have his sure reward, for when he had learned to like it he would hunger for it and never be able to get enough of it. She said that six hours of Wagner was by no means too much. She said that this composer had made a complete revolution in music and was burying the old masters one by one. And she said that Wagner's operas differed from all others in one notable respect, and that was that they were not merely spotted with music here and there but were *all* music, from the first strain to the last. This surprised me. I said I had attended one of his insurrections and found hardly *any* music in it except the Wedding Chorus. She said *Lohengrin* was noisier than Wagner's other operas but that if I would keep going to see it I would find by and by that it was all music and therefore would then enjoy it. I *could* have said, "But would you advise a person to deliberately practice having the toothache in the pit of his stomach for a couple of years in order that he might then come to enjoy it?" But I reserved that remark.

This lady was full of the praises of the head-tenor who had performed in a Wagner opera the night before, and went on to enlarge upon his old and prodigious fame and how many honors had been lavished upon him by the princely houses of Germany. Here was another surprise. I had attended that very opera . . . and had made close and accurate observations. So I said:

"Why madam, *my* experience warrants me in stating that that tenor's voice is not a voice at all but only a shriek—the shriek of a hyena."

"That is very true," she said. "He cannot sing now. It is already many years that he has lost his voice, but in other times he sang, yes, divinely! So whenever he comes now, you shall see, yes, that the theater will not hold the people. *Jawohl bei Gott!* His voice is *wunderschön* in that past time."

I said she was discovering to me a kindly trait in the Germans which was worth emulating. I said that over the water we were not quite so generous; that with us, when a singer had lost his voice and a jumper had lost his legs, these parties ceased to draw. I said I had been to the opera in Hanover once and in Mannheim once and in Munich . . . once, and this large experience had nearly persuaded me that the Germans *preferred* singers who couldn't sing. This was not such a very extravagant speech, either, for that burly Mannheim tenor's praises had been the talk of all Heidelberg for a week before his performance took place—yet his voice was like the distressing noise which a nail makes when you screech it across a window-pane. I said so to Heidelberg friends the next day, and they said in the calmest and simplest way that that was very true but that in earlier times his voice *had* been wonderfully fine. And the tenor in Hanover was just another example of this sort. The English-speaking German gentleman who went with me to the opera there was brimming with enthusiasm over that tenor. He said:

"*Ach Gott!* A great man! You shall see him. He is so celebrate in all Germany—and he has a pension, yes, from the government. He not obliged to sing now, only twice every year. But if he not sing twice each year they take him his pension away."

Very well, we went. When the renowned old tenor appeared, I got a nudge and an excited whisper:

"Now you see him!"

But the "celebrate" was an astonishing disappointment to me. If he had been behind a screen I should have supposed they were performing a surgical operation on him. I looked at my friend—to my great surprise he seemed intoxicated with pleasure, his eyes were dancing with eager delight. When the curtain fell at last he burst into the stormiest applause, and kept it up—as did the whole house—until the afflictive tenor had come three times before the curtain to make his bow. While the glowing enthusiast was swabbing the perspiration from his face, I said:

"I don't mean the least harm, but really, now, do you think he can sing?"

"Him? *No*! *Gott in Himmel, aber*, how he has been able to sing twenty-five years ago?" (Then pensively.) "*Ach*, no, now he not sing any more, he only cry. When he think he sing, now, he not sing at all, no, he only make like a cat which is unwell."

Where and how did we get the idea that the Germans are a stolid, phlegmatic race? In truth, they are widely removed from that. They are warm-hearted, emotional, impulsive, enthusiastic, their tears come at the mildest touch, and it is not hard to move them to laughter. They are the very children of impulse. We are cold and self-contained, compared to the Germans. They hug and kiss and cry and shout and dance and sing. And where we use one loving, petting expression they pour out a score. Their language is full of endearing diminutives. Nothing that they love escapes the application of a petting diminutive—neither the house, nor the dog, nor the horse, nor the grandmother, nor any other creature, animate or inanimate.

# A Raft Trip on the Neckar River

The river was full of logs—long, slender, barkless pine logs—and we leaned on the rails of the bridge and watched the men put them together into rafts. These rafts were of a shape and construction to suit the crookedness and extreme narrowness of the Neckar. They were from fifty to one hundred yards long, and they gradually tapered from a nine-log breadth at their stern to a three-log breadth at their bow-ends. The main part of the steering is done at the bow, with a pole. The three-log breadth there furnishes room for only the steersman, for these little logs are not larger around than an average young lady's waist. The connections of the several sections of the raft are slack and pliant, so that the raft may be readily bent in any sort of curve required by the shape of the river.

The Neckar is in many places so narrow that a person can throw a dog across it, if he has one. When it is also sharply curved in such places, the raftsman has to do some pretty nice snug piloting to make the turns. The river is not always allowed to spread over its whole bed—which is as much as thirty and sometimes forty yards wide—but is split into three equal bodies of water by stone dikes which throw the main volume, depth and current into the central one. In low water these neat narrow-edged dikes project four or five inches above the surface, like the comb of a submerged roof, but in high water they are overflowed. A hatful of rain makes high water in the Neckar, and a basketful produces an overflow.

There are dikes abreast the Schloss Hotel, and the current is violently swift at that point. I used to sit for hours in my glass cage, watching the long, narrow rafts slip along through the central channel, grazing the right-bank dike and aiming carefully for the middle arch of the stone bridge below. I watched them in this way and lost all this time hoping to see one of them hit the bridge-pier and wreck itself sometime or other but was always disappointed. One was smashed there one morning, but I had just stepped into my room a moment to light a pipe, so I lost it.

While I was looking down upon the rafts that morning in Heilbronn, the daredevil spirit of adventure came suddenly upon me, and I said to my comrades:

"*I* am going to Heidelberg on a raft. Will you venture with me?"

Their faces paled a little, but they assented with as good a grace as they could. Harris[28] wanted to cable his mother—thought it his duty to do that, as he was all she had in this world—so, while he attended to this I went down to the longest and finest raft and hailed the captain with a hearty "Ahoy, shipmate!" which put us on pleasant terms at once, and we entered upon business. I said we were on a pedestrian tour to Heidelberg and would like to take passage with him. I said this partly through young Z, who spoke German very well, and partly through Mr. X, who spoke it peculiarly. I can *understand* German as well as the maniac that invented it, but I *talk* it best through an interpreter.

The captain hitched up his trousers, then shifted his quid thoughtfully. Presently he said just what I was expecting he would say—that he had no license to carry passengers and therefore was afraid the law would be after him in case the matter got noised

[28] Fictitious name of M.T.'s traveling companion and good friend, the Reverand Joseph Twichell of Hartford, Connecticut.

about or any accident happened. So I *chartered* the raft and the crew and took all the responsibility on myself.

With a rattling song the starboard watch bent to their work and hove the cable short, then got the anchor home, and our bark moved off with a stately stride and soon was bowling along at about two knots an hour.

Our party were grouped amidships. At first the talk was a little gloomy and ran mainly upon the shortness of life, the uncertainty of it, the perils which beset it, and the need and wisdom of being always prepared for the worst. This shaded off into low-voiced references to the dangers of the deep and kindred matters. But as the gray east began to redden and the mysterious solemnity and silence of the dawn to give place to the joy-songs of the birds, the talk took a cheerier tone and our spirits began to rise steadily.

Germany in the summer is the perfection of the beautiful, but nobody has understood and realized and enjoyed the utmost possibilities of this soft and peaceful beauty unless he has voyaged down the Neckar on a raft. The motion of a raft is the needful motion. It is gentle and gliding and smooth and noiseless, it calms down all feverish activities, it soothes to sleep all nervous hurry and impatience. Under its restful influence all the troubles and vexations and sorrows that harass the mind vanish away, and existence becomes a dream, a charm, a deep and tranquil ecstasy. How it contrasts with hot and perspiring pedestrianism, and dusty and deafening railroad rush, and tedious jolting behind tired horses over blinding white roads!

We went slipping silently along between the green and fragrant banks, with a sense of pleasure and contentment that grew and grew all the time. Sometimes the banks were overhung with thick masses of willows that wholly hid the ground behind. Sometimes we had noble hills on one hand, clothed densely with foliage to their tops, and on the other hand open levels blazing with poppies or clothed in the rich blue of the corn-flower. Sometimes we drifted in the shadow of forests and sometimes along the margin of long stretches of velvety grass, fresh and green and bright, a tireless charm to the eye. And the birds!—they were everywhere. They swept back and forth across the river constantly, and their jubilant music was never stilled.

It was a deep and satisfying pleasure to see the sun create the new morning, and gradually, patiently, lovingly clothe it on with splendor after splendor and glory after glory till the miracle was complete. How different is this marvel observed from a raft from what it is when one observes it through the dingy windows of a railway station in some wretched village while he munches on a petrified sandwich and waits for the train.

* * *

Men and women and cattle were at work in the dewy fields by this time. The people often stepped aboard the raft as we glided along the grassy shores and gossiped with us and with the crew for a hundred yards or so, then stepped ashore again, refreshed by the ride.

Only the men did this. The women were too busy. The women do all kinds of work on the continent. They dig, they hoe, they reap, they sow, they bear monstrous burdens on their backs, they shove similar ones long distances on wheelbarrows, they drag the cart when there is no dog or lean cow to drag it—and when there is, they assist the dog or cow. Age is no matter—the older the woman, the stronger she is, apparently. On the farm a woman's duties are not defined—she does a little of everything. But in the towns it is different; there she does only certain things, the men do the rest. For instance, a hotel chambermaid has nothing to do but make beds and fires in fifty or sixty rooms, bring towels and candles, and fetch several tons of water up several flights of stairs, a hundred pounds at a time, in prodigious metal pitchers. She does not have to work more than eighteen or twenty hours a day, and she can always get down on her knees and scrub the floors of halls and closets when she is tired a needs a rest.

As the morning advanced and the weather grew hot, we took off our outside clothing and sat in a row along the edge of the raft and enjoyed the scenery, with our sun-umbrellas over our heads and our legs dangling in the water. Every now and then we plunged in and had a swim. Every projecting grassy cape had its joyous group of naked children, the boys to themselves and the girls to themselves, the latter usually in care of some motherly dame who sat in the shade of a tree with her knitting. The little boys swam out to us sometimes, but the little maids stood knee-deep in the water and stopped their splashing and frolicking to inspect the raft with their innocent eyes as it drifted by. Once we turned a corner suddenly and surprised a slender girl of twelve years or upwards, just stepping into the water. She had not time to run, but she did what answered just as well. She promptly drew a lithe young willow bough athwart her white body with one hand, and then contemplated us with a simple and untroubled interest. Thus she stood while we glided by. She was a pretty creature, and she and her willow bough made a very pretty picture, and one which could not offend the modesty of the most fastidious spectator. Her white skin had a low bank of fresh green willows for background and effective contrast—for she stood against them—and above and out of them projected the eager faces and white shoulders of two smaller girls.

Towards noon we heard the inspiriting cry:

"Sail ho!"

"Where away?" shouted the captain.

"Three points off the weather bow!"

We ran forward to see the vessel. It proved to be a steamboat—for they had begun to run a steamer up the Neckar for the first time in May. She was a tug, and one of very peculiar build and aspect. I had often watched her from the hotel and wondered how she propelled herself, for apparently she had no propeller or paddles. She came churning along now, making a deal of noise of one kind and another, and aggravating it every now and then by blowing a hoarse whistle. She had nine keel-boats hitched on behind and following after her in a long, slender rank. We met her in a narrow place between dikes, and there was hardly room for us both in the cramped passage. As she went grinding and groaning by, we perceived the secret of her moving impulse. She did not drive herself up the river with paddles or propeller, she pulled herself by hauling on a great chain. This chain is laid in the bed of the river and is only fastened at the two ends. It is seventy miles long. It comes in over the boat's bow, passes around a drum, and is payed out astern. She pulls on that chain and so drags herself up the river or down it. She has neither bow nor stern, strictly speaking, for she has a long-bladed rudder on each end and she never turns around. She uses both rudders all the time, and they are powerful enough to enable her to turn to the right or the left and steer around curves in spite of the strong resistance of the chain. I would not have believed that that impossible thing could be done, but I saw it done and therefore I know that there is one impossible thing which *can* be done. What miracle will man attempt next?

We met many big keel-boats on their way up, using sails, mule power and profanity—a tedious and laborious business. A wire rope led from the foretopmast to the file of mules on the tow-path a hundred yards ahead, and by dint of much banging and swearing and urging, the detachment of drivers managed to get a speed of two or three miles an hour out of the mules against the stiff current. The Neckar has always been used as a canal and thus has given employment to a great many men and animals. But now that this steamboat is able, with a small crew and a bushel or so of coal, to take nine keel-boats farther up the river in one hour than thirty men and thirty mules can do it in two, it is believed that the old-fashioned towing industry is on its death-bed. . . .

At noon we stepped ashore and bought some bottled beer and got some chickens cooked while the raft waited. Then we immediately put to sea again and had our dinner while the beer was cold and the chickens hot. There is no pleasanter place for a meal than a raft that is gliding down the winding Neckar past green meadows and wooded hills and slumbering villages and craggy heights graced with crumbling towers and battlements.

In one place we saw a nicely dressed German gentleman without any spectacles. Before I could come to anchor he had got away. It was a great pity. I so wanted to make a sketch of him. The captain comforted me for my loss, however, by saying that the man was without any doubt a fraud who had spectacles but kept them in his pocket in order to make himself conspicuous.

Below Hassmersheim we passed Hornberg, Götz von Berlichingen's[29] old castle. It stands on a bold elevation two hundred feet above the surface of the river; it has high, vine-clad walls enclosing trees, and a peaked tower about seventy-five feet high. The steep hillside, from the castle clear down to the water's edge, is terraced and clothed thick with grape vines. This is like farming a mansard roof. All the steeps along that part of the river which furnish the proper exposure are given up to the grape. That region is a great producer of Rhine wines. The Germans are exceedingly fond of Rhine wines; they are put up in tall, slender bottles and are considered a pleasant beverage. One tells them from vinegar by the label.

* * *

A mile or two above Eberbach we saw a peculiar ruin projecting above the foliage which clothed the peak of a high and very steep hill. This ruin consisted of merely a couple of crumbling masses of masonry which bore a rude resemblance to human faces; they leaned forward and touched foreheads, and had the look of being absorbed in conversation. This ruin had nothing very imposing or picturesque about it, and there was no great deal of it, yet it was called the "Spectacular Ruin."

[29] A sixteenth-century soldier and knight romanticized as the German Robin Hood and the subject of a play by Goethe.

## *THE LEGEND OF THE "SPECTACULAR RUIN"*

The captain of the raft, who was as full of history as he could stick, said that in the Middle Ages a most prodigious fire-breathing dragon used to live in that region and made more trouble than a tax collector. He was as long as a railway-train and had the customary impenetrable green scales all over him. His breath bred pestilence and conflagration, and his appetite bred famine. He ate men and cattle impartially, and was exceedingly unpopular. The German emperor of that day made the usual offer: he would grant to the destroyer of the dragon any one solitary thing he might ask for; for he had a surplusage of daughters, and it was customary for dragon-killers to take a daughter for pay.

So the most renowned knights came from the four corners of the earth and retired down the dragon's throat one after the other. A panic arose and spread. Heroes grew cautious. The dragon became more destructive than ever. The people lost all hope of succor, and fled to the mountains for refuge.

At last Sir Wissenschaft, a poor and obscure knight, out of a far country, arrived to do battle with the monster. A pitiable object he was, with his armor hanging in rags about him, and his strange-shaped knapsack strapped upon his back. Everybody turned up their noses at him, and some openly jeered him. But he was calm. He simply inquired whether the emperor's offer was still in force. The emperor said it was—but charitably advised him to go and hunt hares and not endanger so precious a life as his in an attempt which had brought death to so many of the world's most illustrious heroes.

But this tramp only asked—"Were any of these heroes men of science?" This raised a laugh, of course, for science was despised in those days. But the tramp was not in the least ruffled. He said he might be a little in advance of his age, but no matter—science would come to be honored, some time or other. He said he would march against the dragon in the morning. Out of compassion, then, a decent spear was offered him, but he declined, and said, "Spears were useless to men of science." They allowed him to sup in the servants' hall and gave him a bed in the stables.

When he started forth in the morning, thousands were gathered to see. The emperor said:

"Do not be rash, take a spear, and leave off your knapsack."

But the tramp said:

"It is not a knapsack," and moved straight on.

The dragon was waiting and ready. He was breathing forth vast volumes of sulphurous smoke and lurid blasts of flame. The ragged knight stole warily to a good position, then he unslung his cylindrical knapsack—which was simply the common fire-extinguisher known to modern times—and the first chance he got he turned on his hose and shot the dragon square in the center of his cavernous mouth. Out went the fires in an instant, and the dragon curled up and died.

This man had brought brains to his aid. He had reared dragons from the egg, in his laboratory; he had watched over them like a mother, and patiently studied them and experimented upon them while they grew. Thus he had found out that fire was the life principle of a dragon; put out the dragon's fires and it could make steam no longer, and must die. He could not put out a fire with a spear, therefore he invented the extinguisher. The dragon being dead, the emperor fell on the hero's neck and said:

"Deliverer, name your request," at the same time beckoning out behind with his heel for a detachment of his daughters to form and advance. But the tramp gave them no observance. He simply said:

"My request is, that upon me be conferred the monopoly of the manufacture and sale of spectacles in Germany."

The emperor sprang aside and exclaimed:

"This transcends all the impudence I ever heard! A modest demand, by my halidome! Why didn't you ask for the imperial revenues at once, and be done with it?"

But the monarch had given his word, and he kept it. To everybody's surprise, the unselfish monopolist immediately reduced the price of spectacles to such a degree that a great and crushing burden was removed from the nation. The emperor, to commemorate this generous act, and to testify his appreciation of it, issued a decree commanding everybody to buy this benefactor's spectacles and wear them, whether they needed them or not.

So originated the widespread custom of wearing spectacles in Germany; and as a custom once established in these old lands is imperishable, this one remains universal in the empire to this day. Such is the legend of the monopolist's once stately and sumptuous castle, now called the "Spectacular Ruin."

* * *

On the right bank, two or three miles below the Spectacular Ruin, we passed by a noble pile of castellated buildings overlooking the water from the crest of a lofty elevation. A stretch of two hundred yards of the high front wall was heavily draped with ivy, and out of the mass of buildings within rose three picturesque old towers. The place was in fine order, and was inhabited by a family of princely rank. This castle had its legend, too, but I should not feel justified in repeating it because I doubted the truth of some of its minor details.

Along this region a multitude of Italian laborers were blasting away the frontage of the hills to make room for the new railway. They were fifty or a hundred feet above the river. As we turned a sharp corner they began to wave signals and shout warnings to us to look out for the explosions. It was all very well to warn us, but what could *we* do? You can't back a raft upstream; you can't hurry it downstream; you can't scatter out to one side when you haven't any room to speak of; you won't take to the perpendicular cliffs on the other shore when they appear to be blasting there, too. Your resources are limited, you see. There is simply nothing for it but to watch and pray.

For some hours we had been making three and a half or four miles an hour and we were still making that. We had been dancing right along until those men began to shout; then for the next ten minutes it seemed to me that I had never seen a raft go so slowly. When the first blast went off we raised our sun-umbrellas and waited for the result. No harm done; none of the stones fell in the water. Another blast followed, and another and another. Some of the rubbish fell in the water just astern of us.

We ran that whole battery nine blasts in a row, and it was certainly one of the most exciting and uncomfortable weeks I ever spent, either aship or ashore. Of course we frequently manned the poles and shoved earnestly for a second or so, but every time one of those spurts of dust and debris shot aloft, every man dropped his pole and looked up to get the bearings of his share of it. It was very busy times along there for a while. It appeared certain that we must perish, but even that was not the bitterest thought; no, the abjectly unheroic nature of the death—that was the sting—that and the bizarre wording of the resulting obituary: "*Shot with a rock, on a raft.*" There would be no poetry written about it. None *could* be written about it. Example:

*Not* by war's shock, or war's shaft—
*Shot,* with a rock, on a raft.

No poet who valued his reputation would touch such a theme as that. I should be distinguished as the only "distinguished dead" who went down to the grave unsonneted, in 1878.

But we escaped, and I have never regretted it. The last blast was a particularly strong one, and after the small rubbish was done raining around us and we were just going to shake hands over our deliverance, a later and larger stone came down amongst our little group of pedestrians and wrecked an umbrella. It did not other harm, but we took to the water just the same.

It seems that the heavy work in the quarries and the new railway gradings is done mainly by Italians. That was a revelation. We have a notion in our country that Italians never do heavy work at all, but confine themselves to the lighter arts, like organ-grinding, operatic singing, and assassination. We have blundered, that is plain.

* * *

As the night shut down, the captain wanted to tie up, but I thought maybe we could make Hirschhorn, so we went on. Presently the sky became overcast, and the captain came aft looking uneasy. He cast his eye aloft, then shook his head, and said it was coming on to blow. My party wanted to land at once—therefore I wanted to go on. The captain said we ought to shorten sail anyway, out of common prudence. Consequently, the larboard watch was ordered to lay in his pole. It grew quite dark, now, and the wind began to rise. It wailed through the swaying branches of the trees and swept our decks in fitful gusts. Things were taking on an ugly look. The captain shouted to the steersman on the forward log:

"How's she heading?"

The answer came faint and hoarse from far forward:

"Nor'-east-and-by-nor'—east-by-east, half-east, sir."

"Let her go off a point!"

"Aye-aye, sir!"

"What water have you got?"

"Shoal, sir. Two foot large, on the stabboard, two and a half scant on the labboard!"

"Let her go off another point!"

"Aye-aye, sir!"

"Forward, men, all of you! Lively, now! Stand by to crowd her round the weather corner!"

"Aye, aye, sir!"

Then followed a wild running and trampling and hoarse shouting, but the forms of the men were lost in the darkness, and the sounds were distorted and confused by the roaring of the wind through the shingle-bundles. By this time the sea was running inches high, and threatening every moment to engulf the frail bark. Now came the mate, hurrying aft, and said, close to the captain's ear, in a low, agitated voice:

"Prepare for the worst, sir—we have sprung a leak!"

"Heavens! Where?"

"Right aft the second row of logs."

"Nothing but a miracle can save us! Don't let the men know, or there will be panic and mutiny! Lay her in shore and stand by to jump with the stern-line the moment she touches. Gentlemen, I must look to you to second my endeavors in this hour of peril. You have hats—go forward and bail for your lives!"

Down swept another mighty blast of wind, clothed in spray and thick darkness. At such a moment as this came from away forward that most appalling of all cries that are ever heard at sea:

*"Man overboard!"*

The captain shouted:

"Hard a-port! Never mind that man! Let him climb aboard or wade ashore!"

Another cry came down the wind:

"Breakers ahead!"

"Where away?"

"Not a log's length off her port fore-foot!"

We had groped our slippery way forward, and were bailing with the frenzy of despair, when we heard the mate's terrified cry, from far aft:

"Stop that dashed bailing, or we shall be aground!"

But this was immediately followed by the glad shout:

"Land aboard the starboard transom!"

"Saved!" cried the captain. "Jump ashore and take a turn around a tree and pass the bight aboard!"

The next moment we were all on shore weeping and embracing for joy, while the rain poured down in torrents. The captain said he had been a mariner for forty years on the Neckar, and in that time had seen storms to make a man's cheek blanch and his pulses stop, but he had never, never seen a storm that even approached this one. How familiar that sounded! For I have been at sea a good deal and have heard that remark from captains with a frequency accordingly.

We framed in our minds the usual resolution of thanks and admiration and gratitude, and took the first opportunity to vote it, and put it in writing and present it to the captain, with the customary speech.

We tramped through the darkness and the drenching summer rain full three miles, and reached "The Naturalist Tavern" in the village of Hirschhorn just an hour before midnight, almost exhausted from hardship, fatigue, and terror. I can never forget that night.

* * *

[The next day] we got to sea in season to make the eight-mile run to Heidelberg before the night shut down. We sailed by the hotel in the mellow glow of sunset, and came slashing down with the mad current into the narrow passage between the dikes. I believed I could shoot the bridge myself, so I went to the forward triplet of logs and relieved the pilot of his pole and his responsibility.

We went tearing along in a most exhilarating way, and I performed the delicate duties of my office very well indeed for a first attempt; but perceiving, presently, that I really was going to shoot the bridge itself instead of the archway under it, I judiciously stepped ashore. The next moment I had my long-coveted desire: I saw a raft wrecked. It hit the pier in the center and went all to smash and scatteration like a box of matches struck by lightning.

I was the only one of our party who saw this grand sight; the others were attitudinizing, for the benefit of the long rank of young ladies who were promenading on the bank, and so they lost it. But I helped to fish them out of the river, down below the bridge, and then described it to them as well as I could.

They were not interested, though. They said they were wet and felt ridiculous and did not care anything for descriptions of scenery. The young ladies, and other people, crowded around and showed a great deal of sympathy, but that did not help matters, for my friends said they did not want sympathy, they wanted a back alley and solitude.

# Walking and Talking

We were satisfied that we could walk to Oppenau in one day, now that we were in practice; so we set out next morning after breakfast determined to do it. It was all the way downhill, and we had the loveliest summer weather for it. So we set the pedometer and then stretched away on an easy, regular stride, down through the cloven forest, drawing in the fragrant breath of the morning in deep refreshing draughts, and wishing that we might never have anything to do but walk to Oppenau and keep on doing it and then doing it over again.

Now, the true charm of pedestrianism does not lie in the walking, or in the scenery, but in the talking. The walking is good to time the movement of the tongue by, and to keep the blood and the brain stirred up and active; the scenery and the woodsy smells are good to bear in upon a man an unconscious and unobtrusive charm and solace to the eye and soul and sense; but the supreme pleasure comes from the talk. It is no matter whether one talks wisdom or nonsense, the case is the same; the bulk of the enjoyment lies in the wagging of the gladsome jaw and the flapping of the sympathetic ear.

And what a motley variety of subjects a couple of people will casually rake over in the course of a day's tramp! There being no constraint, a change of subject is always in order, and so a body is not likely to keep pegging at a single topic until it grows tiresome. We discussed everything we knew, during the first fifteen or twenty minutes, that morning, and then branched out into the glad, free, boundless realm of things we were not certain about.

Harris said that if the best writer in the world once got the slovenly habit of doubling up his "haves" he could never get rid of it while he lived. That is to say, if a man gets the habit of saying "I should have liked to have known more about it" instead of saying simply and sensibly, "I should have liked to know more about it," that man's disease is incurable. Harris said that this sort of lapse is to be found in every copy of every newspaper that has ever been printed in English, and in almost all of our books. He said he had observed it in Kirkham's grammar and in Macaulay. Harris believed that milk-teeth are commoner in men's mouths than those "doubled-up haves."

That changed the subject to dentistry. I said I believed the average man dreaded tooth-pulling more than amputation, and that he would yell quicker under the former operation than he would under the latter. The philosopher Harris said that the average man would not yell in either case if he had an audience. Then he continued:

"When our brigade first went into camp on the Potomac, we used to be brought up standing, occasionally, by an ear-splitting howl of anguish. That meant that a soldier was getting a tooth pulled in a tent. But the surgeons soon changed that; they instituted open-air dentistry. There never was a howl afterward—that is, from the man who was having the tooth pulled. At the daily dental hour there would always be about five hundred soldiers gathered together in the neighborhood of that dental chair waiting to see the performance—and help; and the moment the surgeon took a grip on the candidate's tooth and began to lift, every one of those five hundred rascals would clap his hand to his jaw and begin to hop around on one leg and howl with all the lungs he had! It was enough to raise your hair to hear that variegated and enormous unanimous caterwaul burst out! With so big and so derisive an audience as that, a sufferer wouldn't emit a sound though you pulled his head off. The surgeons said that pretty often a patient was compelled to laugh, in the midst of his pangs, but that they never caught one crying out, after the open-air exhibition was instituted."

Dental surgeons suggested doctors, doctors suggested death, death suggested skeletons—and so by a logical process the conversation melted out of one of these subjects and into the next, until the topic of skeletons raised up Nicodemus Dodge out of the deep grave in my memory where he had lain buried and forgotten for twenty-five years. When I was a boy in a printing-office in Missouri, a loose-jointed, long-legged, tow-headed, jeans-clad, countrified cub of about sixteen lounged in one day, and without removing his hands from the depths of his trousers pockets or taking off his faded ruin of a slouch hat, whose broken rim hung limp and ragged about his eyes and ears like a bug-eaten cabbage leaf, stared indifferently around, then leaned his hip against the editor's table, crossed his mighty brogans, aimed at a distant fly from a crevice in his upper teeth, laid him low, and said with composure:

"Whar's the boss?"

"I am the boss," said the editor, following this curious bit of architecture wonderingly along up to its clock-face with his eye.

"Don't want anybody fur to learn the business, 'tain't likely?"

"Well, I don't know. Would you like to learn it?"

"Pap's so po' he cain't run me no mo', so I want to git a show somers if I kin, 'tain't no diffunce what—I'm strong and hearty, and I don't turn my back on no kind of work, hard nur soft."

"Do you think you would like to learn the printing business?"

"Well, I don't re'ly k'yer a durn what I *do* learn, so's I git a chance fur to make my way. I'd jist as soon learn print'n's anything."

"Can you read?"

"Yes—middlin'."

"Write?"

"Well, I've seed people could lay over me thar."

"Cipher?"

"Not good enough to keep store, I don't reckon, but up as fur as twelve-times-twelve I ain't no slouch. T'other side of that is what gits me."

"Where is your home?"

"I'm f'm old Shelby."

"What is your father's religious denomination?"

"Him? Oh, he's a blacksmith."

"No, no—I don't mean his trade. What's his *religious* denomination?"

"*Oh*—I didn't understand you befo.' He's a Freemason."

"No, no, you don't get my meaning yet. What I mean is, does he belong to any *church*?"

"*Now* you're talkin'! Couldn't make out what you was a tryin' to git through yo' head no way. B'long to a *church*! Why, boss, he's the pizenest kind of Free-will Baptis' for forty year. They ain't no pizener ones 'n what *he* is. Mighty good man, pap is. Everybody says that. If they said any diffrunt they wouldn't say it whar *I* wuz—not *much* they wouldn't."

"What is your own religion?"

"Well, boss, you've kind o' got me thar—and yit you hain't got me so mighty much, nuther. I think 't if a feller he'ps another feller when he's in trouble, and don't cuss, and don't do no mean things, nur noth'n' he ain' no business to do, and don't spell the Saviour's name with a little g, he ain't runnin' no resks—he's about as saift as if he b'longed to a church."

"But suppose he did spell it with a little g—what then?"

"Well, if he done it a-purpose, I reckon he wouldn't stand no chance—he *oughtn't* to have no chance, anyway, I'm most rotten certain 'bout that."

"What is your name?"

"Nicodemus Dodge."

"I think maybe you'll do, Nicodemus. We'll give you a trial, anyway."

"All right."

"When would you like to begin?"

"Now."

So, within ten minutes after we had first glimpsed this nondescript he was one of us, and with his coat off and hard at it.

Beyond that end of our establishment which was furthest from the street was a deserted garden, pathless, and thickly grown with the bloomy and villainous "jimpson" weed and its common friend the stately sunflower. In the midst of this mournful spot was a decayed and aged little "frame" house with but one room, one window, and no ceiling—it had been a smokehouse a generation before. Nicodemus was given this lonely and ghostly den as a bedchamber.

The village smarties recognized a treasure in Nicodemus, right away—a butt to play jokes on. It was easy to see that he was inconceivably green and confiding. George Jones had the glory of perpetrating the first joke on him; he gave him a cigar with a firecracker in it and winked to the crowd to come; the thing exploded presently and swept away the bulk of Nicodemus's eyebrows and eyelashes. He simply said:

"I consider them kind of seeg'yars dangersome"—and seemed to suspect nothing. The next evening Nicodemus waylaid George and poured a bucket of ice-water over him.

One day, while Nicodemus was swimming, Tom McElroy "tied" his clothes. Nicodemus made a bonfire of Tom's by way of retaliation.

A third joke was played upon Nicodemus a day or two later—he walked up the middle aisle of the village church, Sunday night, with a staring hand-bill pinned between his shoulders. The joker spent the remainder of the night, after church, in the cellar of a deserted house, and Nicodemus sat on the cellar door till toward breakfast-time to make sure that the prisoner remembered that if any noise was made, some rough treatment would be the consequence. The cellar had two feet of stagnant water in it, and was bottomed with six inches of soft mud.

But I wander from the point. It was the subject of skeletons that brought this boy back to my recollection. Before a very long time had elapsed, the village smarties began to feel an uncomfortable consciousness of not having made a very shining success out of their attempts on the simpleton from "old Shelby." Experimenters grew scarce and chary. Now the young doctor came to the rescue. There was delight and applause when he proposed to scare Nicodemus to death, and explained how he was going to do it. He had a noble new skeleton—the skeleton of the late and only local celebrity, Jimmy Finn, the village drunkard—a grisly piece of property which he had bought of Jimmy Finn himself, at auction, for fifty dollars, under great competition, when Jimmy lay very sick in the tan-yard a fortnight before his death. The fifty dollars had gone promptly for whisky and had considerably hurried up the change of ownership in the skeleton. The doctor would put Jimmy Finn's skeleton in Nicodemus's bed!

This was done—about half past ten in the evening. About Nicodemus's usual bedtime—midnight—the village jokers came creeping stealthily through the jimpson weeds and sunflowers toward the lonely frame den. They reached the window and peeped in. There sat the long-legged pauper, on his bed, in a very short shirt, and nothing more; he was dangling his legs contentedly back and forth, and wheezing the music of "Camptown Races" out of a paper-overlaid comb which he was pressing against his mouth; by him lay a new jewsharp, a new top, a solid india-rubber ball, a handful of painted marbles, five pounds of "store" candy, and a well-gnawed slab of gingerbread as big and as thick as a volume of sheet-music. He had sold the skeleton to a traveling quack for three dollars and was enjoying the result!

Just as we had finished talking about skeletons and were drifting into the subject of fossils, Harris and I heard a shout, and glanced up the steep hillside. We saw men and women standing away up there looking frightened, and there was a bulky object tumbling and floundering down the steep slope toward us. We got out of the way, and when the object landed in the road it proved to be a boy. He had tripped and fallen, and there was nothing for him to do but trust to luck and take what might come.

When one starts to roll down a place like that, there is no stopping till the bottom is reached. Think of people *farming* on a slant which is so steep that the best you can say of it—if you want to be fastidiously accurate—is that it is a little steeper than a ladder and not quite so steep as a mansard roof. But that is what they do. Some of the little farms on the hillside opposite Heidelberg were stood up "edgeways." The boy was wonderfully jolted up, and his head was bleeding from cuts which it had got from small stones on the way.

Harris and I gathered him up and set him on a stone, and by that time the men and women had scampered down and brought his cap.

Men, women, and children flocked out from neighboring cottages and joined the crowd; the pale boy was petted, and stared at, and commiserated, and water was brought for him to drink and bathe his bruises in. And such another clatter of tongues! All who had seen the catastrophe were describing it at once, and each trying to talk louder than his neighbor; and one youth of superior genius ran a little way up the hill, called attention, tripped, fell, rolled down among us, and thus triumphantly showed exactly how the thing had been done.

Harris and I were included in all the descriptions; how we were coming along; how Hans Gross shouted; how we looked up startled; how we saw Peter coming like a cannon-shot; how judiciously we got out of the way and let him come; and with what presence of mind we picked him up and brushed him off and set him on a rock when the performance was over. We were as much heroes as anybody else, except Peter, and were so recognized; we were taken with Peter and the populace to Peter's mother's cottage, and there we ate bread and cheese, and drank milk and beer with everybody, and had a most sociable good time; and when we left we had a handshake all around, and were receiving and shouting back *Leb' wohl's* until a turn in the road separated us from our cordial and kindly new friends forever.

We accomplished our undertaking. At half past eight in the evening we stepped into Oppenau, just eleven hours and a half out from Allerheiligen—one hundred and forty-six miles. This is the distance by pedometer; the guidebook and the Imperial Ordnance maps make it only ten and a quarter—a surprising blunder, for these two authorities are usually singularly accurate in the matter of distances.

# Part Eight

## *The Alps*

*We located ourselves at the Jungfrau Hotel, one of those huge establishments which the needs of modern travel have created in every attractive spot on the continent. There was a great gathering at dinner, and as usual one heard all sorts of languages.*

*The table d'hôte was served by waitresses dressed in the quaint and comely costume of the Swiss peasants. This consists of a simple gros de laine, trimmed with ashes of roses, with an overskirt of sacre bleu ventre saint gris, cut bias on the off side, with facings of petit polonaise and narrow insertions of pâte de fois gras backstitched to the mise en scène in the form of a jeu d' esprit. It gives the wearer a singularly piquant and alluring aspect.*

from *A Tramp Abroad*

# An Alpine Sunrise

The Rigi-Kulm is an imposing Alpine mass, six thousand feet high, which stands by itself and commands a mighty prospect of blue lakes, green valleys, and snowy mountains—a compact and magnificent picture three hundred miles in circumference. The ascent is made by rail or horseback or on foot, as one may prefer. I and my agent panoplied ourselves in walking-costume one bright morning and started down the lake on the steamboat. We got ashore at the village of Wäggis, three-quarters of an hour distant from Lucerne. The village is at the foot of the mountain.

We were soon tramping leisurely up the leafy mule-path, and then the talk began to flow, as usual. It was twelve o'clock noon, and a breezy, cloudless day. The ascent was gradual, and the glimpses, from under the curtaining boughs, of blue water and tiny sailboats and beetling cliffs were as charming as glimpses of dreamland. All the circumstances were perfect—and the anticipations, too, for we should soon be enjoying for the first time that wonderful spectacle, an Alpine sunrise—the object of our journey. There was (apparently) no real need to hurry, for the guidebook made the walking distance from Wäggis to the summit only three hours and a quarter. I say "apparently," because the guidebook had already fooled us once—about the distance from Allerheiligen to Oppenau—and for aught I knew it might be getting ready to fool us again. We were only certain as to the altitudes—we calculated to find out for ourselves how many hours it is from the bottom to the top. The summit is six thousand feet above the sea but only forty-five hundred feet above the lake. When we had walked half an hour, we were fairly into the swing and humor of the undertaking, so we cleared for action. That is to say, we got a boy whom we met to carry our alpenstocks and satchels and overcoats and things for us. That left us free for business.

I suppose we must have stopped oftener to stretch out on the grass in the shade and take a bit of a smoke than this boy was used to, for presently he asked if it had been our idea to hire him by the job or by the year? We told him he could move along if he was in a hurry. He said he wasn't in such a very particular hurry, but he wanted to get to the top while he was young. We told him to clear out then and leave the things at the uppermost hotel and say we should be along presently. He said he would secure us a hotel if he could, but if they were all full he would ask them to build another one and hurry up and get the paint and plaster dry against we arrived. Still gently chaffing us, he pushed ahead up the trail and soon disappeared. By six o'clock we were pretty high up in the air, and the view of the lake and mountains had greatly grown in breadth and interest. We halted awhile at a little public house, where we had bread and cheese and a quart or two of fresh milk, out on the porch, with the big panorama all before us—and then moved on again.

Ten minutes afterward we met a hot, red-faced man plunging down the mountain with mighty strides, swinging his alpenstock ahead of him and taking a grip on the ground with its iron point to support these big strides. He stopped, fanned himself with his hat, swabbed the perspiration from his face and neck with a red handkerchief, panted a moment or two, and asked how far it was to Wäggis. I said three hours. He looked surprised and said:

"Why, it seems as if I could toss a biscuit into the lake from here, it's so close by. Is that an inn, there?"

I said it was.

"Well," said he, "I can't stand another three hours; I've had enough for today. I'll take a bed there."

I asked:

"Are we nearly to the top?"

"Nearly to the *top*! Why, bless your soul, you haven't really started yet."

I said we would put up at the inn, too. So we turned back and ordered a hot supper and had quite a jolly evening of it with this Englishman.

The German landlady gave us neat rooms and nice beds, and when I and my agent turned in, it was with the resolution to be up early and make the utmost of our first Alpine sunrise. But of course we were dead tired and slept like policemen. So when we awoke in the morning and ran to the window it was already too late, because it was half past eleven. It was a sharp disappointment. However, we ordered breakfast and told the landlady to call the Englishman, but she said he was already up and off at daybreak—and swearing mad about something or other. We could not find out what the matter was. He had asked the landlady the altitude of her place above the level of the lake, and she had told him fourteen hundred and ninety-five feet. That was all that was said. Then he lost his temper. He said that between —— fools and guidebooks, a man could acquire ignorance enough in twenty-four hours in a country like this to last him a year. Harris believed our boy had been loading him up with misinformation, and this was probably the case, for his epithet described that boy to a dot.

We got underway about the turn of noon and pulled out for the summit again with a fresh and vigorous step. When we had gone about two hundred yards and stopped to rest, I glanced to the left while I was lighting my pipe, and in the distance detected a long worm of black smoke crawling lazily up the steep mountain. Of course that was the locomotive. We propped ourselves on our elbows at once to gaze, for we had never seen a mountain railway yet. Presently we could make out the train. It seemed incredible that that thing should creep straight up a sharp slant like the roof of a house—but there it was, and it was doing that very miracle.

In the course of a couple of hours we reached a fine breezy altitude where the little shepherd huts had big stones all over their roofs to hold them down to the earth when the great storms rage. The country was wild and rocky about here, but there were plenty of trees, plenty of moss, and grass.

Away off on the opposite shore of the lake we could see some villages, and now for the first time we could observe the real difference between their proportions and those of the giant mountains at whose feet they slept. When one is in one of those villages it seems spacious and its houses seem high and not out of proportion to the mountain that overhangs them—but from our altitude, what a change! The mountains were bigger and grander than ever as they stood there thinking their solemn thoughts with their heads in the drifting clouds, but the villages at their feet—when the painstaking eye could trace them up and find them—were so reduced, so almost invisible, and lay so flat against the ground that the exactest simile I can devise is to compare them to ant-deposits of granulated dirt overshadowed by the huge bulk of a cathedral. The steamboats skimming along under the stupendous precipices were diminished by distance to the daintiest little toys, the sailboats and rowboats to shallops proper to fairies that keep house in the cups of lilies and ride to court on the backs of bumblebees.

Presently we came upon half a dozen sheep nibbling grass in the spray of a stream of clear water that sprang from a rock wall a hundred feet high, and all at once our ears were startled with a melodious "Lul . . . l . . . l . . . lul-lul-*la*hee-o-o-o!" peeling joyously from a near but invisible source, and recognized that we were hearing for the first time the famous Alpine *jodel* in its own native wilds. And we recognized also that it was that sort of quaint commingling of baritone and falsetto which at home we call "Tyrolese warbling."

The jodeling (pronounced y*o*deling—emphasis on the o) continued and was very pleasant and inspiriting to hear. Now the jodeler appeared—a shepherd boy of sixteen—and in our gladness and gratitude we gave him a franc to jodel some more. So he jodeled and we listened. We moved on presently, and he jodeled us out of sight. After about fifteen minutes we came across another shepherd boy who was jodeling, and gave him half a franc to keep it up. He also jodeled us out of sight. After that we found a jodeler every ten minutes. We gave the first one eight cents, the second one six cents, the third one four, the fourth one a penny, contributed nothing to Nos. 5, 6, and 7, and during the remainder of the day hired the rest of the jodelers, at a franc apiece, not to jodel any more. There is somewhat too much of this jodeling in the Alps.

About the middle of the afternoon we passed through a prodigious natural gateway called the Felsenthor, formed by two enormous upright rocks, with a third lying across the top. There was a very attractive little hotel close by, but our energies were not conquered yet, so we went on. Three hours afterward we came to the railway-track. It was planted straight up the mountain with the slant of a ladder that leans against a house, and it seemed to us that a man would need good nerves who proposed to travel up it or down it either.

During the latter part of the afternoon we cooled our roasted interiors with ice-cold water from clear streams, the only really satisfying water we had tasted since we left home, for at the hotels on the continent they merely give you a tumbler of ice to soak your water in, and that only modifies its hotness, doesn't make it cold. Water can only be made cold enough for summer comfort by being prepared in a refrigerator or a closed ice-pitcher. Europeans say ice-water impairs digestion. How do they know?—they never drink any.

At ten minutes past six we reached the Kaltbad station, where there is a spacious hotel with great verandas which command a majestic expanse of lake and mountain scenery. We were pretty well fagged out now, but as we did not wish to miss the Alpine sunrise, we got through our dinner as quickly as possible and hurried off to bed. It was unspeakably comfortable to stretch our weary limbs between the cool, damp sheets. And how we did sleep!—for there is no opiate like Alpine pedestrianism.

In the morning we both awoke and leaped out of bed at the same instant and ran and stripped aside the window-curtains; but we suffered a bitter disappointment again: it was already half past three in the afternoon.

We dressed sullenly and in ill spirits, each accusing the other of oversleeping. Harris said if we had brought the courier[30] along, as we ought to have done, we should not have missed these sunrises. I said he knew very well that one of us would have had to sit up and wake the courier. And I added that we were having trouble enough to take care of ourselves on this climb, without having to take care of a courier besides.

During breakfast our spirits came up a little, since we found by the guidebook that in the hotels on the summit the tourist is not left to trust to luck for his sunrise, but is roused betimes by a man who goes through the halls with a great Alpine horn, blowing blasts that would raise the dead. And there was another consoling thing: the guidebook said that up there on the summit the guests did not wait to dress much, but seized a red bed-blanket and sailed out arrayed like an Indian. This was good. This would be romantic. Two hundred and fifty people grouped on a windy summit with their hair flying and their red blankets flapping in the solemn presence of the snowy ranges and the messenger splendors of the coming sun would be a striking and memorable spectacle. So it was good luck, not ill luck, that we had missed those other sunrises.

[30] A continental factotum.

We were informed by the guidebook that we were now 3,228 feet above the level of the lake—therefore full two-thirds of our journey had been accomplished. We got away at a quarter past four, P.M. A hundred yards above the hotel the railway divided. One track went straight up the steep hill, the other one turned square off to the right, with a very slight grade. We took the latter and followed it more than a mile, turned a rocky corner, and came in sight of a handsome new hotel. If we had gone on, we should have arrived at the summit, but Harris preferred to ask a lot of questions—as usual, of a man who didn't know anything—and he told us to go back and follow the other route. We did so. We could ill afford this loss of time.

We climbed and climbed and we kept on climbing. We reached about forty summits, but there was always another one just ahead. It came on to rain, and it rained in dead earnest. We were soaked through, and it was bitter cold. Next a smoky fog of clouds covered the whole region densely, and we took to the railway-ties to keep from getting lost. Sometimes we slopped along in a narrow path on the left-hand side of the track, but by and by when the fog blew aside a little and we saw that we were treading the rampart of a precipice and that our left elbows were projecting over a perfectly boundless and bottomless vacancy, we gasped and jumped for the ties again.

The night shut down, dark and drizzly and cold. About eight in the evening the fog lifted and showed us a well-worn path which led up a very steep rise to the left. We took it, and as soon as we had got far enough from the railway to render the finding of it again an impossibility, the fog shut down on us once more.

We were in a bleak unsheltered place now and had to trudge right along in order to keep warm, though we rather expected to go over a precipice sooner or later. About nine o'clock we made an important discovery—that we were not in any path.

We groped around a while on our hands and knees but could not find it, so we sat down in the mud and the wet scant grass to wait.

We were terrified into this by being suddenly confronted with a vast body which showed itself vaguely for an instant and in the next instant was smothered in the fog again. It was really the hotel we were after, monstrously magnified by the fog, but we took it for the face of a precipice and decided not to try to claw up it.

We sat there an hour with chattering teeth and quivering bodies, and quarreled over all sorts of trifles, but gave most of our attention to abusing each other for the stupidity of deserting the railway-track. We sat with our backs to that precipice because what little wind there was came from that quarter. At some time or other the fog thinned a little. We did not know when, for we were facing the empty universe and the thinness could not show, but at last Harris happened to look around and there stood a huge, dim, spectral hotel where the precipice had been. One could faintly discern the windows and chimneys and a dull blur of lights. Our first emotion was deep, unutterable gratitude; our next was a foolish rage born of the suspicion that possibly the hotel had been visible three-quarters of an hour while we sat there in those cold puddles quarreling.

Yes, it was the Rigi-Kulm hotel—the one that occupies the extreme summit and whose remote little sparkle of lights we had often seen glinting high aloft among the stars from our balcony away down yonder in Lucerne. The crusty portier and the crusty clerks gave us the surly reception which their kind deal in in prosperous times, but by mollifying them with an extra display of obsequiousness and servility we finally got them to show us to the room which our boy had engaged for us.

We got into some dry clothing, and while our supper was preparing we loafed forsakenly through a couple of vast cavernous drawing-rooms, one of which had a stove in it. This stove was in a corner, and densely walled around with people. We could not get near the fire, so we moved at large in the arctic spaces among a multitude of people who sat silent, smileless, forlorn, and shivering—thinking what fools they were to come, perhaps. There were some Americans and some Germans, but one could see that the great majority were English.

We lounged into an apartment where there was a great crowd, to see what was going on. It was a memento-magazine. The tourists were eagerly buying all sorts and styles of paper-cutters marked "Souvenir of the Rigi," with handles made of the little curved horn of the ostensible chamois. There were all manner of wooden goblets and such things, similarly marked. I was going to buy a paper-cutter, but I believed I could remember the cold comfort of the Rigi-Kulm without it, so I smothered the impulse.

Supper warmed us, and we went immediately to bed—but first, as Mr. Baedeker requests all tourists to call to his attention to any errors which they might find in his guidebooks, I dropped him a line to inform him that when he said the foot journey from Wäggis to the summit was only three hours and a quarter, he missed it by just about three days. I had previously informed him of his mistake about the distance from Allerheiligen to Oppenau, and had also informed the Ordnance Department of the German government of the same error in the imperial maps. I will add here that I never got an answer to these letters or any thanks from either of those sources. And, what is still more discourteous, these corrections have not been made, either in the maps or the guidebooks. But I will write again when I get time, for my letters may have miscarried.

We curled up in the clammy beds and went to sleep without rocking. We were so sodden with fatigue that we never stirred or turned over till the booming blasts of the Alpine horn aroused us. It may well be imagined that we did not lose any time. We snatched on a few odds and ends of clothing, cocooned ourselves in the proper red blankets, and plunged along the halls and out into the whistling wind bareheaded. We saw a tall wooden scaffolding on the very peak of the summit a hundred yards away and made for it. We rushed up the stairs to the top of this scaffolding and stood there above the vast outlying world with hair flying and ruddy blankets waving and cracking in the fierce breeze.

"Fifteen minutes too late, at last!" said Harris in a vexed voice. "The sun is clear above the horizon."

"No matter," I said, "it is a most magnificent spectacle, and we will see it do the rest of its rising, anyway."

In a moment we were deeply absorbed in the marvel before us and dead to everything else. The great cloud-barred disk of the sun stood just above a limitless expanse of tossing whitecaps—so to speak—a billowy chaos of massy mountain domes and peaks draped in imperishable snow and flooded with an opaline glory of changing and dissolving splendors, while through rifts in a black cloud-bank above the sun, radiating lances of diamond dust shot to the zenith. The cloven valleys of the lower world swam in a tinted mist which veiled the ruggedness of their crags and ribs and ragged forests and turned all the forbidding region into a soft and rich and sensuous paradise.

We could not speak. We could hardly breathe. We could only gaze in drunken ecstasy and drink it in. Presently Harris exclaimed:

"Why—nation, it's going *down*!"

Perfectly true. We had missed the *morning* horn-blow and slept all day. This was stupefying. Harris said:

"Look here. The sun isn't the spectacle—it's *us*—stacked up here on top of this gallows in these idiotic blankets, and two hundred and fifty well-dressed men and women down here gawking up at us and not caring a straw whether the sun rises or sets as long as they've got such a ridiculous spectacle as this to set down in their memorandum-books. They seem to be laughing their ribs loose, and there's one girl there that appears to be going all to pieces. I never saw such a man as you before. I think you are the very last possibility in the way of an ass."

"What have *I* done?" I answered with heat.

"What have you done? You've got up at half past seven o'clock in the evening to see the sun rise, that's what you've done."

"And have you done any better, I'd like to know? I always used to get up with the lark till I came under the petrifying influence of your turgid intellect."

"*You* used to get up with the lark—oh, no doubt—you'll get up with the hangman one of these days. But you ought to be ashamed to be jawing here like this in a red blanket on a forty-foot scaffold on top of the Alps. And no end of people down here to boot. This isn't any place for an exhibition of temper."

And so the customary quarrel went on. When the sun was fairly down, we slipped back to the hotel in the charitable gloaming and went to bed again. We had encountered the horn-blower on the way, and he had tried to collect compensation not only for announcing the sunset, which we did see, but for the sunrise, which we had totally missed. But we said no, we only took our solar rations on the "European plan"—pay for what you get. He promised to make us hear his horn in the morning if we were alive.

* * *

He kept his word. We heard his horn and instantly got up. It was dark and cold and wretched. As I fumbled around for the matches, knocking things down with my quaking hands, I wished the sun would rise in the middle of the day when it was warm and bright and cheerful and one wasn't sleepy. We proceeded to dress by the gloom of a couple of sickly candles, but we could hardly button anything, our hands shook so. I thought of how many happy people there were in Europe, Asia, and America and everywhere who were sleeping peacefully in their beds and did not have to get up and see the Rigi sunrise—people who did not appreciate their advantage, as like as not, but would get up in the morning wanting more boons of Providence. While thinking these thoughts I yawned in an ample way, and my upper teeth got hitched on a nail over the door, and while I was mounting a chair to free myself, Harris drew the window-curtain and said:

"Oh, this is luck! We sha'n't have to go out at all—yonder are the mountains, in full view."

That was glad news indeed. It made us cheerful right away. One could see the grand Alpine masses dimly outlined against the black firmament, and one or two faint stars blinking through the rifts in the night. Fully clothed, and wrapped in blankets, we huddled ourselves up by the window with lighted pipes and fell into chat while we waited in exceeding comfort to see how an Alpine sunrise was going to look by candlelight. By and by a delicate, spiritual sort of effulgence spread itself by imperceptible degrees over the loftiest altitudes of the snowy wastes—but there the effort seemed to stop. I said presently:

"There is a hitch about this sunrise somewhere. It doesn't seem to go. What do you reckon is the matter with it?"

"I don't know. It appears to hang fire somewhere. I never saw a sunrise act like that before. Can it be that the hotel is playing anything on us?"

"Of course not. The hotel merely has a property interest in the sun; it has nothing to do with the management of it. It is a precarious kind of property, too. A succession of total eclipses would probably ruin this tavern. Now what can be the matter with this sunrise?"

Harris jumped up and said:

"I've got it! I know what's the matter with it! We've been looking at the place where the sun *set* last night!"

"It's perfectly true! Why couldn't you have thought of that sooner? Now we've lost another one! And all through your blundering. It was exactly like you to light a pipe and sit down to wait for the sun to rise in the west."

"It was exactly like me to find out the mistake, too. You never would have found it out. I find out all the mistakes."

"You make them all, too, else your most valuable faculty would be wasted on you. But don't stop to quarrel, now—maybe we are not too late yet."

But we were. The sun was well up when we got to the exhibition ground.

# Climbing Mont Blanc

I had always had a deep and reverent compassion for the sufferings of the "prisoner of Chillon," whose story Byron has told in such moving verse; so I took the steamer and made pilgrimage to the dungeons of the Castle of Chillon, to see the place where poor Bonnivard endured his dreary captivity three hundred years ago. I am glad I did that, for it took away some of the pain I was feeling on the prisoner's account. His dungeon was a nice, cool, roomy place, and I cannot see why he should have been so dissatisfied with it. If he had been imprisoned in a St. Nicholas private dwelling, where the fertilizer prevails, and the goat sleeps with the guest, and the chickens roost on him, and the cow comes in and bothers him when he wants to muse, it would have been another matter altogether; but he surely could not have had a very cheerless time of it in that pretty dungeon. It has romantic window-slits that let in generous bars of light, and it has tall, noble columns, carved apparently from the living rock; and what is more, they are written all over with thousands of names; some of them—like Byron's and Victor Hugo's—of the first celebrity. Why didn't he amuse himself reading these names? Then there are the couriers and tourists—swarms of them every day—what was to hinder him from having a good time with them? I think Bonnivard's sufferings have been overrated.

Next, we took the train and went to Martigny, on the way to Mont Blanc. Next morning we started, about eight o'clock, on foot. We had plenty of company, in the way of wagon-loads and mule-loads of tourists—and dust. This scattering procession of travelers was perhaps a mile long. The road was uphill—interminably uphill—and tolerably steep. The weather was blistering hot, and the man or woman who had to sit on a creeping mule, or in a crawling wagon, and broil in the beating sun, was an object to be pitied. We could dodge among the bushes and have the relief of shade, but those people could not. They paid for a conveyance, and to get their money's worth they rode.

We went by the way of Tête Noir, and after we reached high ground there was no lack of fine scenery. In one place the road was tunneled through a shoulder of the mountain; from there one looked down into a gorge with a rushing torrent in it, and on every hand was a charming view of rocky buttresses and wooded heights. There was a liberal allowance of pretty waterfalls, too, on the Tête Noir route.

About half an hour before we reached the village of Argentière a vast dome of snow with the sun blazing on it drifted into view and framed itself in a strong V-shaped gateway of the mountains, and we recognized Mont Blanc, the "monarch of the Alps." With every step, after that, this stately dome rose higher and higher into the blue sky, and at last seemed to occupy the zenith.

* * *

We made the tramp from Martigny to Argentière in eight hours. We beat all the mules and wagons; we didn't usually do that. We hired a sort of open baggage-wagon for the trip down the valley to Chamonix, and then devoted an hour to dining. This gave the driver time to get drunk. He had a friend with him, and this friend also had had time to get drunk.

When we drove off, the driver said all the tourists had arrived and gone by while we were at dinner; "but," said he, impressively, "be not disturbed by that—remain tranquil—give yourselves no uneasiness—their dust rises far before us, you shall see it fade and disappear far behind us—rest you tranquil, leave all to me—I am the king of drivers. Behold!"

Down came his whip, and away we clattered. I never had such a shaking up in my life. The recent flooding rains had washed the road clear away in places, but we never stopped, we never slowed down for anything. We tore right along, over rocks, rubbish, gullies, open fields—sometimes with one or two wheels on the ground, but generally with none. Every now and then that calm, good-natured madman would bend a majestic look over his shoulder at us and say, "Ah, you perceive? It is as I have said—I am the king of drivers." Every time we just missed going to destruction, he would say, with tranquil happiness, "Enjoy it, gentlemen, it is very rare, it is very unusual—it is given to few to ride with the king of drivers—and observe, it is as I have said, *I* am he."

He spoke in French, and punctuated with hiccups. He friend was French, too, but spoke in German—using the same system of punctuation, however. The friend called himself the "Captain of Mont Blanc," and wanted us to make the ascent with him. He said he had made more ascents than any other man—forty-seven—and his brother had made thirty-seven. His brother was the best guide in the world, except himself—but he, yes, observe him well—he was the Captain of Mont Blanc"—that title belonged to none other.

The "king" was as good as his word—he overtook that long procession of tourists and went by it like a hurricane. The result was that we got choicer rooms at the hotel in Chamonix than we should have done if his majesty had been a slower artist—or rather, if he hadn't most providentially got drunk before he left Argentière.

* * *

Everybody was out-of-doors; everybody was in the principal street of the village—not on the sidewalks, but all over the street; everybody was lounging, loafing, chatting, waiting, alert, expectant, interested—for it was train-time. That is to say, it was diligence-time—the half-dozen big diligences would soon be arriving from Geneva, and the village was interested, in many ways, in knowing how many people were coming and what sort of folk they might be. It was altogether the livest-looking street we had seen in any village on the continent.

The hotel was by the side of a booming torrent, whose music was loud and strong; we could not see this torrent, for it was dark, now, but one could locate it without a light. There was a large enclosed yard in front of the hotel, and this was filled with groups of villagers waiting to see the diligences arrive, or to hire themselves to excursionists for the morrow. A telescope stood in the yard, with its huge barrel canted up toward the lustrous evening star. The long porch of the hotel was populous with tourists, who sat in shawls and wraps under the vast overshadowing bulk of Mont Blanc, and gossiped or meditated.

Never did a mountain seem so close; its big sides seemed at one's very elbow, and its majestic dome, and the lofty cluster of slender minarets that were its neighbors, seemed to be almost over one's head. It was night in the streets, and the lamps were sparkling everywhere; the broad bases and shoulders of the mountains were in a deep gloom, but their summits swam in a strange rich glow which was really daylight, and yet had a mellow something about it which was very different from the hard white glare of the kind of daylight I was used to. Its radiance was strong and clear, but at the same time it was singularly soft, and spiritual, and benignant. No, it was not our harsh, aggressive, realistic daylight; it seemed properer to an enchanted land—or to heaven.

I had seen moonlight and daylight together before, but I had not seen daylight and black night elbow to elbow before. At least I had not seen the daylight resting upon an object sufficiently close at hand, before, to make the contrast startling and at war with nature.

The daylight passed away. Presently the moon rose up behind some of those sky-piercing fingers or pinnacles of bare rock of which I have spoken—they were a little to the left of the crest of Mont Blanc, and right over our heads—but she couldn't manage to climb high enough toward heaven to get entirely above them. She would show the glittering arch of her upper third, occasionally, and scrape it along behind the comblike row; sometimes a pinnacle stood straight up, like a statuette of ebony, against that glittering white shield, then seemed to glide out of it by its own volition and power, and become a dim specter, while the next pinnacle glided into its place and blotted the spotless disk with the black exclamation-point of its presence. The top of one pinnacle took the shapely, clean-cut form of a rabbit's head, in the inkiest silhouette, while it rested against the moon. The unilluminated peaks and minarets, hovering vague and phantomlike above us while the others were painfully white and strong with snow and moonlight, made a peculiar effect.

But when the moon, having passed the line of pinnacles, was hidden behind the stupendous white swell of Mont Blanc, the masterpiece of the evening was flung on the canvas. A rich greenish radiance sprang into the sky from behind the mountain, and in this some airy shreds and ribbons of vapor floated about, and being flushed with that strange tint, went waving to and fro like pale green flames. After a while, radiating bars—vast broadening fan-shaped shadows—grew up and stretched away to the zenith from behind the mountain. It was a spectacle to take one's breath, for the wonder of it, and the sublimity.

Indeed, those mighty bars of alternate light and shadow streaming up from behind that dark and prodigious form and occupying the half of the dull and opaque heavens, was the most imposing and impressive marvel I had even looked upon. There is no simile for it, for nothing is like it. If a child had asked me what it was, I should have said, "Humble yourself, in this presence; it is the glory flowing from the hidden head of the Creator." One falls shorter of the truth than that, sometimes, in trying to explain mysteries to the little people. I could have found out the cause of this awe-compelling miracle by inquiring, for it is not infrequent at Mont Blanc—but I did not wish to know. We have not the reverent feeling for the rainbow that a savage has, because we know how it is made. We have lost as much as we gained by prying into that matter.

We took a walk down street, a block or two, and at a place where four streets met and the principal shops were clustered, found groups of men in the roadway thicker than ever—for this was the Exchange of Chamonix. These men were in the costumes of guides and porters, and were there to be hired.

The office of that great personage, the Guide-in-Chief of the Chamonix Guild of Guides, was nearby. This guild is a close corporation, and is governed by strict rules. There are many excursion routes, some dangerous and some not, some that can be made safely without a guide, and some that cannot. The bureau determines these things. Where it decides that a guide is necessary, you are forbidden to go without one. Neither are you allowed to be a victim of extortion; the law states what you are to pay. The guides serve in rotation; you cannot select the man who is to take your life into his hands, you must take the worst in the lot, if it is his turn. . . .

We went into the Chief's office. There were maps of the mountains on the walls; also one or two lithographs of celebrated guides, and a portrait of the scientist De Saussure.

In glass cases were some labeled fragments of boots and batons, and other suggestive relics and remembrances of casualties on Mont Blanc. In a book was a record of all the ascents which have ever been made, beginning with Nos. 1 and 2—being those of Jacques Balmat and De Saussure, in 1787, and ending with No. 685, which wasn't cold yet. In fact No. 685 was standing by the official table waiting to receive the precious official diploma which should prove to his German household and to his descendants that he had once been indiscreet enough to climb to the top of Mont Blanc. He looked happy when he got his document; in fact, he spoke up and said he *was* happy.

I tried to buy a diploma for an invalid friend at home who had never traveled, and whose desire all his life has been to ascend Mont Blanc, but the Guide-in-Chief rather insolently refused to sell me one. I was very much offended. I said I did not propose to be discriminated against on account of my nationality; that he had just sold a diploma to this German gentleman, and my money was as good as his; I would see to it that he couldn't keep shop for Germans and deny his produce to Americans; I would have his license taken away from him at the dropping of a handkerchief; if France refused to break him, I would make an international matter of it and bring on a war; the soil should be drenched with blood; and not only that, I would set up and opposition shop and sell diplomas at half price.

For two cents I would have done these things, too, but nobody offered me the two cents. I tried to move that German's feelings, but it could not be done; he would not give me his diploma, neither would he sell it to me. I *told* him my friend was sick and could not come himself, but he said he did not care a *verdammtes pfennig*, he wanted his diploma for himself—did I suppose that he was going to risk his neck for that thing and then give it to a sick stranger? Indeed he wouldn't, so he wouldn't. I resolved, then, that I would do all I could to injure Mont Blanc.

* * *

As we strolled along the road we looked up and saw a red signal light glowing in the darkness of the mountainside. It seemed but a trifling way up—perhaps a hundred yards, a climb of ten minutes. It was a lucky piece of sagacity in us that we concluded to stop a man whom we met and get a light for our pipes from him instead of continuing the climb to that lantern to get a light, as had been our purpose. The man said that that lantern was on the Grand Mulets, some sixty-five hundred feet above the valley! I know by our Riffleberg experience that it would have taken us a good part of a week to go up there. I would sooner not smoke at all than to take all that trouble for a light.

Even in the daytime the foreshortening effect of the mountain's close proximity creates curious deceptions. For instance, one sees with the naked eye a cabin up there beside the glacier, and a little above and beyond he sees the spot where that red light was located; he thinks he could throw a stone from one place to the other. But he couldn't, for the difference between the two altitudes is more than three thousand feet. It looks impossible, from below, that this can be true, but it is true, nevertheless.

While strolling about we kept the run of the moon all the time, and we still kept an eye on her after we got back to the hotel portico. I had a theory that the gravitation of refraction, being subsidiary to atmospheric compensation, the refrangibility of the earth's surface would emphasize this effect in regions where great mountain ranges occur, and possibly so evenhandedly impact the odic and idyllic forces together, the one upon the other, as to prevent the moon from rising higher than 12,200 feet above sea level. This daring theory has been received with frantic scorn by some of my fellow-scientists, and with an eager silence by others. Among the former I may mention Prof. H____y; and among the latter Prof. T____l. Such is professional jealousy; a scientist will never show any kindness for a theory which he did not start himself. There is no feeling of brotherhood among these people. Indeed, they always resent it when I call them brother. To show how far their ungenerosity can carry them, I will state that I offered to let Prof. H____y publish my great theory as his own discovery; I even begged him to do it; I even proposed to print it myself as his theory. Instead of thanking me, he said that if I tried to fasten that theory on him, he would sue me for slander. I was going to offer it to Mr. Darwin, whom I understand to be a man with no prejudices, but it occurred to me that perhaps he would not be interested in it since it did not concern heraldry.

* * *

After breakfast, that next morning in Chamonix, we went out in the yard and watched the gangs of excusionizing tourists arriving and departing with their mules and guides and porters; then we took a look through the telescope at the snowy hump of Mont Blanc. It was brilliant with sunshine, and the vast smooth bulge seemed hardly five hundred yards away. With the naked eye we could dimly make out the house at the Pierre Pointue, which is located by the side of the great glacier and is more than three thousand feet above the level of the valley; but with the telescope we could see all its details. While I looked a woman rode by the house on a mule, and I saw her with sharp distinctness; I could have described her dress. I saw her nod to the people of the house, and rein up her mule, and put her hand up to shield her eyes from the sun. I was not used to telescopes; in fact, I had never looked through a good one before; it seemed incredible to me that this woman could be so far away. I was satisfied that I could see all these details with my naked eye; but when I tried it, that mule and those vivid people had wholly vanished, and the house itself had become small and vague. I tried the telescope again, and again everything was vivid. The strong black shadows of the mule and the woman were flung against the side of the house, and I saw the mule's silhouette wave its ears.

The telescopulist—or the telescopulariat—I do not know which is right—said a party were making the grand ascent and would come in sight on the remote upper heights, presently; so we waited to observe this performance.

Presently I had a superb idea. I wanted to stand with a party on the summit of Mont Blanc, merely to be able to say I had done it, and I believed that the telescope could set me within seven feet of the uppermost man. The telescoper assured me that it could. I then asked him how much I owed him for as far as I had got. He said, one franc. I asked him how much it would cost me to make the entire ascent. Three francs. I at once determined to make the entire ascent. But first I inquired if there was any danger. He said no—not by telescope; said he had taken a great many parties to the summit, and never lost a man. I asked what he would charge to let my agent go with me, together with such guides and porters as might be necessary. He said he would let Harris go for two francs, and that, unless we were unusually timid, he should consider guides and porters unnecessary; it was not customary to take them, when going by telescope, for they were rather an encumbrance than a help. He said that the party now on the mountain were approaching the most difficult part, and if we hurried we should overtake them within ten minutes, and could then join them and have the benefit of their guides and porters without their knowledge, and without expense to us.

I then said we would start immediately. I believe I said it calmly, though I was conscious of a paling cheek, in view of the nature of the exploit I was so unreflectingly engaging in. But the old daredevil spirit was upon me, and I said that as I had committed myself I would not back down; I would ascend Mont Blanc if it cost me my life. I told the man to slant his machine in the proper direction and let us be off.

Harris was afraid and did not want to go, but I heartened him up and said I would hold his hand all the way; so he gave his consent, though he trembled a little at first. I took a last pathetic look upon the pleasant summer scene about me, then boldly put my eye to the glass and prepared to mount among the grim glaciers and the everlasting snows.

We took our way carefully and cautiously across the great Glacier des Bossons, over yawning and terrific crevasses and amongst imposing crags and buttresses of ice which were fringed with icicles of gigantic proportions. The desert of ice that stretched far and wide about us was wild and desolate beyond description, and the perils which beset us were so great that at times I was minded to turn back. But I pulled my pluck together and pushed on.

We passed the glacier safely and began to mount the steeps beyond, with great celerity. When we were seven minutes out from the starting point, we reached an altitude where the scene took on a new aspect; an apparently limitless continent of gleaming snow was tilted heavenward before our faces. As my eye followed that awful acclivity far away up into the remote skies, it seemed to me that all I had ever seen before of sublimity and magnitude was small and insignificant compared to this.

We rested a moment and then began to mount with speed. Within three minutes we caught sight of the party ahead of us and stopped to observe them. They were toiling up a long, slanting ridge of snow—twelve persons, roped together some fifteen feet apart, marching in single file, and strongly marked against the clear blue sky. One was a woman. We could see them lift their feet and put them down; we saw them swing their alpenstocks forward in unison, like so many pendulums, and then bear their weight down upon them; we saw the lady wave her handkerchief. They dragged themselves upward in a worn and weary way, for they had been climbing steadily from the Grand Mulets, on the Glacier des Bossons, since three in the morning, and it was eleven now. We saw them sink down in the snow and rest and drink something from a bottle. After a while they moved on, and as they approached the final short dash of the home-stretch, we closed up on them and joined them.

Presently we all stood together on the summit! What a view was spread out below! Away off under the northwestern horizon rolled the silent billows of the Farnese Oberland, their snowy crests glinting softly in the subdued lights of distance; in the north rose the giant form of the Wobblehorn, draped from peak to shoulder in sable thunderclouds; beyond him, to the right, stretched the grand processional summits of the Cisalpine Cordillera, drowned in a sensuous haze; to the east loomed the colossal masses of the Yodelhorn, the Fuddlehorn, and the Dinnerhorn, their cloudless summits flashing white and cold in the sun; beyond them shimmered the faint far line of the Ghauts of Jubbelpore and the Aiguilles des Alleghenies; in the south towered the smoking peak of

Popocatapetl and the unapproachable altitudes of the peerless Scrabblehorn; in the west-south-west the stately range of the Himalayas lay dreaming in the purple gloom; and thence all around the curving horizon the eye roved over a troubled sea of sun-kissed Alps, and noted, here and there, the noble proportions and soaring domes of the Bottlehorn, and the Saddlehorn, and the Powderhorn, all bathed in the glory of noon and mottled with softly-gliding blots, the shadows flung from drifting clouds.

Overcome by the scene, we all raised a triumphant, tremendous shout, in unison. A startled man at my elbow said:

"Confound you, what do you yell like that for, right here in the street?"

That brought me down to Chamonix, like a flirt. I gave the man some spiritual advice and disposed of him, and then paid the telescope man his full fee and said that we were charmed with the trip and would remain down and not reascend and require him to fetch us down by telescope. This pleased him very much, for of course we could have stepped back to the summit and put him to the trouble of bringing us home if we had wanted to.

I judged we could get diplomas now, anyhow; so we went after them, but the Chief Guide put us off, with one pretext or another, during all the time we stayed in Chamonix, and we ended up by never getting them at all. So much for his prejudice against people's nationality. However, we worried him enough to make him remember us and our ascent for some time. He even said, once, that he wished there was a lunatic asylum in Chamonix. This shows that he really had fears that we were going to drive him mad. It was what we intended to do, but lack of time defeated it.

I cannot venture to advise the reader one way or another as to ascending Mont Blanc. I say only this: if he is at all timid, the enjoyments of the trip will hardly make up for the hardships and sufferings he will have to endure. But if he has good nerve, youth, health, and a bold, firm will, and could leave his family comfortably provided for in case the worst happened, he would find the ascent a wonderful experience, and the view from the top a vision to dream about, and tell about, and recall with exultation all the days of his life.

While I do not advise such a person to attempt the ascent, I do not advise him against it. But if he elects to attempt it, let him be warily careful of two things: choose a calm, clear day, and do not pay the telescope man in advance. There are dark stories of his getting his advance-payers on the summit and then leaving them there to rot.

# Part Nine

## *A Few Days in Paris*

*In Paris they simply opened their eyes and stared at us when we spoke to them in French! We never did succeed in making those idiots understand their own language. One of our passengers said to a shopkeeper in reference to a proposed return to buy a pair of gloves, "Along restay trankeel—maybe ve coom Moonday"; and, would you believe it, that shopkeeper, a born Frenchman, had to ask what it was that had been said.*

from *The Innocents Abroad*

# Bloody Deeds in Paris

We have come five hundred miles by rail through the heart of France. What a bewitching land it is! What a garden! Surely the leagues of bright green lawns are swept and brushed and watered every day and their grasses trimmed by the barber. Surely the hedges are shaped and measured and their symmetry preserved by the most architectural of gardeners. Surely the long straight rows of stately poplars that divide the beautiful landscape like the squares of a checkerboard are set with line and plummet, and their uniform height determined with a spirit level. Surely the straight, smooth, pure white turnpikes are jack-planed and sandpapered every day. How else are these marvels of symmetry, cleanliness, and order attained? It is wonderful. There are no unsightly stone walls and never a fence of any kind. There is no dirt, no decay, no rubbish anywhere—nothing that even hints at untidiness—nothing that even suggests neglect. All is orderly and beautiful—everything is charming to the eye.

We had such glimpses of the Rhone gliding along between its grassy banks; of cozy cottages buried in flowers and shrubbery; of quaint old red-tiled villages with mossy medieval cathedrals looming out of their midst; of wooded hills with ivy-grown towers and turrets of feudal castles projecting above the foliage. Such glimpses of Paradise, it seemed to us, such visions of fabled fairyland!

We knew then what the poet meant when he sang of:

> —thy cornfields green,
>
> and sunny vines,
>
> O pleasant land of France!

And it *is* a pleasant land. No word describes it so felicitously as that one. They say there is no word for "home" in the French language. Well, considering that they have the article itself in such an attractive aspect, they ought to manage to get along without the word. Let us not waste too much pity on "homeless" France. I have observed that Frenchmen abroad seldom wholly give up the idea of going back to France some time or other. I am not surprised at it now.

We are not infatuated with these French railway cars, though. We took first-class passage, not because we wished to attract attention by doing a thing which is uncommon in Europe but because we could make our journey quicker by so doing. It is hard to make railroading pleasant in any country. It is too tedious. Stagecoaching is infinitely more delightful. Once I crossed the plains and deserts and mountains of the West in a stagecoach, from the Missouri line to California, and since then all my pleasure trips must be measured to that rare holiday frolic. Two thousand miles of ceaseless rash and rattle and clatter, by night and by day, and never a weary moment, never a lapse of interest! The first seven hundred miles a level continent, its grassy carpet greener and softer and smoother than any sea and figured with designs fitted to its magnitude—the shadows of the clouds. Here were no scenes but summer scenes, and no disposition inspired by them but to lie at full length on the mail sacks in the grateful breeze and dreamily smoke the pipe of peace—what other, where all was repose and contentment? In cool mornings, before the sun was fairly up, it was worth a lifetime of city toiling and moiling to perch in the foretop with the driver and see the six mustangs scamper under the sharp snapping of the whip that never touched them; to scan the blue distances of a world that knew no lords but us; to cleave the wind with uncovered head and feel the sluggish pulses rousing to the spirit of a speed that pretended to the resistless rush of a typhoon! Then thirteen hundred miles of desert solitudes; of limitless panoramas of bewildering perspective; of mimic cities, of pinnacled cathedrals, of massive fortresses, counterfeited in the eternal rocks and splendid with the crimson and gold of the setting sun; of dizzy altitudes among fog-wreathed peaks and never-melting snows, where thunders and lightnings and tempests warred magnificently at our feet and the storm clouds above swung their shredded banners in our very faces!

But I forgot. I am in elegant France now, and not skurrying through the great South Pass and the Wind River Mountains, among antelopes and buffaloes and painted Indians on the warpath. It is not meet that I should make too disparaging comparisons between humdrum travel on a railway and that royal summer flight across a continent in a stagecoach.

* * *

From earliest infancy it had been a cherished ambition of mine to be shaved some day in a palatial barbershop in Paris. I wished to recline at full length in a cushioned invalid chair, with pictures about me and sumptuous furniture; with frescoed walls and gilded arches above me and vistas of Corinthian columns stretching far before me; with perfumes of Araby to intoxicate my senses and the slumberous drone of distant voices to soothe me to sleep. At the end of an hour I would wake up regretfully and find my face as smooth and as soft as an infant's. Departing, I would lift my hands above that barber's head and say, "Heaven bless you, my son!"

So we searched high and low, for a matter of two hours, but never a barbershop could we see. We saw only wigmaking establishments, with shocks of dead and repulsive hair bound upon the heads of painted waxen brigands who stared out from glass boxes upon the passerby with their stony eyes and scared him with the ghostly white of their countenances. We shunned these signs for a time, but finally we concluded that the wigmakers must of necessity be the barbers as well, since we could find no single legitimate representative of the fraternity. We entered and asked, and found that it was even so.

I said I wanted to be shaved. The barber inquired where my room was. I said never mind where my room was, I wanted to be shaved—there, on the spot. The doctor said he would be shaved also. Then there was an excitement among those two barbers! There was a wild consultation, and afterwards a hurrying to and fro and a feverish gathering up of razors from obscure places and a ransacking for soap. Next they took us into a little mean, shabby back room; they got two ordinary sitting-room chairs and placed us in them with our coats on. My old, old dream of bliss vanished into thin air!

I sat bolt upright, silent, sad, and solemn. One of the wigmaking villains lathered my face for ten terrible minutes and finished by plastering a mass of suds into my mouth. I expelled the nasty stuff with a strong English expletive and said, "Foreigner, beware!" Then this outlaw strapped his razor on his boot, hovered over me ominously for six fearful seconds, and then swooped down upon me like the genius of destruction. The first rake of his razor loosened the very hide from my face and lifted me out of the chair. I stormed and raved, and the other boys enjoyed it. Their beards are not strong and thick. Let us draw the curtain over this harrowing scene. Suffice it that I submitted and went through with the cruel infliction of a shave by a French barber; tears of exquisite agony coursed down my cheeks now and then, but I survived. Then the incipient assassin held a basin of water under my chin and slopped its contents over my face, and into my bosom, and down the back of my neck, with a mean pretense of washing away the soap and blood. He dried my features with a towel and was going to comb my hair, but I asked to be excused. I said, with withering irony, that it was sufficient to be skinned—I declined to be scalped.

I went away from there with my handkerchief about my face, and never, never, never desired to dream of palatial Parisian barbershops anymore. The truth is, as I believe I have since found out, that they have no barbershops worthy of the name in Paris—and no barbers, either, for that matter. The imposter who does duty as a barber brings his pans and napkins and implements of torture to your residence and deliberately skins you in your private apartments. Ah, I have suffered, suffered, suffered, here in Paris, but never mind—the time is coming when I shall have a dark and bloody revenge. Someday a Parisian barber will come to my room to skin me, and from that day forth that barber will never be heard of more.

# A Parisian Ferguson

The next morning we were up and dressed at ten o'clock. We went to the *commissionaire* of the hotel—I don't know what a *commissionaire* is, but that is the man we went to—and told him we wanted a guide. He said the great International Exposition had drawn such multitudes of Englishmen and Americans to Paris that it would be next to impossible to find a good guide unemployed. He said he usually kept a dozen or two on hand, but he only had three now. He called them. One looked so like a very pirate that we let him go at once. The next one spoke with a simpering precision of pronunciation that was irritating and said:

"If ze zhentlemans will to me make ze grande honneur to me rattain in hees serveece, I shall show to him everysing zat is magnifique to look upon in ze beautiful Parree. I speaky ze Angleesh pairfaitemaw."

He would have done well to have stopped there, because he had that much by heart and said it right off without making a mistake. But his self-complacency seduced him into attempting a flight into regions of unexplored English, and this reckless experiment was his ruin. Within ten seconds he was so tangled up in a maze of mutilated verbs and torn and bleeding forms of speech that no human ingenuity could ever have gotten him out of it with credit. It was plain enough that he could not "speaky" the English quite as "pairfaitemaw" as he had pretended he could.

The third man captured us. He was plainly dressed, but he had a noticeable air of neatness about him. He wore a high silk hat which was a little old, but had been carefully brushed. He wore second-hand kid gloves, in good repair, and carried a small rattan cane with a curved handle—a female leg—of ivory. He stepped as gently and as daintily as a cat crossing a muddy street; and oh, he was urbanity; he was quiet, unobtrusive self-possession; he was deference itself! He spoke softly and guardedly, and when he was about to make a statement on his sole responsibility or offer a suggestion, he weighed it by drachms and scruples first, with the crook of his little stick placed meditatively to his teeth. His opening speech was perfect. It was perfect in construction, in phraseology, in grammar, in emphasis, in pronunciation—everything. He spoke little and guardedly after that. We were charmed. We were more than charmed—we were overjoyed. We hired him at once. We never even asked him his price. This man—our lackey, our servant, our unquestioning slave though he was—was still a gentleman—we could see that—while of the other two one was coarse and awkward and the other was a born pirate. We asked our man Friday's name. He drew from his pocket-book a snowy little card and passed it to us with a profound bow:

A. Billfinger
Guide to Paris, France, Germany,
Spain, &c., &c.
*Grande Hotel du Louvre*

"Billfinger! Oh, carry me home to die!"

That was an "aside" from Dan. The atrocious name grated harshly on my ear, too. The most of us can learn to forgive, and even to like, a countenance that strikes us unpleasantly at first, but few of us, I fancy, become reconciled to a jarring name so easily. I was almost sorry we had hired this man, his name was so unbearable. However, no matter. We were impatient to start. Billfinger stepped to the door to call a carriage, and then the doctor said:

"Well, the guide goes with the barbershop . . . and maybe with many another pretty romance of Paris. I expected to have a guide named Henri de Montmorency or Armand de la Chartreuse or something that would sound grand in letters to the villagers at home, but to think of a Frenchman by the name of Billfinger! Oh! This is absurd, you know. This will never do. We can't say Billfinger; it is nauseating. Name him over again; what had we better call him? Alexis du Caulaincourt?"

"Alphonse Henri Gustave de Hauteville," I suggested.

"Call him Ferguson," said Dan.

That was practical, unromantic good sense. Without debate, we expunged Billfinger *as* Billfinger and called him Ferguson.

The carriage—an open barouche—was ready. Ferguson mounted beside the driver, and we whirled away to breakfast. As was proper, Mr. Ferguson stood by to transmit our orders and answer questions. By and by, he mentioned casually—the artful adventurer—that he would go and get his breakfast as soon as we had finished ours. He knew we could not get along without him and that we would not want to loiter about and wait for him. We asked him to sit down and eat with us. He begged, with many a bow, to be excused. It was not proper, he said; he would sit at another table. We ordered him peremptorily to sit down with us.

Here endeth the first lesson. It was a mistake.

As long as we had that fellow after that, he was always hungry; he was always thirsty. He came early; he stayed late; he could not pass a restaurant; he looked with lecherous eyes upon every wineshop. Suggestions to stop, excuses to eat and to drink, were forever on his lips. We tried all we could to fill him so full that he would have no room to spare for a fortnight, but it was a failure. He did not hold enough to smother the cravings of his superhuman appetite.

He had another "discrepancy" about him. He was always wanting us to buy things. On the shallowest pretenses he would inveigle us into shirt stores, boot stores, tailor shops, glove shops—anywhere under the broad sweep of the heavens that there seemed a chance of our buying anything. Anyone could have guessed that the shopkeepers paid him a percentage on the sales, but in our blessed innocence we didn't until this feature of his conduct grew unbearably prominent. One day Dan happened to mention that he thought of buying three or four silk dress patterns for presents. Ferguson's hungry eye was upon him in an instant. In the course of twenty minutes the carriage stopped.

"What's this?"

"Zis is ze finest silk *magasin* in Paris—ze most celebrate."

"What did you come here for? We told you to take us to the palace of the Louvre."

"I suppose ze gentleman say he wish to buy some silk."

"You are not required to 'suppose' things for the party, Ferguson. We do not wish to tax your energies too much. We will bear some of the burden and heat of the day ourselves. We will endeavor to do such 'supposing' as is really necessary to be done. Drive on."

So spake the doctor.

Within fifteen minutes the carriage halted again, and before another silk store. The doctor said:

"Ah, the palace of the Louvre—beautiful, beautiful edifice! Does the Emperor Napoleon live here now, Ferguson?"

"Ah, Doctor! You do jest; zis is not ze palace; we come there directly. But since we pass right by zis store, where is such beautiful silk—"

"Ah! I see, I see. I meant to have told you that we did not wish to purchase any silks today, but in my absentmindedness I forgot it. I also meant to tell you that we wished to go directly to the Louvre, but I forgot that also. However, we will go there now. Pardon my seeming carelessness, Ferguson. Drive on."

Within the half hour we stopped again—in front of another silk store. We were angry; but the doctor was always serene, always smooth-voiced. He said:

"At last! How imposing the Louvre is, and yet how small! How exquisitely fashioned! How charmingly situated! Venerable, venerable pile—"

"Pairdon, Doctor, zis is not ze Louvre—it is—"

"*What* is it?"

"I have ze idea—it come to me in a moment—zat ze silk in zis *magasin*—"

"Ferguson, how heedless I am. I fully intended to tell you that we did not wish to buy any silks today, and I also intended to tell you that we yearned to go immediately to the palace of the Louvre, but enjoying the happiness of seeing you devour four breakfasts this morning has so filled me with pleasurable emotions that I neglect the commonest interests of the time. However, we will proceed now to the Louvre, Ferguson."

"But, Doctor" (excitedly), "it will take not a minute—not but one small minute! Ze gentleman need not to buy if he not wish to—but only *look* at ze silk—*look* at ze beautiful fabric. (Then pleadingly.) *Sair*—just only one *leetle* moment!"

Dan said, "Confound the idiot! I don't want to see any silks today, and I *won't* look at them. Drive on."

And the doctor: "We need no silks now, Ferguson. Our hearts yearn for the Louvre. Let us journey on—let us journey on."

"But, *Doctor*! It is only one moment—one leetle moment. And ze time will be save—entirely save! Because zere is nothing to see now—it is too late. It want ten minute to four and ze Louvre close at four—*only* one leetle moment, Doctor!"

The treacherous miscreant! After four breakfasts and a gallon of champagne, to serve us such a scurvy trick. We got no sight of the countless treasures of art in the Louvre galleries that day, and our only poor little satisfaction was in the reflection that Ferguson sold not a solitary silk dress pattern.

# Epilogue
# Heading Home

*We . . . made the homeward passage in the Cunarder,* Gallia, *a very fine ship. I was glad to get home—immeasurably glad; so glad, in fact, that it did not seem possible that anything could ever get me out of the country again. I had not enjoyed a pleasure abroad which seemed to me to compare with the pleasure I felt in seeing New York harbor again.*

from *A Tramp Abroad*

*It seemed a fine and large thing to have accomplished—the circumnavigation of this great globe in that little time, and I was privately proud of it. Then came one of those vanity-snubbing astronomical reports from the Observatory-people, whereby it appeared that another great body of light had lately flamed up in the remoteness of space which was traveling at a gait which would enable it to do all that I had done in a minute and a half. Human pride is not worthwhile; there is always something lying in wait to take the wind out of it.*

from *Following the Equator*

# *Selected Major Works by Mark Twain*

## Fiction

*The Celebrated Jumping Frog of Calaveras County and Other Sketches* (1867)

*The Gilded Age* (1873)

*Sketches, New and Old* (1875)

*The Adventures of Tom Sawyer* (1876)

*The Prince and the Pauper* (1881)

*Adventures of Huckleberry Finn* (1885)

*A Connecticut Yankee in King Arthur's Court* (1889)

*Merry Tales* (1892)

*The American Claimant* (1892)

*The One Million Pound Bank Note and Other New Stories* (1893)

*Tom Sawyer Abroad* (1894)

*The Tragedy of Pudd'nhead Wilson* (1894)

*Personal Recollections of Joan of Arc* (1896)

*The Stolen White Elephant and Other Detective Stories* (1896)
*The Man That Corrupted Hadleyburg and Other Stories and Essays* (1900)
*The Diaries of Adam and Eve* (1904)
*What is Man?* (1906)
*The $30,000 Bequest and Other Stories* (1906)
*Extract from Captain Stormfield's Visit to Heaven* (1909)
*Letters from the Earth* (1962)

## Non-Fiction

*The Innocents Abroad* (1869)
*Roughing It* (1872)
*A Tramp Abroad* (1880)
*Life on the Mississippi* (1883)
*How To Tell a Story and Other Essays* (1897)
*Following the Equator* (1897)
*Christian Science* (1907)
*1601, and Is Shakespeare Dead?* (1909)
*Speeches* (1910)
*Autobiography* (1917)